LAW GUIDE FOR THE HOSPITALITY INDUSTRY

A priority and a must read for existing and potential proprietors,
hospitality personnel, business students
and anyone who aims to start or grow a business.

HEUGHETTE AMMA ASANTE (MIH)

Grosvenor House
Publishing Limited

This book is published by
Grosvenor House Publishing Ltd
Link House
140 The Broadway, Tolworth, Surrey, KT6 7HT.
www.grosvenorhousepublishing.co.uk

A CIP record for this book
is available from the British Library

ISBN 978-1-78623-106-2

DEDICATION

I dedicate this book to proprietors in the hospitality industry. I also dedicated this book to my mother Mary Akosua Nuamah Asante and the memory of my late father Robert Yaw Newman Asante. Mum and Dad, your love and support over the years have made this possible.

With affectionate appreciation to Karl, Louis and Christabel whose encouragement proved decisive in the final stages of this work.

ACKNOWLEDGEMENTS

"What shall I render unto my Lord for this great thing He has done, for He has been a force of tectonic good" as Aristotle puts it and I couldn't agree more with Hegel when he referenced Him as the 'Absolute whole'.

"Thank you Lord, for the endowment and the breath of life"

The documentary materials used in these pages have come from many lecture notes, authorities, leading books in the business field as well as my private reflections and experiences as a student, worker and consultant in the field of hospitality. I would like to thank my lecturers in the Department of Science and Technology, University of Middlesex (Hendon, London) for their enlightenment and encouragement.

I am also grateful to all those who helped me in my quest for information and answered all my queries. Your exchanges with me helped to bounce off ideas and shape this academic piece.

ABOUT THE AUTHOR

Heughette Amma Asante was initially trained as a nurse. She later switched to study Hospitality Management. She is currently registered as a Hospitality Management Consultant with many years of experience.

Her affinity with the hospitality industry is as old as her insatiable quest for reforms and changes to improve it. This has undoubtedly found her in several spheres of the industry, as a student, worker and a tutoring consultant.

As a student, she read National Diploma in Hotel and Catering Operations at the Middlesex Polytechnic (now Middlesex University, Hendon, London), where the course content and modules heightened her curiosity. This led her to enrol to study Hotel, Catering and Institutional Management at the same institution. Upon completion of the course, she set herself another challenge; to turn the classroom theory into practice, she therefore set out to work. As a worker she found herself working in restaurants and hotels in London as a catering assistant, bar attendant, room attendant etc. On completion of her course, she worked as a Catering Supervisor with the Civil Service Catering Organization in London. She was also recommended for company training by the Civil Service Catering Organization. Her quest to be an all-rounder in the industry inspired her to alternate various positions and roles in the respective hotels, restaurants and other areas she worked in the industry.

She later went to Ghana and worked with the Inspectorate and Training Division of the Ghana Tourist Board respectively. After sometime, she left the Ghana Tourist Board and established her own business as a registered consultant offering advice to proprietors in the industry. She also trained staff on and off the job, organizing workshops several times for all categories of personnel in the industry.

In the last few years, she has spent more time travelling, and undertaking more research to update her knowledge on the latest developments in the industry. This was to enable her to offer quality assistance to the industry through consultation and book writing. She is also a member of the Institute of Hospitality in the United Kingdom.

PREFACE

The pursuit of law and order has led men to sit down four times to re-order the world; the treaty of Westphalia – after the thirty years' war, the Vienna convention – after the Napoleonic wars, the Paris declaration – after World War One and San Francisco – after World War Two. Also in the long march of mankind from the cave to the computer, law has played a central role in times of chaos – to bring stability, and also in times of stability – to bring progress. Law exists to bring order in daily activities and behaviour. As such the search to fashion out a body of law to regulate activities and define what is permissible and forbidden cannot be overemphasized.

Law itself consists of a series of rules regulating behaviour and reflecting to some extent, the ideas and preoccupations of the society within which it functions. Law is the element, which binds communities and business entities like hotels and guest houses together in their adherence to recognized values and standards. To help increase global tourism receipts, the hospitality industry must continuously instil in their daily operations, canons and laws of the trade.

The focus of this book is to equip personnel in the hospitality trade with the laws governing the industry, so as to help them avoid fines, imprisonment and endless litigation and thus save many from defamation and potential insolvency.

Lucidly, unambiguously and with no equivocation the author has laid out all the laws in the hospitality industry in clear terms, including the use of diagrams to create a mind-map for pictorial illustrations and to offer a deeper understanding.

The law, rights and liabilities in the hospitality industry have been covered under subject themes like: contracts, misrepresentation and procedure for the acquisition of property, food regulation, employment and the doctrine of respondeat superior. It also considers perceived potential and actual or legally recognized negligence at the workplace and how to avoid them. There is also the adherence to health and safety laws, which every employer and employee in the industry must abide by.

Case histories and questions on the law of contract have been added as a bonus package. In the light of the aforementioned areas covered by the scope of this book, proprietors in the hospitality industry, managers, receptionists, housekeepers, stewards, maintenance and those who handle health and safety issues in hotels, guesthouses, apartments and all forms of commercial accommodation will find this book worth purchasing and reading.

Tour operators and travel agents will also find this book useful; some pages have been devoted to the law of agency; which specifically delves into the law regarding tour operations and travel agency. Business owners and organizations will find reading of this book quite refreshing. Provisions of what to consider when setting up a limited liability, private and public companies have all been discussed here.

Students in the hospitality industry will also see this book as an important resource material; it offers clear and simple definitions to terminologies in the field as well as case histories and questions to help them prepare for examinations.

Finally, for the curious mind that craves law and order, it certainly will rekindle your reading pleasure. The book "*LAW GUIDE FOR THE HOSPITALITY INDUSTRY*" remains a priority and a must read for operators in the hospitality industry and all those who aim to grow and own a business.

The author's enthusiasm for the canons and laws in the industry is as encouraging as it is infectious and it is hoped that you will catch the law bug in the hospitality industry as well. When it happens do spread the word!!!

May the reading of this book help to instil the respect, practice and knowledge of law that upholds the way in the industry. May it save the next manager or housekeeper from trouble, may it fiercely push back self-inflicted negligence with no recourse to the law. May it make ignorance of the law of the hospitality industry a thing of the past. Above all, may this book be a precursor in the bid to make the hospitality industry a place of warmth, friendliness and of law.

CONTENTS

Chapter Two

DIFFERENTIATION BETWEEN HOTELS AND OTHER CATERING ESTABLISHMENTS

Chapter Four

Chapter Ten

EMPLOYMENT OF STAFF

Chapter One

UNDERSTANDING THE BASIC PRINCIPLES OF LAW

1.1 INTRODUCTION

Law is a set of rules made by Parliament to be observed by everyone in the territory. Every nation in the world today has a Parliament where laws are made by the authorities [The Prime Minister and his or her cabinet, lawyers, judges, the House of Commons and the House of Lords]. These laws are used to govern the people for which everyone is expected to comply. The legal structure of two countries has been used as examples in this book, namely United Kingdom and Ghana. Some countries may be using either a similar or a different legal structure and different ways of dealing with some types of offences. Some countries still use capital punishment for serious offences. For example, **some offenders face death sentences when they commit murder, while other countries give life sentences for the same offence. We will be dealing more with civil offences.**

Criminal offences are punishable by the state, but in the case of civil offences, compensation is normally paid by the defendant to the plaintiff for non-compliance of the law. Civil offences could be settled out of court when there is an agreement between the parties involved. Certain civil offences can be treated under criminal law.

Food sellers, supermarkets, restaurants and takeaway shops must clearly let consumers know what ingredients their food contains. Consumers have the right to know what they are buying. Where this is breached, consumers can report the organisation to the Food

Standards Agency. If a company fails to properly describe the ingredients of a product, it can also face criminal prosecution. This offence would be under the Food Safety Act. Breaching it can be punished with up to two years in prison and or an unlimited fine.

The Consumer Protection Act states that you can bring a claim against a producer, importer or supplier if there is something wrong with a product.

In this book, we shall be mainly concerned with the law of contract, which is very important in the running of any business. It is a priority for every organization, big or small, to have a basic knowledge of contract law. Whenever there is an exchange of goods and services for reward, it means that there has been an agreement, an offer and acceptance, plus the intention to create legal relations. The parties involved may be dealing with either visible goods, or rendering services that are invisible. The hospitality industry offers services that are intangible; i.e. offering accommodation at the reception or serving food and beverage in the restaurant. Proprietors buy assets like furniture and fittings etc. for their establishments, which are visible goods that are purchased on contract. When a breach of contract occurs, the offender may have to compensate the other party.

In any organization, there are policies and procedures provided to keep staff within the law. For example, staff must acquaint themselves with Health and Safety law. Fire training is considered a priority and a necessity for staff working in sleeping accommodations i.e. hotels, hostels, boarding houses, motels, etc. A breach of the Health and Safety Act by employers or employees will be a criminal offence. An employee at work, has a duty to take reasonable care for the health and safety of himself and the people who may be affected by his acts and omissions at work, and to cooperate with either his employer or others so far as is necessary to see that statutory duties are performed.

In the hotel and catering industry, there are various departments with departmental heads. They are normally given the authority to enter into contracts by purchasing various items from suppliers. They can also decide to change and nominate suppliers. Departmental heads may recruit and dismiss staff. The chef in the kitchen may order and purchase food items, the restaurant manager may order and purchase beverages, crockery, glasses etc.

Larger hotel companies normally have a human resource department who deals with staff records and sometimes recruitment. They also have a purchasing department who deals with ordering, purchasing, receiving, storing, issuing and control of items. The managers in these larger hotel companies may be qualified and experienced enough to confidently handle all departments where need be. Unfortunately, majority of the hotel and catering outlets are small establishments and cannot afford either a human resource department or a purchasing department. The manager therefore finds himself engaged in duties such as recruiting, purchasing, as well as entering into contracts all by himself with little or no previous training.

Lack of basic legal knowledge in an industry could cost any business a fortune, more importantly a bad reputation, fines, bankruptcy, loss of licence, closure of the business, and worst of all imprisonment.

Employers are often held vicariously liable for negligence of duty by their staff. So if employees have a fair knowledge of the law, it goes a long way to help the employer. An employer can then have a peace of mind so as to support the company well, maximise profit and maintain the company's position in the market and in turn help the company to employ more people to help decrease unemployment.

We must not forget that, the law has dominion over man as long as he lives. The law is there for us all to let everyone fight for their rights. So consumers will sue the company when a breach of contract occurs and that can affect the business.

There are real case studies, which have been compiled globally at the end of this book to confirm how negligence and ignorance of the law have caused problems to some businesses.

1.1.1 Definitions of Law

The following are various definitions of law by five prominent authors:

1)

    a. "A set of rules that become known to the society that they govern through a number of originating sources. For example the court from decided cases, and parliament through legislation made by Parliament as in the case of Acts of Parliament."

    b. "The agreement of the members of the particular society involved to be bound by and follow rules laid down. The agreement is generally not expressed by the members of the society governed by the rules, but is signified by living in the society and obeying its rules and yet could not point to any specific agreement to comply with them. When a society has rules in place and an implied obedience, then it may be said to conduct its affair under the rule of law."

Keenan, D. (Law for Business)

2) "All law is the law of a group of individuals or of groups made up of individuals. No one can make a law purely for himself. He may form a resolution, frame an ambition, or adopt a rule, but these are private prescriptions, not law."

Honore, T. (Making Law Blind)

3) It will help to distinguish three senses of the word 'law':

    a. "The first is law as a distinctive social institution; that is, the sense invoked when we ask whether primitive law is really law".

    b. "The law as a collection or set of propositions, the set we refer to as antitrust law, the law of torts, the statute of frauds and so on."

c. "The third is law as a source of rights, duties and powers, as in the sentence."

Posner, A.R. (Problems of Jurisprudence)

4)

a. "The regime that orders human activities and relations through systematic application of the force of politically organised society or through social pressure, backed by force in such a society."

b. "The aggregate of legislation, judicial precedents and accepted legal principles, the body of authoritative grounds of judicial and administrative action, especially the body of rules and standards, and principles that the courts of a particular jurisdiction apply in deciding controversies brought before them (the law of the land)."

c. "The set of rules or principles dealing with a specific area of a legal system. The judicial and administrative process; legal action and proceedings. When settlement negotiations fail, they submit their dispute to the law."

Garner, B.A. – Editor in Chief, (Black's Law Dictionary, 8th edition)

5) "Law is a collection of man-made rules to be observed by all human beings who reside within the territory to which those rules are intended to apply."

Richard, M. and Stewart, S.W. – (Legal Aspects of the Hotel and Catering Operations)

1.1.2 Sources and Development of English Law

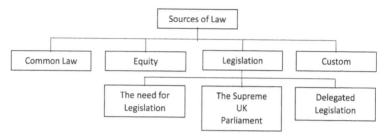

Fig 1.1.2 A Diagram of Sources and Development of English Law

1.1.2.1 The meaning of the word 'Source'

The word 'source' has various meanings when applied to law. One may treat the word 'source as referring to the historical origins of law and trace the development of the Common Law, equity, legislation, delegated legislation, custom, the law merchant, canon law and legal treatises. One treats the word 'source' as referring to the methods by which laws are made and brought into existence and considering the current processes of legislation, delegated legislation, judicial precedent and to a limited extent, custom. We shall be concerned with the methods by which laws are made with particular reference to the laws made in the UK Parliament and how they are interpreted by the judiciary.

1.1.2.2 The need for Law

There can be a state of insecurity and anarchy in the absence of the law. Since the creation of the world, there has been some sort of law to help govern the people (from ancient times to modern times). In the ancient times, Kings or rulers were settling disputes amongst their subjects. They relied on the Common Law to judge cases. It appeared there were some defects with the Common Law. In an attempt to help bring fairness into the system, Parliament was created so that cases could be fairly dealt with by professionals such as judges, lawyers, magistrates etc. Power was then taken from the Kings or rulers and given to the courts. In England for example, the

Queen only gives the Royal Assent after the law or new laws are made by the Houses of Parliament.

Common Law is the basis of our law today. It is the unwritten law that developed from customs and judicial decisions. The phrase 'Common Law' is still used to distinguish laws that have been created by statute or other legislation. Common Law also has another meaning, in that it is used to distinguish between rules of equity which were developed by the Lord Chancellor and the Chancery Courts.

Common Law, as the body of law, was derived from judicial decisions rather than statutes and constitutions. It was one of the three main historical sources of English law. The other two were legislation and equity. The Common Law was the body of law created by and administered by the King's Court.

1.1.2.3 Local customs as the basis for judging cases

When Henry II 1154–89 came to the throne, the local courts were managed by the local Lords. Justice was also administered by the County Sheriffs, often sitting with the Earl and the Bishop in the Courts of the Shires. They judged cases that came before them, based on local customs.

Many customary rules of law were similar in all parts of the country, but some parts of the country applied different customary rules of law. For example, it was the right of the eldest son to inherit the whole of his father's land where there was no will, i.e. on intestacy. This was applied throughout England. But in Kent, with respect to intestacy, all the sons inherited equally. In Nottingham and Bristol, under the custom of the borough, the property passed to the youngest son.

These customs were finally abolished by Statutory Instrument and part IV of Administration of Estates Act 1925, and replaced by the rule that, the deceased's estate must be distributed amongst near relatives and in most cases to the wife and children.

There was a royal court named the *Curia Regis* or the King's Council, which was generally used by the wealthy people. Those who wish to send their cases to this court spent so much money and went through great frustration by following the King and his council for years before their cases are heard and judged.

There was the need to establish a place where cases could be heard. However, S.17 of the statute of 1215, Magna Carta, provided that what was then the High Court should not follow the King but should be held 'in some certain place'. This turned out to be Westminster, which was in central London. Steps were also taken to ensure that royal justice would go out to the Shires and be opened to all.

The introduction of the General "Eyre" (which simply means a journey), was whereby representatives of the King were sent from Westminster on a tour of the Shires (a rural area with an elected council) to check on the local Shire administration. On these visits, they would sit with the local court and judge cases. Due to their judicial functions, they were called the "Justices of the Eyre". Those suspected of serious crimes were brought before the General Eyre when it arrived in their area. Civil cases; for example, land cases, were brought before the General Eyre as well. The introduction of the General Eyre ensured uniformity in English Law.

During the reign of Edward the third, 1327–77, the Judges in Eyre were substituted by more formally trained lawyers to shape existing local customary laws into one uniform law common to the whole Kingdom.

However, there was no complete unification as at 1389, while in some areas a husband was not liable for his wife's trading debts; the Common Law elsewhere regarded him as liable. Also, the right to make a will of personal property was not regarded in the whole of England until1724. Land could still not be left by will to the heir by law. But it later became possible to leave land by will, which is still the case today. Half of the deceased man's personal property went to the wife and children and the other half to the church.

1.1.2.4 The Common Law

Many new rules were created and applied by the royal judges as they went on the circuit, and these were added to local customary law to make one uniform body of law called the 'Common Law'. When a judge decided on a new problem in a case brought before him, this became a new rule of law and was followed by subsequent judges. Later on, this practice became more definite and was known as the binding force of judicial precedent, and the judges felt bound to follow previous decisions instead of merely looking to them for guidance. By these means, the Common Law earned the status of a system. The Common Law is a judge-made system of law, originating in ancient customs, which were clarified, much extended and used in all places by the judges.

1.1.2.5 Equity

The basic meaning of equity is the quality of being impartial; fairness. It is a system of using principles of natural justice and fair conduct to reach a judgement when Common Law is inadequate or inappropriate. Equity grew up to supply the defects and correct injustices of the Common Law.

Judges came to be chosen exclusively from the legal profession instead of a wider variety of royal officials, as had been the case in the thirteenth century.

The Common Law courts became more aware of what they were doing and attempted to become more systematic. Also people were greatly concerned about things being done properly. Yet, it appeared they were used to their old ways and reluctant to depart from what had become established.

The Common Law initially developed one major remedy available to claimants, i.e. monetary damages. Assuming that you acquire a new building for your business, but the owner breaks the contract and refuses to complete the sale. The Common Law would grant you damages, but what is required is a remedy that will make the owner convey the property to you. The Common Law has no such remedy.

Since the judiciary was following precedent and not seeming to develop remedies other than damages, frustrated claimants petitioned the King who appeared to be the only person who could change legal rules to provide for a wide range of remedies. The King referred such petitions to his chief legal advisor, the Lord Chancellor. He began to hear complaints in what was called the Court of Chancery and created new rights and remedies. The law administered by the chancellor was called equity, and is the remedy of injunction that can stop an offensive activity, and specific performance that can make a person perform a contract. People are made to carry out what is required of them when an injunction of specific performance is ordered against them. Since they are orders of court, a failure to carry them out is a contempt of court, for which the defaulter can be imprisoned. The threat of this or the imposition of the penalty usually makes the defaulter obey the order.

For some time, the Common Law judges dispensed their justice in separate courts from the court of chancery where equity was dispensed. However, in the late nineteenth century, the Judicature Acts 1873–75 united the courts. Today we still have a chancery division of the high court. The remedies devised by the chancellor and later the judges of the court of chancery can be administered in all divisions of the high court and in the taking of appeals from the high court.

Common Law and equity have been developed and continue to some extent to be developed by the system of court precedents (Case Law). Equity's greatest contribution to law is the trust. A trust arises where one or more persons hold a property, e.g. land or company shares, for the benefit of other persons called beneficiaries. People sometimes wish to provide for their children or grandchildren when they die or during their lifetime. They may leave some of their property in trust, particularly where the beneficiary was under the age of eighteen. They can appoint trustees who will look after the property till the beneficiary attains the age of eighteen years. The dishonest trustees could do what they liked with the trust property and ignore the rights of the beneficiaries until the system of legal rules called equity came along. Equity recognizes the equitable interest of the beneficiaries and will enforce them against defaulting trustees.

1.1.2.6 Mercantile Law

When the merchants and the seamen needed quicker solutions to their disputes at their destinations, they set up their own courts.

The Common Law courts were slow to show an interest in dealing with commercial matters. Furthermore, they were formal and slow to the needs of merchants who required a quicker justice in administering the rules with which they were familiar. Again it appeared the Common Law courts were too preoccupied with disputes concerning more problems arising from disputes about the possession and ownership of land.

The rules of the European Law Merchant developed over the years were from the customary practices of the merchants. The jury was often made up of merchants presided over by the mayor or his deputy. The mercantile law was developed independently from the Common Law. These merchants were traders who used the ships involved in commercial trade. Disputes between local and foreign merchants at an exhibition or fair, where most important commercial business was conducted in the fourteenth century, were heard at the courts of the fair. The borough was known as 'courts of powder' after the dusty feet of the merchants who used courts at the harbour.

The major ports, such as Bristol, established their own courts where disputes were heard. They also applied special European Customary Law from the customary practices of the seamen.

When the Court of Admiralty developed, it took over much of the work of the merchants' courts. From the seventeenth century onwards, the Common Law courts began to hear the commercial cases, and many rules of the law merchant were included in the Common Law. The most important mercantile customs recognized were that a bill of exchange was negotiable and that mere agreements should be binding as contracts. In this way, the custom of merchants relating to negotiable formal legal document and contracts including the sale of goods became part of the Common Law, and later, an established method of statute law in the Bills of Exchange Act 1882, and the Sale of Good Act 1979.

1.1.2.7 Canon Law

Canon law is a body of laws of a Christian church. A set of church decrees regulating morals or religious practices. Before 1857 the church courts dealt with offences against the church doctrine and morality. The church courts also dealt with other matters such as matrimonial legitimacy and the inheritance of property when a person died. Many of these matters were eventually transferred to the civil courts. In 1970, the civil courts concerned were combined with the Family Division of the High Court. Today, the church courts deal with disciplinary and moral offences committed by the clergy, parish clerks, churchwardens and certain other matters.

1.1.2.8 Early Writers in Law

Great jurists have written law books over the years, which have contributed to the development of law and the legal profession.

Sir Edward Coke (1552–1624) contributed a lot to legal literature. His writings covered many aspects of law. His first book, which was published in 1628, was concerned with Land Law. His second, published in 1642 was written on the Principal Statutes. The third, in 1644, on Criminal Law, and the fourth, also published in 1644 was on the Jurisdiction and History of the Courts. During his lifetime, Sir Edward Coke was a Recorder in London, Solicitor-General, Speaker of the House of Commons, Attorney General and finally Chief Justice of Common Pleas.

Other prominent writers like Sir William Blackstone (1723–80), published his commentaries in 1765. He wrote on various aspects of law, which were based on his lectures at Oxford. He was also the first Professor of English Law to lecture in any English Universities.

The works of older and modern writers are sometimes quoted when fresh or new points of law are being discussed in the courts.

1.2 THE LAW-MAKING PROCESS

1.2.1 The Law-Making Body

Much of United Kingdom Law is contained in the Acts of Parliament. Parliament consists of two chambers – the House of Lords and the House of Commons. The House of Commons consists of 651 members, each of whom represents a geographical area in the country called a constituency. They are Members of Parliament (MP's) who are elected at general elections. The House of Lords on the other hand consists of peers. Under the provisions of the Life Peerages Act 1958, there has been an addition of distinguished people from various walks of life who hold life peerages, but whose descendants will have no right to a seat when the life peers are dead.

In addition to the Lord's Temporal, there are also the Lord's Spiritual e.g. the Archbishops of Canterbury and York and certain other Bishops. Over one thousand people are eligible to sit in the House of Lords. When Parliament is in session (usually a year), a large number of Bills become Law, most of which are Government Bills. The government is formed by the parliamentary party, having an overall majority; the government is led by the Prime Minister who appoints a variety of other ministers such as the Chancellor of the Exchequer, the Home Secretary, the Foreign Secretary and others to manage various departments of the state. A group of these ministers (called the Cabinet), meet frequently under the Chairmanship of the Prime Minister and formulate the policy of the government. An important part of this policy consists of presenting Bills to Parliament with a view of them becoming Law.

Such Bills are usually presented by the minister of the department concerned with their contents. Most government bills are introduced in the House of Commons, going later to the House of Lords and finally for the Royal Assent.

1.2.2 The Procedure for making the Bill

An Act of Parliament begins as a Bill. The legal meaning of the Bill is a draft of a proposed new law presented by a law making body (Parliament) for discussion. Before it can become law, any Bill introduced into the House of Commons must go through five distinct procedures. They consist of the first reading, second reading, committee stage, report stage and then the third reading.

Bills are divided into public and private. A Public and Private Members' Bill follow the same procedures in Parliament. Bills may be introduced in either house. A Finance Bill is a Public Bill certified by the speaker as one containing provision relating to taxations or loans. It must be introduced in the Commons by a minister and not by a private member. The following procedure relates to a Private or Public Bill introduced in the Commons.

The Bill is normally read three times and debated on in Parliament. It may be accepted or rejected. On its introduction, the Bill first receives a formal reading. Only the title of the Bill is read out by the clerk of the House. The purpose of this stage is to tell members that the Bill exists and that the date is set for the second reading. It is then printed and published. It is later given a second reading, at which point its general merits may be debated, but no amendments are proposed to the various clauses it contains. There is an alternative procedure for the second reading of Public Bills, which is designed to save Parliamentary time.

Having survived the second reading, the Bill passes to the committee stage. Here, details are discussed by the Standing Committee of members chosen from the various parties in the House of Commons. Amendments to the clauses are proposed and if not accepted by the government are voted on. The Bills return to the

House at the report stage. If the legislation is quite important, the Bill may return to a committee of the whole House. Certain Bills in the Commons may be sent to a Special Standing Committee, which is given power to hear evidence from outsiders, thus following to some extent the procedure for Private Bills.

At the report stage, the amendments may be debated and the Bills may in some cases be referred back to the House for further consideration. After passing the third reading, the Bill is said to have 'Passed the House'. It is then sent to the House of Lords where it goes through a similar procedure. If the Lords propose amendment, the Bill is sent to the Commons for approval. At one time, the House of Lords had the power to reject the Bills sent to them by the Commons. Now, under the provisions of the Parliament Acts 1911 and 1949, this power amounts to no more than an ability to delay a Public Bill for a period of one year. A Finance Bill may be delayed for one month only.

A Bill requires a Royal Assent after passing through the Commons and the Lords. It is not customary for the monarch to consent in person. In practice, consent is given by a committee of three peers; including the Lord Chancellor. The Royal Assent Act 1967 provides that an Act is duly enacted and becomes law if the Royal Assent is notified to each House of Parliament, sitting separately by the Speaker of that House or the acting Speaker.

The Bill is then referred to as an Act or Statute or as a source of law. An Act may specify a future date for its coming into operation, or it may be brought into operation by ministerial order. The courts have no power to examine proceedings in Parliament as to whether the passing of the Act or delegated legislation has been obtained by means of any irregularity.

Each Act has under the provisions of the Short Titles Act 1896, a short title to enable easy reference to be made. The Act of Parliament Numbering and Citation Act 1962, provides that chapter numbers assigned to Acts of Parliament passed in 1963 and after shall be assigned by reference to the calendar year and not the session in which they are passed. For example, the official reference of the Sale of Goods Act 1979, c 54, means the fifty-fourth statute.

1.2.3 The Origin of the Acts of Parliament (Legislation)

Parliamentary legislation became more general in the fourteenth century. Parliament first asked the king to legislate, but later it presented a bill in its own wording. The development of modern procedure in particular became more popular during the Tudor times, in the reign of the English royal house that ruled from 1485 to1603.

From the Tudor period onwards, parliament became more and more independent and the practice of law making by statute increased. Parliament's increasing involvement with economic and social affairs increased the need for statutes. A statute is the most significant source of law, and even if a statute is incompatible with the Common Law or equity, the statute should succeed. It is such an important source that it has been said; "A statute can do anything except to turn a man into a woman," and no court can dispute the validity of the Act of Parliament.

Right from the start, the Common Law was not sufficient. What was once a good rule is not necessarily a good rule today. So a means of altering the Common Law was required. This was done in Parliament where bills were brought in to say that instead of the law being this it will now be that. Once a bill is passed, it becomes an Act of Parliament. Whereas the Common Law is only to be in the principles on which past cases were decided. An Act of Parliament sets out a new law in so many words. However, no matter how carefully an Act of Parliament is worded, when it comes to be applied to particular situations, it is not always quite clear what its words mean. So it becomes necessary to interpret the act as it applies to the particular circumstances. Once this has been done, the meaning of that bit of the act becomes clearer and the decision is a precedent (previous case or legal decision etc., taken as a guide for subsequent cases).

Acts of Parliament are also known as statutes. They frequently provide that in matters of detail, a minister of the crown can make specific regulations. Statute Law and Common Law are interpreted by the judges. They deal with individual cases, in many of which there is an argument about what the law is. One side will say the law is so and so, supporting their argument by referring to previous cases on similar points. His adversary in the case will argue the other way, and will also refer to previous cases. The judge will then give his decision, stating his reasons in detail. His decision then becomes part of the law and will be referred to as a precedent in future cases when a similar point comes to be argued. If the case ends up as one of the few that is determined by the Supreme Court (the ultimate appeal court), it will almost certainly be a precedent of importance. We still have the Common Law, but some branches of it have been considerably altered by Parliament.

Much of the law that affects consumers is derived from Acts of Parliament and decisions of courts on their interpretation. Some of it are derived from the Common Law, untouched by Acts of Parliament. No court or any other body can dispute the validity of an Act of Parliament.

Statute law can be used to abolish Common Law rules which have outlived their usefulness, or to amend the Common Law to cope with the changing circumstances and values of the society. Once enacted, statutes even if obsolete do not cease to have the force of law but common sense usually prevents most obsolete laws from being invoked. In addition, statutes which are no longer of practical utility are repealed from time to time by Statute Law Repeal Acts. A statute stands as law until it is specifically repealed by Parliament.

An Act of Parliament is absolutely binding on everyone within the sphere of its jurisdiction. All Acts of Parliament can be repealed by the same or subsequent Parliaments; and this is the only exception to the rule of the absolute sovereignty of Parliament – it cannot bind itself or its successors.

1.2.4 Delegated Legislation (Subordinate Legislation)

This is where a duty of responsibility is given to someone who is chosen to represent a group of people. For example, (a government minister to the civil servant).under the authority of the government minister, the civil servant under his ministry is entrusted with duties and powers to work on statutes and interpret them in the light of the parent act and implement them in his department. The legislation only gives a general provision of a complex nature, and a large number of the detailed regulations have to be made by civil servants under the authority of the Minister. The regulations when made and approved are considered as law.

This form of law is known as delegated or subordinate legislation. Delegated Legislation has many advantages:

- Delegated Legislation saves parliamentary time in that ministers are left with the civil service to make detailed rules. Parliament concerns itself with the broad framework of the legislation.
- The parliamentary procedure for enacting bills is slow whereas rules and orders can be put more rapidly, particularly in times of national emergency.
- Parliament may not foresee all the problems that may arise after an act has become law. Delegated Legislation can deal with these when they arise.
- Delegated Legislation is less rigid in that it can be withdrawn quickly by another statutory instrument if it proves impossible to put into practice.

1.2.5 Types of Delegated Legislation

In modern statutes, delegated powers are used by four main bodies as follows:

(a) <u>Statutory Instruments:</u> Most powers given to ministers in modern statutes can be put into use by ministerial or departmental regulations or orders called collective instruments.

(b) <u>Orders in Council:</u> Powers of special importance relating to constitutional issues. The powers are in fact exercised by Cabinet who are all Privy Councillors.

(c) <u>Bye-laws of local authorities:</u> These are made by authorities under powers given to them in Acts of Parliament and require the approval of the appropriate minister.

(d) <u>Rules of the Supreme Court and County Court:</u> These are made by Rules Committees set up by statute specifically to make rules concerning the practice and procedures of the courts. The Rules Committees are made up of judges and senior members of the legal profession.

1.3 THE MAIN CLASSIFICATION OF ENGLISH LAW

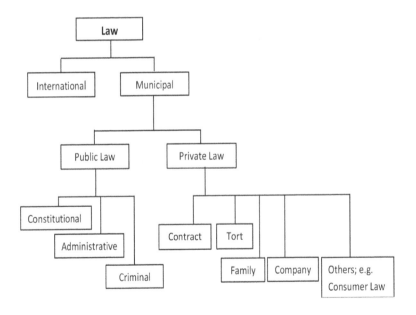

1.3.1 Public Law

Public Law concerns itself with those branches of law which involve the state. It is concerned with the constitution and functions of the many different kinds of governmental organizations, including central and local government departments of authorities. Obviously, a business may become involved in a public law dispute, for example in a case of a planning matter where the business requires additional premises for expansion. Public law is also concerned with crime, which involves the state's relationship with the power of control over individuals. Civil law includes the whole of private law and all divisions of public law except criminal law.

1.3.1.1 Constitutional Law

This branch of law controls the constitution and the structure of the organs of central and local government. Constitutional Law therefore comprises the law which relates to such topics as the method of electing the Sovereign and defines his or her powers and the status of ministers and their relationship with the civil service through which they act.

1.3.1.2 Administrative Law

There is no firm line between constitutional and administrative law. The latter comprises the rules that govern the exercise of executive functions by authorities and officers to whom such functions have been entrusted by the constitution. It is particularly important in the context of the subject matter of this book with respect to the powers of local authorities etc., in the exercise of their duties of granting alcohol licences and the powers of supervision granted to them.

1.3.1.3 Criminal Law

The state has recognized from very early times that certain types of human behaviour which cause injury or loss to individuals are detrimental to the community as well as to the individual concerned. An acknowledged definition of a criminal offence is that, it is a wrong whose sanction is punitive and in no way remissible by the court. A criminal proceeding can only be abandoned by the courts, if at all. A civil action can only be settled out of court even after proceedings have commenced. The original idea of a criminal offence was that the relevant behaviour involved an extreme breach of a moral rule.

1.3.2 Private Law

Private law deals with the legal relationships between a business and its employees and customers and with individuals who are not in either of these categories but who may be injured in a physical or financial way by its activities. It is concerned with the legal relationships of ordinary persons in everyday transactions. A person injured by the negligent driving of a vehicle belonging to a business has an action against the business under private law.

Private law in its numerous branches exists to enable private, as opposed to state, redress to be taken against individuals who cause personal injury, damage to property or in any other way infringe upon the public rights of other persons. The redress obtainable through the courts is usually in a form of damages to compensate the injured party for the loss he has suffered. Although in appropriate cases the court can award an equitable remedy, which can have the effect of ordering action by the offending party to restore the original position between the parties. The branches of private law, which relate to the practices of a hotelier or a caterer are the law of tort and the law of contract. Private law includes contract and commercial law, the law of tort, family law e.g. divorce, adoption, guardianship, trusts and the law of property, which involves a consideration of the rights which can exist in property and how property can be transferred from one person to another.

1.3.2.1 Tort

A tort is a civil wrong independent of contract. It arises out of a duty imposed by law, and a person who commits a tortious act does not voluntarily undertake the liabilities that the law imposes on him. That an individual living within a community has a duty to be careful with regard to the person, property and rights of his fellow citizens has been recognized since the earliest forms of society emerged. The Law of Tort is therefore the earliest form of law, and it is the root from which criminal law and the law of contract eventually emerged. There are many kinds of tort with common characteristics: injury of some kind inflicted by one person on another. Nuisance, trespass, slander and libel are well known civil wrongs.

1.3.2.2 Contract Law

A contract comes into existence when two or more parties enter into an agreement, through which each will gain or expect to gain an advantage from the others, and the agreement is intended to have legal consequences. So if a breach occurs, the unsatisfied party can take action in the appropriate court. Sometimes this possibility is eliminated by a qualification in the agreement that it will be a gentleman's agreement. Again, it is obvious that this branch of law governs agreements made between a hotelier and his customers as well as a hotelier and his employees.

1.3.2.3 Family Law

Family Law deals with matrimonial cases as well as wardship and adoption of children.

1.3.2.4 Company Law

The High Court deals with company cases.

1.3.2.5 Consumer Law

The law is vast and complex, more so nowadays than ever before. All branches of the law tend to merge and overlap. The legal protection of the consumer is derived from both the criminal law and the civil law. For example, the Food and Drugs Act contains provisions of vital importance to consumers. Suppose a caterer sells to you a mouldy meat pie and you eat it and become ill, under the Food and Drugs Act, it is a criminal offence to sell food that is unfit for human consumption. The caterer may therefore be prosecuted in the magistrate court. If the court is satisfied that the meat pie sold to you was unfit for human consumption, the caterer will be found guilty of the offence under the act and probably fined.

The court where all these take place cannot give you any compensation. You will have to bring a civil action against him in a County Court or the High Court. For the Food and Drugs Act is concerned with criminal matters and these courts deal with civil ones only. However, you will nevertheless probably be awarded damages, because the caterer has infringed your right as the buyer to get food that is edible.

1.4 CIVIL AND CRIMINAL LAW

1.4.1 Civil and Criminal wrongs

The Supreme Court of Judicature established a two-tier system of supreme courts. The courts are divided into two streams: those administering Civil Justice as well as those administering Criminal Justice. The rules have the authority of the Supreme Body in the state. That supreme body should have the ability to enforce their observance and give punishment through a court when a breach of the law occurs. Breach of certain legal rules is visited by punishment of the lawbreaker. We call these the 'rules of criminal law'.

Breach of other rules of law however, does not lead to punishment, but entitles the person who has some interest in the observance of the rule to have his right protected by a court of law. This is done by having either monetary damages awarded to him or by receiving a court order, which requires the rule breaker to rectify their breach by other means. These are the rules of civil law. No individual can escape the operation of law and perhaps that is why it is important for the proprietors of the hospitality industry to have a working knowledge of the technical areas of law that are concerned with food, drink and accommodation etc.

It is worthless to say that you must not steal, without going on to say that if you do, you will be punished. Some people would appreciate it if they were not made uncomfortable to disobey. Sometimes, both set of rules apply, because the same circumstances can amount to a criminal offence and also be the subject matter of a civil claim. For example, being injured by dangerous driving – a matter of criminal law under the Road Traffic Act. At the same time, the driver can be sued for compensation for the injuries, which the passenger suffered – a matter of civil law.

There are some criminal offences which cannot give rise to civil claim, because in theory, no individual is harmed by them. Examples of these are treason and perjury. There are matters which only give rise to civil claims and not criminal offences, such as failure to pay a debt. The law aims at protecting the whole community and the civil law gives rights to the individual.

1.4.2 Civil and Criminal Proceedings

In criminal proceedings, a prosecutor prosecutes a defendant. If he is successful, it results in the conviction of the defendant. After the conviction, the court may deal with the defendant by giving him a custodial sentence, e.g. prison or a non-custodial sentence, e.g. probation. In rare cases, the court may discharge the defendant without sentence.

As regards to civil proceedings, a plaintiff sues (brings action against) a defendant. If the plaintiff is successful, this leads to the court entering judgement ordering the defendant to pay a debt owed to the plaintiff or money damages.

Alternatively, it may require the defendant to transfer property to the plaintiff or to do or not to do something (injunction) or to perform a contract (specific performance). Some of these remedies are legal and others equitable.

1.5 THE COURTS OF LAW IN ENGLAND AND WALES

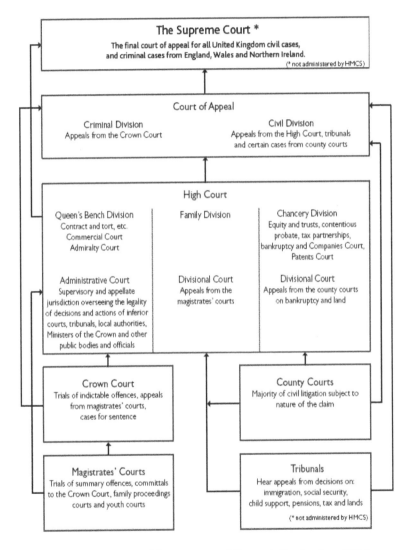

Fig. 1.5.1 A diagram of the structure of Courts in England and Wales

1.5.1 Supreme Court (The House of Lords)

The House of Lords comprises of the Lord Chancellor, nine specially appointed Lords of Appeal in Ordinary and peers who hold or have held high judicial office. The court hears appeals from both divisions of the court of appeal. An appeal to the House of Lords requires a certificate from the lower court qualifying the case as an appropriate one for examination by the House of Lords, that is, concerning a point of law of general public importance.

1.5.2 Court of Appeal

In Britain, not until 1966, the court of appeal considered appeals from courts of civil jurisdiction only. The Criminal Appeal Act 1966 merged the Court of Criminal Appeal into the Court of Appeal forming two divisions in that court. They include the Civil Division and the Criminal Division. Judges who are entitled to sit in both divisions of the court are the Lord Chancellor, the Lord Chief Justice, the Master of Rolls as well as the Lord of Appeal in Ordinary. But the Master of Rolls is the head of the court and he sits habitually. The permanent judge of the court is the Lord Justices of Appeal in Ordinary. Since incorporation of the Criminal Appeal Division, the Lord Chief Justice sits in that division with Lords of Ordinary and selected judges of the high court. Appeals are heard from the High Court and the County Court in the Civil Division and from the Crown Courts in the Criminal Division.

1.5.3 The High Court

The High Court deals with Common Law litigation such as breaches of contract and actions in tort. It also deals with matters concerning partnerships, mortgages, trusts, companies and some revenue and bankruptcy matters. The High Courts also deal with family matters such as matrimonial disputes and the care, adoption or guardianship of children.

In appeal by case stated, the complete written statements of evidence are submitted to the Divisional Court so that the judges can decide upon the point of law which the Lower Courts are uncertain.

This appellate jurisdiction can be exercised by two judges without a jury.

1.5.4 The Crown Court
In England and Wales, the Crown Court has the power to act anywhere and is in continuous session within six circuits which give complete converge of the whole territory concerned. The act provides that each circuit (the route and places visited regularly by a judge) shall have a High Court Judge allocated to it. Each circuit has within it a number of courts whose jurisdiction is classified into three tiers. First – tier courts deal with both civil and criminal cases and are served by High Court and Circuit Court Judges or Recorders. Second-tier courts whilst supervised by High Court and Circuit Court Judges can hear criminal cases only. The jurisdictions of third-tier courts is limited to less grave criminal cases and are served by Circuit Judges or Recorders.

1.5.5 The County Court
County Courts hear minor civil disputes and relieve pressure in the Common Law Court. Appeals from the County Court are sent to the Court of Appeal (Civil Division).

1.5.6 The Magistrates' Court
The Magistrates' Courts Act 1952 defines a Magistrates' Courts as any justice or justices of the peace acting under any enactment (written law) or by virtue of his or her commission or under Common Law. Most magistrates or justices of the peace are appointed by the Lord Chancellor and on the recommendation of the local authority within whose boundaries they will serve and from lay members of the community. Magistrates' Courts although they have numerous administrative functions and jurisdiction in civil disputes, deal mainly with the trial of criminal offenders. It can try summary offences, which can be tried summarily and can impose sentences of imprisonment of up to six months. It acts as an examining court in connection with more serious cases that is those which have to be tried on indictment before a Crown Court.

This means that all evidence in connection with the case must be presented to the magistrates who must decide whether or not there is a prima facie (Latin) case against the accused person. If they decide that there is a prima facie case (on the face of it), the accused is indicted to stand trial at the Crown Court. If not, the accused must be discharged.

One of the main administrative functions of magistrates is to control the licensing of hotels and other catering establishments through a specially appointed committee.

1.5.7 Tribunals
A board appointed to adjudicate in some matter, especially one appointed by the government to investigate a matter of public concern.

1.6 THE STRUCTURE OF COURTS IN GHANA

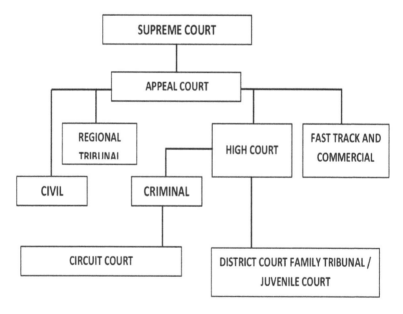

Fig 1.6.1 – A diagram of the Structure of Courts in Ghana

1.6 JUDICIAL SYSTEM (JUDICIAL SERVICE COUNCIL OF GHANA)

1.6.1 The Ghanaian Legal System

Ghana's legal system takes its roots from the British Common Law tradition and it is supplemented by various legislation on specific issues. Accordingly, Ghana's legal system has all the attributes and safeguards for the protection of property and human freedom, all of which are inherent attributes of the Common Law tradition.

1.6.2 The Judicial System

The civil law in force in Ghana is based on Common Law doctrines of equity and general statutes, which were in force in England in 1874, as modified by subsequent ordinances. Ghanaian customary law is however, the basis of most personal, domestic and contractual relationships. Criminal law is based on the criminal procedure code 1960, derived from English criminal law and since amended.

1.6.3 The Court Structure

Since independence in 1957, the court system headed by the Chief Justice has demonstrated extraordinary independence and resilience. The structure and jurisdiction of the courts was defined by the Courts Act of 1971, which established the Supreme Court of Ghana, the Court of Appeal (Appellate Court) with two divisions – ordinary bench and full bench, as well as the High Court of Justice (or simply the High Court) and a Regional Tribunal.

The High Court is a court with both appellate and original jurisdiction. The Act also established the inferior courts which include circuit courts, community tribunal, circuit tribunals and such other courts as may be designed by law, along with the above courts constituted the judiciary of Ghana according to the 1960; 1979 and 1992 constitutions.

Until mid–1993, the inferior courts, in descending order of importance were the circuit courts, the district courts (Magistrate Courts) grade I and II and juvenile courts. Such courts existed mostly in cities and large urban centres. In mid-1993, however, Parliament created a new system of lower courts, consisting of circuit tribunals and community tribunals in place of the former circuit courts and district (magistrate) courts. The traditional courts are the National House of Chiefs, the Regional Houses of Chiefs and traditional councils, the traditional courts are constituted by the judicial committees of the various houses and councils. All courts, both superior and inferior, with the exception of traditional courts are vested with jurisdiction in civil and criminal matters. The traditional courts have the exclusive power to adjudicate any cause or matter affecting chieftaincy as defined by the Chieftaincy Act of 1971.

Judicial appointments are made by the Chief Justice on the advice of the independent judicial council of Ghana and are subject to governmental approval. The PNDC establishment proclamation abolished the judicial council, but it was re-established by the 1992 constitution.

Chapter Two

DIFFERENTIATION BETWEEN HOTELS AND OTHER CATERING ESTABLISHMENTS

2.1 EARLY LEGISLATION DESIGNED TO REGULATE INNS AND OTHER CATERING ESTABLISHMENTS IN THE FOURTEENTH CENTURY

Inns and other catering establishments invited legislation designed to regulate them at quite an early date. Publicans were compelled by law to put up a sign, although with other trades this was optional. In the fourteenth century, concern was expressed at excessive number of taverns.

In the reigns of Edward II and III, many alehouses and taverns were closed and only a limited number allowed. At this time, the people petitioned the Parliament about excessive prices, and the King intervened accordingly. In 1349, Edward III officially declared the introduction of a statute compelling all Inns to make reasonable charges. Offenders shall be liable to pay penalty refund to the cheated guest double the sum taken from him.

Four years later, another stronger law was passed to put an end to the great outrageous cost of food or other provisions charged in the country by innkeepers and other retailers to the great detriment of the people travelling across the country. Mayors and justices were charged to inquire in all places of the "deeds" and outrageous charges of Innkeepers and their kind and to deal with them summarily. This disgraceful behaviour appears to have been settled by the innkeepers themselves.

The predecessor of the Food and Drugs legislation was designed in the fourteenth and fifteen centuries to counter the adulteration of wine and practice of the cheaper cook shops, particularly common in London, of preparing pies and other dishes from an undesirable quality of meat.

2.2 WHAT IS A HOTEL? DEFINITION AND MEANING

We need to know the exact definition and meaning of the word "hotel" to enable us to examine the laws governing hotels.

2.2.1 The Standard Industrial Classification 1968, UK
The Standard Industrial Classification 1968 defines the accommodation sector of the hospitality industry as consisting of hotels, motels, holiday camps, guest houses, boarding houses, hostels and similar establishments providing furnished accommodation with food and service for reward.

2.2.2 The Oxford Dictionary
The Oxford dictionary defines a hotel as a building or establishment where travellers or tourists are provided with overnight accommodation, meals, and other services. Hotels may be distinguished from other forms of temporary lodging for travellers by their larger size and range of facilities, now often being equipped with a restaurant, bar, conference rooms and leisure facilities. The term is also widely used to refer to smaller establishments.

2.2.3 The Business Dictionary
The Business dictionary defines hotel as commercial establishment providing lodging, meals, and other guest services. In general, to be called a hotel, an establishment must have a minimum of six letting bedrooms in which at least three of which must have attached private bathroom facilities.

2.2.4 The Legal Definition of a Hotel

By s.1 (3) of the Hotel Proprietors Act 1956, the word hotel is defined and explained in detail as follows:

'A hotel is an establishment held out by the proprietor as offering food and drink, and if so required, sleeping accommodation without a special contract to any traveller presenting himself, who appears able and willing to pay a reasonable sum for the services and facilities provided, and who is in a fit state to be received.'

This means that only those establishments, who are willing to receive guests at any time of the day or night, can in fact be classified as hotels. Travellers who have not previously booked accommodation (without special contract) are regarded as travellers by law. Other establishments, using the word 'hotel' are not for legal purposes. For an establishment to qualify as a hotel depends upon the following requirements being satisfied.

2.3 EXPLANATION OF TERMS WITHIN THE LEGAL DEFINITION OF THE WORD HOTEL

2.3.1 Definition of a traveller

A traveller is a person who uses the hotel temporarily or for a more permanent stay in order to make use of the services the inn can provide. He may stay an hour, a night, a week or even a few months. At one time the term traveller merely referred to people who stayed at an inn during the course of their journey for food and lodging. But nowadays the meaning is extended and can include local residents who call in just for meal.

Case Law – William v Bush 1951; where a farmer who resided within one mile of the defendant's inn and who frequently called in for a drink was held to be a traveller and as such entitled to the protection given by the Common Law to a guest.

Although a person may be a '*traveller*' when he first arrives at a hotel he may cease to be one at a later stage. He then takes on the character of a lodger or a boarder. Then the Common Law duty of the proprietor to entertain him ceases. The relationship is then based upon the Law of Contract and the lodger can be evicted after being given reasonable notice to leave.

If the rule were otherwise then a guest would have the right to stay provided he pays his bills and complies with the hotel regulations, to stay in the hotel till whenever he wants to leave, while the hotel proprietor would be bound to provide him with boarding and lodging without any right to give him notice to quit .

Case Law – Lamond v. Richmond 1897; A lady of a good character was given notice to quit a hotel where she had been staying for seven months. She had paid her bills regularly but was disturbing the other visitors, as she was under a delusion that enemies were seeking to injure her. She claimed that she had a right to remain in the hotel. Even though the hotel had unoccupied rooms, and her room was not needed for anyone yet, she was told to quit based on what the hotel complained to the court. It was held that she had ceased to be a traveller and that the notice to quit was valid.

All travellers are entitled to be received irrespective of sex, creed or colour. It is submitted that if a proprietor refuses to accept children as such then his establishment cannot be classified as a hotel. The proprietor may not pick and choose his guests. He holds himself out as being willing to receive all visitors.

Case Law – In Constantine v. Imperial Hotels [1944]; Mr. Learie Constantine, the West Indian cricketer was awarded damages by the court after being refused a hotel room without any just cause. The fact that he was able to secure a room into another hotel belonging to the same company was said to be no excuse for its behaviour.

The Common Law rule is now strengthened by s.2 of Race Relations Act 1968 which makes it unlawful for a person to discriminate on the ground of colour, race or ethnic or national origins, in the provision of accommodation in a hotel, boarding house or other similar establishment and in the provision of facilities for refreshment.

2.3.2 Without a special contract
A traveller is entitled to walk into a hotel and make use of the amenities offered without having come to an arrangement with the proprietor in advance. The proprietor only discharges his liability if he has reasonable grounds for refusal. Failure to book in advance is not sufficient justification to refuse service to the traveller. This is one distinguishing feature of a hotel. Private and residential hotels differ in that; they enter into a contract with their guests to accommodate them, the condition under which the guest stays in such a hotel being governed by the terms of contract.

2.3.3 At a reasonable price
The duty of the proprietor is to charge his guests reasonable prices, little if any guidance can be gained from old case law on what is reasonable except that he is entitled to charge such rates as will give him a reasonable profit. However, size, locality and amenities offered by a hotel are all factors to be taken into account.

2.3.4 In a fit state to be received
Any caller suffering from an infectious disease which is noticeable – for example, chicken pox – or any caller who is drunk and behaving disorderly or improperly can certainly be refused. It must not be thought that the Common Law rules were devised solely for the benefit of the traveller. The Innkeeper was given a protection against the dishonest travellers (unless justified in refusing). He did not have to trust them and was entitled to demand a reasonable sum, in advance as payment. This undoubtedly was the forerunner of the present day deposit. In fact, some hotels now go as far as to ask their guests to pay their bill in full, or in advance.

Furthermore Common Law remedies were and still are available to the Innkeeper against the guest who refuses to pay his bill.

2.4 CLASSIFICATION OF HOTELS AND OTHER CATERING ESTABLISHMENTS

2.4.1 Distinguishing between hotels and other catering establishments

The distinction between a hotel and other establishments is not an easy one. The following points explain some of the difficulties.

The fact that the word 'inn' or 'hotel' appears in the name is not a conclusive test neither presumably it is the use of the word 'motel' but it is probable that the very purpose of a motel is mainly to attract the passing motorist. This means that, motels are generally within the definition of a hotel.

The general assumption is that public houses are not hotels: the majority of them do not supply sleeping accommodation. But of course a public house which also provides food and sleeping accommodation could come within the definition.

Private hotels for example, boarding houses, guest houses and hostels are generally excluded. Many of them do have some characteristics of a hotel. For example, they may hold a licence for liquor and they must keep a register, but cannot serve either drinks or give accommodation to casual callers.

A Restaurant is not a 'hotel' as it does not provide sleeping accommodation. However, a restaurant forming part of a hotel and not having a separate entrance is part of the hotel.

Case Law – In Orchard v. Bush 1898, the plaintiff called into the defendant's hotel for a meal, he was not intending to stay overnight. After he had eaten, he discovered his coat, which he hung in the restaurant was missing. The plea by the defendant that the restaurant did not form part of the hotel and therefore the defendant was not liable for the coat failed.

The keeping of a hotel register is not a conclusive test, as occupiers of any premises where lodging or sleeping accommodation is provided for must keep a register.

It can be seen that even though an establishment may have some characteristics of a hotel, unless the proprietor holds himself up as prepared to receive, feed and if necessary accommodate all travellers or casual callers, then the place in question is not a hotel. A hotel must not pick and choose its guest, but a private hotel (boarding houses, guest houses, hostels) can. In fact, every place that takes in occasional guests for bed and breakfast. The private hotelier may choose his guest and can decide which guests to accept together with terms upon which he will receive them. No guest can demand as of right, to be received into a private hotel even though there are vacancies. The hotel proprietor must accept as guests all people who are travellers and entertain them at a reasonable price without any special contract, unless he has some special grounds for refusal.

2.4.2 Classification by the Business Dictionary and the official Hotel Guide

Although hotels are classified into 'star' categories (1 – star to 5-star), there is no standard method of assigning these ratings, and compliance with customary requirements is voluntary.

A hotel based in the United States with a certain rating may look very different from a European or Asian hotel with the same rating and would provide different level of amenities, range of facilities and quality of service. Whereas a chain of hotels can assure uniform standards throughout, non-chain hotels (even within the same country) may not agree on the same standards.

In Germany, only about 30 percent of the hotels choose to comply with the provisions of the rules established by the German Hotels and Restaurants Association. Although both World Tourism Organization [WTO]and ISO have tried to persuade hotels to agree on some minimum requirements as world-wide norms, the entire membership of the Paris-based International Hotel and Restaurant (IH&RA) opposes any such move.

According to IH & RA, to harmonize hotel classification based on a single grading (which is uniform across national boundaries) would be an undesirable and impossible task. As a rough guide:

A **1-Star hotel** provides a limited range of amenities and services, but adheres to a high standard of facility-wide cleanliness.

A **2-Star hotel** provides good accommodation and better equipped bedrooms, each with a telephone and attached private bathroom,

A **3-Star Hotel** has more spacious rooms and adds high-class decorations and furnishings and a colour TV. It also offers one or more bars or lounges.

A **4-Star Hotel** is much more comfortable and larger, and provides excellent cuisine (table d'hôte and àla carte), room service, and other amenities.

A **5-Star Hotel** offers most luxurious premises, widest range of guest services, as well as a swimming pool and sport and exercise facilities.

2.4.3 Classification by the Official Hotel Guide

Published in the United States and followed worldwide, the official Hotel Guide has its own classification scheme that ranks hotel in nine categories as:

(1) Moderate Tourist Class
(2) Tourist Class
(3) Superior Tourist Class
(4) Moderate First Class
(5) Limited Service First Class
(6) First Class
(7) Moderate Deluxe
(8) Deluxe, and
(9) Superior Deluxe.

2.5 BASIS OF CLASSIFICATION

In recent years, hotels and hostels have been on the increase. It appears this is confusing the general public. It is therefore necessary to help classify these establishments.

In the analysis of an industry into its component sectors, establishments are grouped into reasonably homogeneous divisions according to their most important characteristics, which are normally determined by their respective functions. This is an industry in which many establishments engage in a combination of activities, and certainly so with establishments providing hotel and catering services, where there is a two-fold explanation for the lack of clear-cut specialization.

Since some hotel and catering services are often in joint demand, either as food and accommodation, or drink with a meal, it makes it necessary and desirable that they should be provided together. Classification of the hotel and catering industry into its component sectors then becomes a difficult one.

The fact that many establishments engage in a combination of activities, and that it is frequently difficult to determine the main one with any accuracy, would still present problems of some kind. There is, therefore, much to be said for a broad division of the industry into a small number of sectors each comprising units sharing important common characteristics and carrying on broadly comparable activities.

The Standard Industrial Classification 1968 meets the needs of this study by dividing the industry into five sectors:

- Hotels and other residential establishments
- Restaurants, Cafes and Snack bars
- Public houses
- Clubs
- Catering contractors

Each of the sectors is described as follows;

2.5.1 Hotels and other Residential Establishments
The Standard Industrial Classification defines the accommodation sector of the industry as consisting of boarding houses, hostels, holiday camps, hotels, motels, guesthouses and similar establishments providing furnished accommodation with food and service for reward. It excludes licensed or residential clubs, which are classified to the club sector. We are, therefore, principally concerned with

establishments meeting the accommodation demand of travellers and temporary residence.

Three main problems present themselves as described below:
The first is between the accommodation sector of the industry, and the provision of accommodation on a tenancy basis. In order to qualify for inclusion in the scope of the industry, an establishment must provide some food and service for its residents for reward. Although this distinction may be sometimes difficult to draw in practice, it does exclude establishments whose primary function is the letting of flats and similar accommodation, whether furnished or not, and whether either for holiday or other use, which places them in the property ownership and management sector, rather than in the hotel and catering industry.

The second difficulty arises with an establishment with a small amount of sleeping accommodation to let, which merges into something else, because the provision of meals and refreshment constitutes its principal activity, to which the letting of a few beds is merely ancillary, and which may be called a hotel, an inn, a public house among others. In most countries, a minimum accommodation capacity is adopted in defining an accommodation unit although the minimum requirement varies.

The third problem is to find a point at which the private house, letting rooms to visitors should be regarded as being either a guesthouse or a boarding house, and thus a part of the accommodation sector of the industry.

On this issue, the Catering Wages Commission felt that the minimum accommodation of four or eight should be ordinarily available as sleeping accommodation for guest or lodgers.

Another line of demarcation is provided by the Fire Precaution's Order which covers premises providing sleeping accommodation for more than six persons, guests or staff.

The variety of establishments within this sector is considerable. Moreover, as there are no rules of law prohibiting the use of various designations unless certain conditions are satisfied, the name given to the establishment does not necessarily provide a reliable guide to its nature.

The Legal Definition of Hotel

The legal definition of a hotel which has been embodied in the Hotel Proprietors Act, 1956 for instance, describes a *'hotel as an establishment held out by the proprietor as offering food, drink and, if so required, sleeping accommodation, without special contract, to any traveller presenting himself who appears able and willing to pay a reasonable sum for the services and facilities provided, and who is in a fit state to be received.'*

Thus in law, all residential establishments fall into one of two classes, hotels within the meaning of the Act on the one hand, and others which are usually for convenience described as 'private hotels'.

The distinction is of importance mainly in determining the proprietor's duty to receive travellers and his responsibility for guests' property. The Act does not make it impossible to use the name 'hotel' and its use does not make an establishment an hotel in the legal sense. The proprietor can choose to call his establishment whatever name and manage it as he chooses. If he decides to conduct it as a hotel within the meaning of the 1956 Act subject to certain exception he must receive all travellers and accept responsibility for their property; he also has a lien on his guests' property in respect of unpaid bills. A private hotelier on the other hand has no such obligations; neither can he detain his guests' property for unpaid bills. However, subject to this qualification, the hotel usually provides accommodation, meals, and refreshments for irregular periods of time for those who may reserve the accommodation in advance and also to casual callers. An establishment must meet the demands of the modern traveller.

Hostels and Boarding Houses

Hostels are even more distinguished from hotels by the length of stay of their residents, which tends to be still greater than in the case of a boarding house. The same is true of lodging houses. In practice, many of these become boarding houses for a part of the year, only to go back to their former character as lodging houses for the remainder of the year. As far as hostels are concerned, accommodation in them is in many cases provided by arrangement with an organization with which the resident is an associate; for example, by an employer for his employees or by an educational institution for its students.

Motels

Motels represent the most recent addition to this sector of the industry in providing accommodation usually built by the roadside with catering facilities. Their facilities are geared to the needs of motorists, and they cater almost exclusively for highly transient customers. Whether or not a place constitutes a hotel depends upon all these requirements being satisfied; it is essentially a question of fact in each case. It is probable that the very purpose of a motel is mainly to attract the passing motorist, means that motels are generally within the definition of a hotel.

2.5.2 Restaurants, Cafes and Snack Bars

These are non-residential catering establishments which supply food for consumption on the premises in which the supply of alcoholic liquor (if any)is a supplement. They are grouped into a separate sector of the hotel and catering industry, and are normally called restaurants, cafes, refreshment rooms, tea rooms, tea shops, snack bars, milk bars, coffee bars and so on. Fast food shops also fall within this category.

The common characteristic of all these units is that they supply food to the general public who consume it on the premises, and they do not provide sleeping accommodation. They may be divided into silver service or selfservice establishments. In the case of silver service, food is served at tables whilst with self-service, the customer plates and collects his own food. Seating accommodation is either provided at tables or food is consumed at the counter. The list of dishes may range on one hand from a variety of cooked dishes and on the other to light refreshment according to the type of establishment.

Most difficulties of demarcation arise because a combination of catering and other activities is being carried on, and because of the similarities between the catering establishment and a retail shop. Such difficulties arise for instance, in connection with fast food shops, which fall into three broad groups:

- Shops from which all meals are taken away off the premises for consumption
- Shops, which also provide facilities for consumption on the premises, and
- Shops which sell for consumption only on the premises.

It is generally accepted that restaurants in common with retail shops, represent one of the most volatile sectors of the economy. The ease of entry into the restaurant business, its frequent closures and changes in ownership and its responsiveness to demand in providing catering services readily where the demand becomes apparent, are some of the reasons why an assessment of the size of this sector of the industry can be made only in broad terms.

2.5.3 Public Houses

Public houses or drinking bars represent a reasonably homogeneous group of establishments either wholly or mainly engaged in supplying alcoholic liquor to the general public for consumption either on or off the premises to which the supply of food, if any, is merely ancillary.

The most important economic characteristic of establishments that sell alcoholic beverages is the requirement of a magistrates' licence, which enables it to carry on its activities. Whilst this requirement is common also to other establishments such as hotels and restaurants, if they wish to sell alcoholic liquor, in no other section of the industry is it universal. The business of a public house cannot be carried out without a licence and in this sense there is a restriction on entry into this sector of the hotel and catering industry, as it exists whenever a statutory authority makes a licence a pre-requisite of carrying on an activity.

2.5.4 Clubs

Clubs, as a sector of the hotel and catering industry, comprise of establishments providing food and drink and sometimes also accommodation to members and their guests. Club membership may be the only common ground between the users, but many have been established by and for persons associated together for the promotion of either cultural, political, social or other objects for members of sports clubs and for employees of firms.

The nature and characteristic of clubs varies considerably. They may be residential (with letting bedrooms), restaurants with entertainment or merely bars; they range from those with substantial numbers employed to those in which the management and operation of the club are shared by members. Their revenue normally consists of more than one element; some charge entrance fees to those becoming members, most levy subscriptions, and all derive the greater part of their income from supplying services to members. Most of the English licensed clubs tend to resemble licensed restaurants, and a high proportion of their income is derived from the sale of meals; the sales mix of registered clubs approximates more closely to that of public houses in that a high proportion of their income is derived from the supply of drink. Since they sell alcohol on the premises for consumption the law requires the club to have a licence to operate.

2.5.5 Catering Contractors

The four industrial sectors described so far – hotels, restaurants, public houses and clubs cover organizations whose main activity is in providing accommodation, food and drink. Substantial catering services are also provided in organizations whose main activity is in some other fields to which catering is ancillary.

Two main approaches may be discerned in providing catering services in these circumstances: under *direct management* or under *contract*. In the former case, the parent organization operates the catering service under its own management (as one of its operating services), with its own personnel, (employees of the parent organization). In the latter case, the parent organization contracts with a specialist catering organization for the provision of its catering services. For the organizations which run their own catering, it is an ancillary function. For the catering contractors, catering is their main activity. Those organization which operate their own catering units as a service, do so on a non-profit making basis, and in fact, subsidize them to a varying extent.

2.5.6 Catering Contractors as firms on a profit-making basis

It is rare for them to work on a lump sum contract; the client paying a particular amount and the contractor deriving a profit from operating within the agreed price. The majority of contracts are 'cost plus', the client paying the contractor a fee for operating the catering service in addition to paying the operating costs. Direct management normally 'provides for closer direct control and supervision by the parent organization,' and for more flexibility in operation. The major reason for the employment of a catering contractor is to relieve the parent organization of an unfamiliar service, which enables it to concentrate on its main activity.

Chapter Three

RUNNING OR STARTING A BUSINESS

3.1 SETTING UP A BUSINESS

Setting up a business should be an exciting process and a rewarding path to take, but it is a path littered with challenges. Without the right advice, there can be some hidden dangers, particularly where legal issues are concerned. Often, businesses do not consult a solicitor for fear of large legal bills. Early consultation is advisable in case there is legislation to be complied with, or some important legal documents, such as contracts to be signed. Above all, you will need to be focused on reaching your goal. If you come across a barrier, you will need to find a way round it.

Successful entrepreneurs do not give up at the first sign of problems. To become successful, many hours of hard work will need to be put into your business and a positive attitude will be required.

3.1.1 Buying a ready-made or an existing business

It may occur to you that, it might be simpler to buy a ready-made or an existing business. With an existing business:

- The premises would already exist.
- There may be some staff and stock.
- The company will be registered, and all necessary documentation will have been filed with the registrar and also the certificate of incorporation so that trading can start soon.

- You only have to appoint your own director(s) and the secretary and transfer the shares to your own shareholders.

But think again. Why is the owner selling the business?

Being in business is about responsibility. There is no easy way to establishing your own business. Here is a simple guide to what you should consider when buying a business.

- If you are already in business what are you looking to add?
- Have you money to invest?
- Have you expertise that can be employed in the additional business?
- Have you defined the business profile you would like to acquire?
- What size of business and where it will be located.
- Market research done? Is the location suitable for that kind of business if not the same?
- Obtain help from accountants, bankers, designers, financial planners, surveyors and a solicitor.

Solicitors also specialise, so make sure you get one who can deal with your needs. If you want to choose your own company name, they will check its availability for a fee. If you intend to use the name as a Trade Mark, you should also carry out a search at the Trade Marks Registry in the appropriate class of goods and services.

Company house will send you information packs and guides, and agents will advise you on the necessary initial changes for takeover.

The object clause can be changed but you should ensure that, the existing principal object clause covers your main business activities.

You will then have a company with a current certificate of incorporation, a standard memorandum of association, with an appropriate object and capital clause, standard articles of association, a set of statutory books and a company seal, if this is required by your articles. The existing directors, secretary and shareholders of the ready-made company resign in favour of your nominees. If you wish to make other changes, the Registrar of Companies must be notified in accordance with the Companies Act.

3.1.2 Starting a new business

There are some key areas which need to be considered. These areas are Business Structure – It is worth considering carefully which structures best suit you, how you intend to do business and the likely profits it will make. There are several ways to structure your business, sole trader, partnership, limited company, limited liability partnership, [LLP] etc.

Also, the business name, finance and accounts, tax, employees, use of professionals, insurance, relevant authorities, overhead expenses, etc. Before entering into a business, either large or small, the Hotel and Catering Proprietor must determine the character of the legal organization upon which he will base his venture. There are three main choices open to him, whether he has a small guesthouse, a big hotel, or a chain of hotels, he must decide if they will be in the form of a one-man business, a partnership or a company. All have advantages and disadvantages needing a careful thought.

Many hotels are owned by sole proprietors, and some are small companies. It is important to have some knowledge of the ability of a company to enter into a contract. A company being an artificial person must be negotiated through its directors and employees. Acting through such persons, the company may enter into and be bound by contracts in the same way as human beings. Directors can make contracts on behalf of the company, but they can only make such contracts as they are permitted to make by the documents incorporating the company, that is the article of the association and memorandum.

The law requires hotels and other sleeping accommodations to be registered, classified and graded by the Tourist Board. The Tourist Board also runs a registration scheme which enable hoteliers to have details of their establishments included in a book published for tourists.

In some countries, the Tourist Board has the power to inspect premises, issue certificate of registration, charge registration fees and require proprietors to furnish information and impose penalties for refusing to comply with the order.

3.1.3 Understanding the terms used for the financing of a business

Choosing the right type of finance for the business.
Any small business, whether it is a start-up or well-established firm, needs funding to grow. But finding that money and then choosing the right type of finance is not a simple task. Unless you are lucky enough to be able to fund your entire business through your own savings, it is likely that at some point you will need to raise money elsewhere.

There are of course many different ways to finance a business. Choosing the right type of finance will depend on a variety of factors including what you are financing, how you want to repay and the aims and objectives of your business. So it pays to think carefully about your specific aims and choose the type of finance that is right for your business.

The reasons for looking for new finance can be many and varied. It could be that you need finance to start up the business, buy equipment, launch a new product or perhaps expand the business.

To choose one type of finance may not be appropriate, you may well need to choose different types. And in that case getting the right mix is crucial. But it is also vital to keep an eye on costs. The last thing you will want to do as a small business is to borrow too much and find you have over committed. Before you think about raising finance, check if there is anything you could do to find the funds elsewhere. For example, many businesses could reduce their borrowing requirements substantially if they chased the money they were owed by their debtors more effectively.

3.1.3.1 The meaning of the word Capital

The money called capital, which is needed to run the business, can be obtained from friends and families. Borrowing from a relative or friend, might ease the strain in some sense, but it can leave more scope for things to go wrong.

Arguments over loans are not uncommon, so to avoid things turning sour, you should not enter into any agreement lightly.

Other ways of financing a business are:

- Leasing/Hire Purchase.
- Selling shares in the business
- Grants
- Loans
- Overdrafts
- Debenture is another way of financing a business, which will be explained later in the chapter.

When you are looking for finance, it is well worth taking advice before you make any decisions. Your banker, accountant or business advisor would be a good place to start. Whichever route you choose to finance your business, it is important that you remember the responsibility that comes with borrowing money.

Hopefully, you won't encounter too many problems, but if you do experience difficulties or even if you are simply looking for advice, you should speak to your bank or investor immediately. As always, the earlier you highlight any potential issues, the better.

3.1.3.2 The share capital of a company

The share capital of a company goes under a number of different names. First there is the authorized capital or the nominal capital. This is the capital stated in the memorandum of association and which the company is authorized to issue. It may not, at least initially, issue all its authorized capital and so the capital that has been issued is quite reasonably called issued capital or allotted capital. If some shares are issued only partly paid, then the amount the shareholders have actually paid for is called the paid-up capital. It is not so common nowadays for a company to issue partly paid shares.

3.1.3.3 Other financial terms explained

Shares
A share is a part of a larger amount, which is divided among or contributed by a number of people. Any of the equal parts into which a company's wealth is divided entitles the holder to a proportion of the profits.

A shareholder is an owner of shares in a company.

A dividend is a sum of money that is divided among a number of people such as part of a company's profits paid to its shareholders.

Preference shares
The capital is divided usually into two main classes, preference shares and ordinary shares. The preference shares, as the name implies, give the holder of such shares preference over other shareholders in the payment of dividends and also in the repayment of capital in the event of the company being wound up. Preference shareholders receive a fixed dividend from any profits set aside by the directors for distribution. The dividend never varies and so such shares are usually considered solid and dependable and suitable for trustee investments.

Cumulative Preference Shares
Fixed rate of dividend and arrears must be paid. This means that if no dividend is declared in any particular year, arrears of dividend must be carried forward from year to year until they are all paid; before the ordinary shareholders can receive any dividends.

Redeemable Preference Shares
A company may, however, issue preference shares, which from their inception are redeemable, either at a fixed date or after a certain period of time at the option of the company. Sections 159 and 160 of the Companies Act 1985 lay down conditions to be fulfilled before a company may redeem redeemable preference shares. Basically, these conditions seek to maintain the capital of the company. For example, the redemption must be made out of profits, and only shares which are fully paid may be redeemed.

Ordinary Shares

These normally carry the residue of profits available from distribution as dividend after the preference shareholders, if any, have been paid their fixed dividend. Ordinary shares are sometimes called the risk capital. This is because after the dividend has been paid to preference shareholders, the residue is distributed to the ordinary shareholders and of course the amount will depend on the performance of the company.

In a winding up, if preference shares have priority as to return on capital, the ordinary shares will be entitled to the surplus assets, unless there are deferred shares. Hence ordinary shares are sometimes called the equity share capital of the company because they take what is left (the equity). The ordinary shareholders have a vote at the annual general meeting of the company and so the power to control the company rests with them.

These are the two main types of capital, preference or ordinary. There are other types of shares but these are not so common. By issuing shares, a company acquires money for its activities. However by issuing shares to the people who contribute money, the company is acquiring more shareholders and consequently the control of its existing shareholders is being weakened. An alternative method of acquiring money is for the company to borrow it and in that case it will issue debentures to those people who lend it money.

Debentures

In addition to attracting investment from shareholders a company can borrow money long term by issuing debentures.

A debenture is a document or certificate, which is issued as evidence of a debt. The point about debentures is that the holders of these are not members of the company and do not have the same control over the company as the shareholders. Instead of dividends, debenture holders receive interest on their holdings. However, like shares, debentures may be transferred on the Stock Exchange.

Since debenture holders are assured of their interest even if the company makes a loss (as long as the company does not go into liquidation) they are a safer investment than shares but they represent a greater burden on a company, which is obliged to pay the interest on them whatever the profit and loss situation.

In the event of the company being liquidated, debenture holders would be reimbursed before shareholders. Some debentures are secured against specific company assets; these are known as *mortgage debentures,* and if the company fails, the specified assets are sold to raise money to repay the holders. Others have no charge on any specific assets and are called simple or naked debentures. Debentures may be redeemable i.e. they must be repaid by or on a set date or they may be irredeemable, i.e. they must and continue in existence, like shares, as long as the company is in existence.

Redeemable Debentures
If company fails to pay at a stated period, debenture holders can force company into liquidation.

Irredeemable Debentures: only paid back at company's pleasure.

Loans
Companies are also able to borrow long-term loans from banks, merchant banks, venture capital companies and other financial institutions. These could be anything from a year or two to ten or more years and would be used to finance expansion, new projects and capital expenditure. The lender normally asks for security in the form of a charge on a specific asset.

Retained Profits
Companies do not distribute all their profits to the shareholders but retain some as reserves. This money is invested in assets such as shares in other companies etc. Land can be used in the future to finance expansion without the necessity of raising loans. Internal financing is especially important to small companies who find it difficult to raise capital because they are not well known and cannot offer security.

Governments Grants
Governments in some countries make money available to companies as low interest loans or grants, especially if the companies generate economic activity and provide employment in less developed regions.

Highly geared company
One having a high proportion of fixed loans and other debt instruments.

Cooperative Society
A Cooperative Society is a commercial enterprise owned and run by customers or workers, in which the profits are shared among the members.

Rochdale pioneers started the movement in 1844 where a group of 28 artisans obtained initial capital of £28 and started a trading company which distributed profit to its members in proportion to their purchases.

The minimum shareholding in a co-operative is £1, the maximum £1,000. In the UK, there are mainly consumer co-operatives as opposed to the producer co-operatives i.e. Common Market and Commonwealth countries. The cooperative wholesale societies in Great Britain have four main activities.

- Wholesaling
- Manufacturing
- Importing
- Banking and finance (including building society).

The advantages of a cooperative society are stability of trade and loyalty. They are democratically managed and profits are distributed as dividends in proportion to amount spent.

The disadvantages of the cooperative society are that it tends to be run by amateurs, uninspired management and slow decision-making.

3.2 THE ORIGIN OF COMPANY LAW

A registered or a limited company, is a form of business organization. It is called by these names because such a company is formed by registering certain documents with the Registrar of Companies and it is a limited company because the liability of its shareholders is limited. A company is an artificial legal person. In other words, it is a person in the eyes of the law and has rights and duties like any human person. This point was established in the famous case of Solomon versus Solomon and Co; 1897.

3.2.1 The famous case of solomon versus solomon and company – 1897

Mr. Solomon formed a company to take over his business of manufacturing shoes. The company paid Mr. Solomon for his business partly in cash, partly in shares and partly by a charge over the company's assets. The company was wound up and its debts to creditors were in excess of his company's assets. Therefore the creditors claimed the assets of the company arguing that a person cannot owe money to himself.

And as Mr. Solomon owned the company he and it (the company) were the same person. The court held that the company was a separate person from Mr. Solomon who owned it.

Being artificial, a company cannot be seen, it exists on paper. As a company exists only on paper, the certificate of Incorporation is the document that brings a company into existence and this is a proof of the company's existence. It is issued by the Registrar of Companies when he has examined the documents filed in his office by the promoters of the company.

The concept that a company exists as a single person on its own is the basis of company law. Together with the principle that the liability of the shareholders is limited to the amount due to be paid (if any) for their shares. It is the main difference between a company and a partnership.

The partners contribute money to the assets of the partnership but if this is insufficient to pay the debts of the partnership, then the partners must continue to provide more money, even if that means they are bankrupting themselves.

In the case of a company, the shareholders have contributed to the assets of the company, but if this proves to be insufficient to pay the creditors of the company then the shareholders will lose their money in the company, but will not have to provide more money. The other difference is that the company is a person separate from the person (the shareholder) who owns it. A partnership is not a separate person but consists of all the partners.

As an illustration, it is often said that if all the partners of a partnership are in a room and a bomb explodes killing them all, that would be the end of the firm. But if all the shareholders of a company were killed in the same circumstances that would not be the end of the company. It would continue its existence, but with different shareholders. The law relating to companies is contained mainly in the Companies Act 1985. This document was of the greatest importance to outsiders dealing with the company because it contained the objects clause, which stated the purpose for which the company had been formed and in so doing it established the powers of the company to enter into contracts. The rule was that a company could only enter into a valid and enforceable contract if it had power to do so. If any contract made was outside its powers, (ultra vires) then the contract was null and void. This principle was known as the 'ultra vires doctrine' and was intended to protect investors in the company and those who were considering lending money to it. By consulting the objects clause such people would know the permitted activities of the company.

In practice this was not particularly helpful because the lawyers who drew up a company's documents usually made the object so wide as to cover every possible activity that the company might have wished to enter in the future. Nevertheless if a company entered into a contract and it was discovered that it lacked the power to enter into that particular contract then the contract would be void and the company could not be sued successfully.

The latest position is that, the Companies Act 1989 has amended the companies Act 1985. Sections 108–112 of the 1989 Act have effectively abolished the ultra vires rule Section 35 of the 1985 Act.

3.2.2 The "Ultra Vires Reform Act 1989 (Sections 108–112)

Ultra Vires – Latin (Beyond The Powers)
The provisions of the 1985 Act, which deals with the ultra vires doctrine and the authority of the Board of Directors was amended. (The ultra vires doctrine is a Common Law rule which; in the absence of statutory provision, renders void acts by a company which are beyond its stated objects).

The doctrine in the law of corporations states that if a corporation enters into a contract that is beyond the scope of its corporate powers, the contract is illegal. The doctrine of ultra vires played an important role in the development of corporate powers. Though, largely obsolete in modern private corporation law, the doctrine remains in full force for government entities. The earliest legal view was that such acts were void. Under this approach, a corporation was formed only for limited purposes and could do only what it was authorized to do in its corporate charter.

This early view proved unworkable and unfair. It permitted a corporation to accept the benefits of a contract and then refuse to perform its obligations on the ground that the contract was ultra vires. The doctrine also impaired the security of title to properly and fully executed transactions in which a corporation participated. Therefore, the courts adopted the view that such acts were voidable rather than void. And that, the then facts should dictate whether a corporate act should have effect.

Over time, a body of principles developed that prevented the application of the ultra vires doctrine. The principles included the ability of shareholders to ratify an ultra vires transaction and the application of the doctrine of Estoppel, which prevented the defence of ultra vires when the transaction was fully performed by one party and the prohibition against asserting ultra vires when both parties had fully performed the contract.

The law also held that if an agent of a corporation committed a TORT within the scope of the agent's employment, the corporation could not defend on the ground that the act was ultra vires.

Accordingly, modern corporation law has sought to remove the possibility that the ultra vires acts may occur. Most importantly, multiple purposes, clauses and general clauses that permit corporations to engage in any lawful business are now included in the articles of incorporation. In addition purposes clauses can now be easily amended if the corporation seeks to do business in new areas. For example, under traditional ultra vires doctrine, a corporation that had as its purpose the manufacturing of shoes could not, under its charter, manufacture motorcycles. Under modern corporate law, the purposes clause would either be so general as to allow the corporation to go into the motorcycle business, or the corporation would amend its purposes clause to reflect the new venture.

State laws in almost every jurisdiction have also sharply reduced the importance of the ultra vires. Historically, the ultra vires concept has been used to construe the powers of the government entity narrowly. Failure to observe the statutory limits has been characterized as ultra vires.

The main features of the amended provisions are as follows:

- The validity of a completed act of a company is not to be called into question on the grounds of lack of capacity by reason of anything in the company's memorandum of association.
- In favour of a person dealing with the company in good faith, the power of the board of directors to bind the company or

authorize others to do so is to be free of any limitation in the company's constitution.

- A third party is to have no duty to enquire as to the capacity of a company or the authority of directors to bind the company.
- Transactions which are beyond the authority of the board of directors and to which directors or connected persons are a party are to be voidable in certain circumstances at the instance of the company.
- If a company states that its object is to carry on business as a 'general commercial company' it will have the object of carrying on any business or trade whatsoever, and will have the power to do whatever is incidental or conclusive to that object.
- The provisions on capacity and authority are qualified in the case of charitable companies, so as to maintain current controls on charitable companies and to assist in the recovery of misappropriated charitable property. In order to prevent those provisions on charitable companies undermining the provisions affecting companies generally, charitable companies are required to disclose their charitable states in their official documents if the status is not apparent from their name.
- A company may alter its objects by the passing of a special resolution to that effect. After the resolution has been passed the company must wait for 21 days (before implementing the alteration) to see whether any members who oppose the alteration may apply to the court to have it set aside. An application to cancel the alteration will not be entertained by the court unless it is made by:
  a. At least 15 percent of the members; or
  b. The holder of at least 15 percent of any debentures issued by the company.

The court may on such an application make an order confirming the alteration. If the alteration is confirmed, the company must deliver to the Registrar a printed copy of the memorandum as altered.

Section 110 of the Companies Act 1989 inserts a new section four into the Companies Act 1985. This allows a company to alter its objects for any reason.

3.2.3 What is the Companies Act UK?

The Companies Act 2006 (c 46) is the main piece of legislation which governs company law in the UK and regulating companies within that jurisdiction. The act has the distinction of being the longest in British Parliamentary history with 1,300 sections.

The Companies Act—The series of laws enacted by Parliament governing the establishment and conduct of incorporated business enterprises. The Companies Act 1985 consolidated the Acts that preceded it. It is an important part of UK company law that governs various aspects of the registration and management of Companies.

3.3 FORMATION OF A COMPANY

3.3.1 Companies

This section introduces you to the formation of a company right up to the winding up of the company. A registered company is regarded as a legal person, separate from those members who comprise it. The company can have its own banking account, its own property, incur debts and be a creditor of other people. But it must transact its business through human beings who act as its agents and its policies are controlled by directors.

A public company must have at least two directors whilst a private company can have a sole director. It is usual for directors to be paid a salary. Profits can be used to issue dividends to shareholders or can be ploughed back into the business in order to improve it. In most private companies the directors and the shareholders are usually the same persons.

3.3.2 The Constitution of the Company

The Memorandum of Association

The Memorandum of Association is a legal document required for registering a company under the Companies Act, stating powers and objectives of the company. Those wishing to form companies will have decisions to make in regard to the contents of the company's constitution. This is contained in two documents – the Memorandum of Association and the Articles of Association.

The memorandum is the superior constitutional document and should there be a conflict between the provisions of the memorandum and the articles, it is the memorandum provision that must be followed and applied. The clauses of the memorandum carry material not contained in the articles. However, the exception is shareholders' rights that may sometimes be found in both documents. If the rights are different, those in the memorandum are to be applied.

The Association Clause:

This is the final clause of the memorandum. It is in a company's memorandum of association in which the subscribers declare that, they wish to be formed into a company and agree to take the number of shares recorded opposite their names.

The Article of the Association

This is a document which regulates a company's internal affairs consisting of regulations governing the rights of members and the conduct of the company's business. e.g. the appointments and powers of directors. Articles are subject to the Memorandum of Association and cannot give any power not given by the memorandum. They can be altered by special resolution at a general meeting.

Any alteration must benefit the company as a whole. The alteration is valid as if it was originally contained in the articles.

The following are some of the matters which are provided for in a company's articles:

Calls on its shares
The company's lien on its shares
The transfer of shares
The exercise of the borrowing powers of the company
The delegation of the management of the company to the board of directors
The voting rights of members
The payment of dividends
Variation of the members' rights
The conduct of meetings
The capitalization of profits
The use of company's seal.

When registered, the articles constitute a contract between the members and the company. The contract binds the members to the company but only in their capacity as members (Companies Act Section 14).

The article as a contract

The articles and memorandum when registered bind the company and its members in contract as if these documents had been signed as a deed by each member and contained undertakings on the part of each member to observe the provisions of the memorandum and articles. The main result of this statutory contract, which is relevant mostly in terms of provisions in the articles, is that:

The articles constitute a contract between the company and each member.
The articles constitute a contract between the members and its members.
The articles do not constitute a contract with outsiders but only with the members in respect of rights as members.
The articles may be altered by a special resolution in general meeting or in private companies, by a written resolution. A copy of the resolution altering the articles must be filed with

the Registrar. Copies should be sent to those known to be in possession of the memorandum and articles, e.g. auditors and bankers.

3.3.3 The Passing of Resolution at Meetings

The business of the company is transacted by means of passing resolutions at meetings. The meetings must be properly called and constituted according to the rules contained in the Articles of Association and according to the general law relating to meetings. All persons who have a right to attend a meeting must be notified that one is to take place. Such persons may have to be given a minimum length of notice to attend. Also there must be a minimum number present in order for a valid resolution to be passed – (a quorum).

When a bank sends money to a company and takes security from it, it will require a certified copy of the resolution, which authorizes the change. If a quorum was not present or if it was an invalid quorum then, it would follow that, any resolution passed would itself be invalid. A bank therefore must be on its guard and if it knows that the meeting was invalid then it must reject any resolution made by such a meeting.

Every company must hold annually, a general meeting of shareholders of which the accounts of the company are presented by the directors, who may have to submit to questioning from the shareholders. At this annual meeting of which the shareholder must receive 21 days' notice, it appoints or re-appoints the directors and auditor. They also confirm, or not as the case may be the dividend proposed by the directors to be distributed.

Every company must hold its first general meeting. – The statutory meeting – within six weeks of its formation. Apart from the annual meeting, the directors may either, on their own accord, because they have been so required by members of the company holding not less than one-tenth of the paid-up capital of the company, call an extraordinary general meeting of the shareholders who must be given 14 days' notice. If it is desired to propose a special resolution then 21 days' notice must be given to those persons entitled to attend. At these meetings proposals are made and if accepted, resolutions are passed.

3.3.4 The Director's Powers

As already mentioned, a company is an artificial person, which cannot be seen but only exists on paper. The company operates through human agents called directors. The directors' powers are contained in the articles and so they operate and decide matters on behalf of the company, provided they have the necessary authority to act.

So when one says, 'the company has decided to buy A Co plc.' What that really means is that the directors have taken the decision to buy it. Directors are appointed by the shareholders in general meetings. The shareholders own the company and they appoint the directors to run the company on their behalf. The directors are given certain powers to act without recourse to the shareholders, but of course such powers may be curtailed or extended as the shareholders wish. The directors may only act on behalf of the company within the powers of the company and also within their own powers. The powers are set out in the Articles of Association. Certain matters may need the authority of the shareholders in general meetings, for example, the fixing of a dividend or the appointment of auditors.

As an agent is in a position of trust as regards his principal, so is a director as regards to the company. A director must exercise his powers for the purpose for which they are conferred and for the benefit of the company and must not put himself in a position in which his duties to the company and his personal interests may conflict.

Some directors (called non-executive) are appointed because of the contacts they can bring to the company. They might have been cabinet ministers, trade union leaders, etc. Other directors perform some particular functions within the company, such as financial directors, production directors etc. They are known as managing directors or executive directors.

If a bank is contemplating lending money to a company, it must ascertain the directors' powers to borrow money on behalf of the company by consulting the articles. In some cases the shareholders may desire to restrict the directors' borrowing powers.

Now that the Ultra Vires rule has been abolished, a company will be able to do anything that the directors wish. It will be unnecessary for an outsider to consult the memorandum. Although directors are agents of the company, they do have a greater number of restrictions placed upon them.

The provisions of the 1985 Act which deal with the ultra vires doctrine and the authority of the board of directors are amended. (The Ultra Vires doctrine is a Common Law rule which in the absence of a statutory provision renders void acts by a company which are beyond its stated objects).

A third party is to have no duty to enquire as to the capacity of a company or the authority of the board of directors to bind a company.

If a company states that its object is to carry on business as a "general commercial" company, it will have the object of carrying on any business or trade whatsoever, and will have the power to do whatever is incidental or conclusive to that object.

The provisions on capacity and authority are qualified in the case of charitable companies so as to maintain current controls on charitable companies, and to assist in the recovery of misappropriated charitable property. In order to prevent those provisions on charitable companies undermining the provisions affecting companies generally, charitable companies are required to disclose their charitable status in their official documents if the status is not apparent from their names.

3.3.5 The Names of Directors

The names of directors' need not be shown on business letters, but if they are, it must be all of them. A director may include his name in a letter without infringing this rule.

3.3.6 Company Name

The name chosen must not be undesirable in the opinion of the secretary of State for Trade and Industry. A name is not acceptable if it is either:

- too similar to the name of another company
- Misleading, for example, the name suggests that the company has connections with a government department.

Once the Secretary of State has approved a name for the company, it must be written on the business documents.

A company may alter its name provided the following is adopted:

- the company must pass a special resolution to effect the change, and
- obtain the written consent of the Secretary of State.

Once the alteration of the name has been made, the Registrar will issue an altered Certificate of Incorporation.

3.3.7 Company Bank Account

If the bank's customer is a company, there are certain matters which must be considered. The bank must see the Certificate of Incorporation because this document establishes the existence of the company. The bank must examine the company's Memorandum of Association in order to ascertain the powers of the company. Once the Ultra Vires rule has been abolished presumably it will no longer be necessary for a bank to examine the above mentioned documents. A bank will be able to assume that the company has power to do anything it wants so long as it is not aware of any restriction on the company's authority or on the authority of the directors. If a company wishes to borrow money, the bank must ensure that certain conditions are met:

(a) The company has power to borrow
(b) The directors have the authority to borrow the money on behalf of the company
(c) The bank will wish to see a resolution of the board of directors appointing the bank as bankers of the company
(d) If a company is a public company, the bank will require seeing the certificate to commence business
(e) When the account has been opened, a bank must take the same care in paying cheques as it does in the case of an individual. In collecting the proceeds of a cheque the amount must only be credited to the account of the company.

3.3.8 Disclosure Requirements

A company must disclose its name in accordance with the CA 1985 (Company Act 1985). In addition, if the company is trading under a business name the disclosure must indicate an address at which documents can be served. The disclosure of the fact that a company is running must be stated clearly i.e.:

- Places where the business is carried on, provided that customers or suppliers are dealt with there
- Business letters
- Written orders for the supply of goods and services
- Invoices and receipts
- Written demands for the payment of business debts.

So far as companies are concerned, the above disclosures are required by the Company Act 1985 and so basically the only additional disclosure for a company is the business name itself. An additional disclosure for companies over and above the Company Act 1985 rules is that, when a business is being transacted and the third party asks for it, the name or the company and its address must be given to the third party immediately in writing. The requirement can be satisfied by giving a business card containing the relevant information. It is a criminal offence to use a business name that needs prior approval.

It is also a criminal offence not to disclose the details that the Business Names Act 1985 and Company Act 1985 requires to be disclosed.

3.3.9 Winding Up

Whenever a company decides to finish in business or becomes insolvent, it is wound up. The company goes into liquidation with a liquidator being appointed to wind up its affairs. His job is to sell off any property and other assets belonging to the company in order to meet outstanding debts. Should there be any surplus, this is then distributed amongst the members.

3.4. COMPANY ADMINISTRATION

3.4.1 Company Register

Under the company's legislation, companies must on a continuing basis:

- Maintain registers that are available to the public for inspection. These are normally kept at the registered office of the company:
    1. Register of directors
    2. Register of members (shareholders)

The Companies Act set out the prescribed details that these registers must contain:

- File annual returns. Annual returns are filed with the Registrar of Companies. It provides information about a company. The information includes details on:
- Directors
- Registered Office
- Type of business
- Share capital
- Details of shareholders.

This information is then made available to the public either upon attendance at or by contacting the Registrar of Companies.

3.4.2 Preparing, Approval and Filing of Annual Accounts

Every company has to keep accounting records and from those records prepare a set of accounts consisting of a balance sheet, a profit and loss account together with a director's report and auditor's report (if the accounts are being audited). The content of accounts is prescribed and must be filed with the Registrar of Companies within the appropriate time scale each year. The filing period for accounts begins on or after 6 April which is normally the beginning of the financial year.

3.4.3 Accounting Records

The Companies Act requires companies to keep adequate accounting records to:

- Show and explain the companies transactions
- Disclose with reasonable accuracy the company's current financial position
- Enable the directors to ensure that the accounts comply with the Act. Records must be maintained on a day-to-day basis including:
- Details of cash receipts and payments, including the transactions to which they relate
- Daily entries of cash receipts and expenditures, including transactions to which they relate
- A list of assets and liabilities
- Statement of stock of goods held at the end of each financial year including statements of stocktaking
- A sufficient description of goods and services bought and sold to enable sellers and purchasers to be identified.

The Company's officers are liable to fines and/or up to two years' imprisonment if the accounts or records are inadequate unless they can prove they acted honestly.

They are also liable for up to two years' imprisonment and/or a fine, if records are not available for inspection by company officers for at least three years at the registered office or other places the directors designate. If registered for VAT, records must be retained for six years. All these records must also be available electronically.

Copies of the company's accounts signed by a director or secretary, if any, comprise:

- A profit and loss account
- The balance sheet approved by the board and signed by a director
- If appropriate, a special signed and dated auditors' report
- The director's report signed by a director or the secretary, if any
- Notes to the accounts
- It is vital that all businesses have clear, concise accounts. Banks will insist on them when considering taking loans; Revenue and customs may require sight of them; prospective new investors may want to review them to see if a business is viable
- Suppliers may require them before they give credit. Your accounts show how well your business is doing and whether your debtors and creditors are under control.

Larger business may require regular management accounts throughout the year so that problems can be identified early. Limited companies and LLP's have to file statutory accounts with Companies House every year.

3.4.4 Audit

Auditing is an official inspection of business accounts, conducted by an independent qualified accountant. A person who is qualified to audit accounts is called an auditor.

If your business grows significantly or if you work in a regulated area, your business may require an audit. These can be time consuming and costly, but as long as you keep good financial records and have a good accountant, the process can be quite simple and can actually help show areas of the business that could have processes improved.

3.4.5 Corporation Tax

Corporation tax is payable on the profits of a limited company. Corporation tax returns must be submitted to revenue and customs, again within strict deadlines and with penalties for late submission. Interest is also chargeable on late payment. Corporation tax is charged at a lower rate, income tax is charged on higher rate. Tax is also chargeable on the funds extracted by the directors and shareholders by salary or dividends.

3.4.6 VAT

Once the turnover of a business reaches a certain level, the person or persons running that business will be required to register it for Value Added Tax.

After registration, VAT will need to be charged on most goods and services provided. Vat returns and payments must be made available to the revenue and customs on a regular basis – usually quarterly. There are strict time limits for submission of the returns and payments. Heavy penalties are suffered for non-compliance.

3.4.7 Tax

The sole trader, the partner and the director pay income tax; companies pay corporation tax. The sole trader and the partners pay revenue and customs for tax on their share of business profits. Under the self-assessment rules, retiring partners take their tax liability with them. The partnership, however, has to complete a Partnership (Tax) Return setting out the partnership's profits and losses for tax purposes, and showing how they were divided between the partners. Self-assessment is based on the current tax year instead of the preceding year income. You can 'self-assess' the company's tax bill but you still have to provide account drawn up in accordance with the Companies Acts or computations showing how the figures have been arrived at from the figures in the accounts. Tax on profits is paid nine months after the end of the accounting period and shareholders pay tax on dividends as part of their own liability to income tax. The company is taxed separately for corporation tax on business profit.

3.4.8 Final Account

A limited company prepares a profit and loss account and balance sheet, just like a sole trader and partnership. But these are more complex.

In the United Kingdom, the Companies Acts 1981, 1985 and 1989, require limited companies to disclose certain information and also lay down how the financial statements are to be presented.

This is seen to be necessary because company accounts are published for general information and should be presented in a way that is satisfactory and understandable for interested parties.

The law requires that the accounts presented to shareholders give a 'true and fair' view of the financial affairs of the company. It also required that the fundamental concepts of accounting are followed, i.e., going concern, accruals, consistency and prudence. Any departure from a concept should be mentioned in the accounts and the reasons for doing this should be stated.

3.4.9 Other Common Filings and Returns

- Changes to Memorandum and Articles of Association (those documents are the constitution of the company). Change the company name
- Increase in share capital
- Changes in officers – appointments, resignations, retirements, removals or changes in details.
- Change in accounting reference dates.

3.4.10 Insolvency

Insolvent means not having enough money to pay one's debts. A company is legally insolvent if it is unable to pay its debts and discharge its liabilities as and when they fall due, or the value of its assets is less than its liabilities. In determining liabilities, contingent and prospective liabilities must be taken into account, as well as actual and quantified amounts. Day to day involvement in management often give a false picture of the company's financial position. If customers are slow to pay, plant, machinery and stock have been purchased under credit agreements and the company's bank account is in overdraft, the business may be far from healthy.

Financial problems need not, however lead to liquidation. The procedures introduced by the 1986 Insolvency Act permit a company to reach a compromise agreement with creditors, or to apply for an administration order so that company affairs can be reorganised and supervised, and insolvency avoided.

You should therefore ensure that you have adequate accounting records and proper financial advice so that you are able to consider taking appropriate action.

3.4.11 Procedure for Liquidation

Liquidation is the settling of an obligation by legal proceedings or agreement. It is the winding up of the affairs of a business by identifying and converting assets into cash and paying off liabilities.

The liquidator presents a statement of affairs, which sets out the company's financial position and detailed proposals to creditors and shareholders for a scheme or composition in satisfaction of debts. An insolvency practitioner is required to supervise the arrangement and unless he or she is a liquidator or administrator, he or she must report to the court as to the necessity for shareholders' and creditors' meetings and notify creditors. A liquidator or administrator must call meetings, but need not report to court. The meetings must approve the supervisor and can accept, modify or reject the proposals. Directors, shareholders, creditors and the supervisor can challenge decisions and implementation. The arrangement is carried out by the supervisor who must report to the court.

3.5 PARTNERSHIP

3.5.1 What is meant by Partnership?

A partnership is defined in s.1 of the Partnership Act 1890, as the relationship which subsists between persons carrying on business in common with a view of profit. It will be noted that, there must be a business that must be carried on in common by members and that there must be an intention to earn profits. Two or more persons can combine to form a partnership, which can be brought into existence in a highly formal or a very casual manner.

No legal formalities are essential, but it is desirable and usual for rights and liabilities of the partners to be defined in a formal Deed of Partnership Agreement.

On the other hand, mere oral agreement is equally binding, and in extreme cases a relationship of partnership may be inferred from the conduct of the parties. The partners are at liberty to vary the arrangement made between them and where the conduct of the parties has for a lengthy period been inconsistent with the terms as originally agreed. It will be presumed that the new arrangement shall be binding on them. The partnership Act makes provisions as to contribution of capital, division of profits, rights of partners to participate in active management, and so on, but these only apply in so far as they are not varied by agreement between the partners.

3.5.2 The Formation of Partnership

Section 716 of the Companies Act 1985, prohibits the formation of a partnership consisting of more than 20 persons for the purpose of carrying on the business for gain. The Banking Act 1979, s .51 [2] and Sch. 7 applies the usual limit of 20 to banking partnerships.

However certain partnerships of solicitors, accountants and stockbrokers are exempted from this prohibition by s. 716 of the Companies Act 1985. Regulations made by the Department of Trade and Industry exempt from prohibition in s.716 of the Act of 1985 certain other partnerships, patent agents and also certain partnerships ,i.e., surveyors, auctioneers, valuers, estate agents and town planners.

In partnership, you and your partner [or partners] personally share responsibility for the business.

These include;

- Any losses your business makes
- Bills for things you buy for your business, like stock or equipment
- Partners share the business's profits and each partner pays tax on their share.

When you set up a business partnership, you need to choose a name, choose a 'nominated partner' and register with Revenue and Customs. The 'nominated partner' is responsible for managing the partnership's tax returns and keeping business records.

There are different rules for limited partnerships and limited liability partnerships [LLP's].

A partnership may be formed by a mere verbal agreement. However, a written agreement is the only safe one. The members of a partnership may enter into a written contractual agreement, but such formality is not necessary. Generally, to determine whether a partnership existed, a court will ask whether there was a sharing of profit, and losses, joint administration and control of business, a capital investment by each partner, and common ownership of property. The court will also examine the intentions of the parties.

Partnerships are governed almost exclusively by state law. Tax concerns and jurisdictional issues are the notable exceptions.

The parties to a partnership may be individuals, corporations, and even other partnerships. Partnerships may be general partnerships, where all partners have equal rights and duties.

- In Limited partnership, general partners have broad rights and duties

- In Limited liability partnerships, all parties have certain restrictions on liability.

The principal characters of a general partnership include;

Joint and several liabilities– This means that each partner may be responsible not only for his or her proportion or share of partnership debt, but may be personally liable for all partnership debt.

Unlike a corporation, a partnership does not pay income tax at the business entity level. Instead, the income earned by each partner passes through his or her personal tax return.

There is no limitation on the activities of partners provided these are legal nor is there any limit to the liability of the individual partners for the debts of the firm each being liable to the full extent of his personal estate for any deficiencies of the partnership.

However provision is made for the introduction of limited partners whose liability is limited to the amount of capital they have introduced, though there must always be at least one general partner who is fully liable for the debts of the firm. Such a partnership must be registered as a limited partnership under the Limited Partnership Act 1907.

The partnership was the normal form of business organization for operations on a fairly large scale before the advent of the joint stock company, but it is now largely restricted to the type of enterprise requiring intimate personal collaboration between the members or where incorporation is not possible or desirable, as among doctors, solicitors and accountants, though the increasing control over companies may see some revival of the partnership as a more general organization.

3.5.3 Dissolution of Partnership

A partnership may be dissolved by any partner giving notice to the others at any time unless the partnership is entered into for a fixed period of time. However dissolution by a notice depends upon what the partnership agreement, if any, says.

The partnership agreement will normally provide that the business is to continue under the remaining partners. No one member of a company can wind up the partnership; neither the death, bankruptcy nor insanity of a member can wind up the company.

One of the defects of the partnership is its lack of continuity. On the death of a partner the continuing partners must account to his personal representatives for the amount of his interest in the firm. This difficulty may be met to some extent by providing funds out of the proceeds of an insurance policy on the deceased partner's life, or by arranging for the balance of his capital account to be left in the business as a loan, but failing these measures the sudden withdrawal of a large amount of capital may well cause serious dislocation of the smaller business, or even end its operations. The most serious defect of a partnership, however is the difficulty of providing additional funds for expansion, and this may induce partners to admit new members for the sake of their capital, regardless of their fitness for taking an active part in controlling the business.

3.5.4 The Formation of Limited Liability Partnership
A limited liability partnership (LLP) is created by registration of an incorporation document with the Registrar of Companies.

The LLP is a corporate body and exists as a separate entity from its members in the same way as a limited company does. It has unlimited capacity to act and may enter into contract and hold property. It continues in existence even though its individual members may change. New members may be admitted by agreement with the existing members. Where there is no formal agreement, a person ceases to be a member by giving reasonable notice to the other members. Changes in membership must be notified to the Registrar within two weeks. There is no limit on the number of members in LLP. There is no requirement for management powers to be set out in a formal document but it is usual to have one. In the absence of an agreement, the regulations made under the Act of 2000 set out default provisions under which every member may take part in the management of LLP.

The LLP and its assets are primarily liable for the debts and obligations of the firm and in the ordinary course of business and in respect of debts. For example, the members will not be personally liable. They could, however, lose the capital that they had invested in the LLP if its assets were exhausted in paying its debts.

3.5.5 The Dissolution of a Limited Liability Partnership

A limited liability partnership can be dissolved by agreement of the members. In the situation where the LLP is insolvent; creditors can initiate a winding up. In a winding up, past and present members are liable to contribute to the LLP to the extent that they have agreed to do so in the LLP agreement.

3.5.6 The Advantages and Disadvantages of Incorporation as a Company or Limited Liability Partnership

Advantages

A perpetual succession of the organization despite retirement, bankruptcy, mental disorder or death of a member.

- Liability of members of the organization is limited to the amount of their respective shareholding
- Contractual liability of the organization from all contracts in its name
- Ownership of property vested in the organization is not affected by a change in the members
- The organization or property vested in the organization is not affected by a change in the members
- The organization may obtain finance by creating a floating charge with its undertaking or property as security, yet may realize assets within that property without the concern of the lenders during the normal course of business until completely clear. No other form of business organization can use such charge.

Disadvantages

- There is public inspection of accounts

- There are administrative expenses – filing fees for documents
- There is a compulsory annual audit.

The above advantages outweigh the disadvantages of incorporation as a company or Limited Liability Partnership.

3.5.7 What is a Joint Venture?

A joint venture may be established in a couple of different ways. Often, the parties to a joint venture will set up a new entity to handle all matters relating to a joint effort i.e. a corporation, limited liability company, or partnership. However, no formal structure is necessary. A joint venture may be established when parties agree to work cooperatively toward a common end.

3.5.7.1 What is the Difference between a Joint Venture and a Partnership?

In many respects, a joint venture and a partnership are the same thing. In the U S, joint ventures are governed by state partnership laws, and a joint venture is treated the same as a partnership for tax purposes. The key difference, in most instances, is that a joint venture is typically in place for a single business transaction or a single product line with a temporary intent.

Partnership customarily address long-term business relationships. Another key difference is that, the members of a partnership cannot take actions that benefit them individually to the detriment of the partnership. In a joint venture, the individual parties retain their separate identities, and must only abide by their commitments to the joint venture.

3.6 THE LEGAL FORMS OF BUSINESS OPERATING IN THE HOSPITALITY INDUSTRY

3.6.1 The Structure of the Hospitality Industry

The structure of the hospitality industry is complex because it is made up of a wide variety of interrelated commercial and non-commercial organizations. The hospitality industry is predominantly led by the private sector with the majority of enterprises being small and medium sized.

The private sector is that part of the economy that is not state controlled and is run by individuals or groups for profit.

The structure of the hospitality industry includes:

- Commercial Organizations:
- Non-commercial organizations (including public and voluntary sectors)
- Agencies delivering travel and tourism products and services.

The commercial or private sector of the hospitality industry involves business organizations owned by individuals or groups of people. Business organizations in this sector tend to operate for profit. This means that the money the business receives from trading by selling their goods or services to customers must be more than is spent on buying stock or providing services.

More aggressive private sector organizations may aim to increase their market share in direct competition with similar business organizations offering products or services. For examples, a travel agency may aim to progress from being a local organization based in one town to a regional or national company with many branches by competing with, taking over, or, merging with other travel agencies.

Another aim might be to maintain a constant cash flow, to keep money flowing in and out of the organization, and not allowing debts to pile up.

3.6.2 The Legal Forms of Business Operating in the Private Sector of the Hospitality Industry

3.6.2.1 Commercial – (Have profit as the main aim.)

i. The Sole Proprietor

This business is owned and controlled by one person. He takes the risks, provides the capital either from saving or a loan, keeps the profit and bears the losses. This is known as 'unlimited liability'.

The sole proprietor is able to employ additional brokers if necessary, but is restricted as the business is usually small and cash flow needs to be controlled carefully. Examples of sole proprietor enterprises in the hospitality industry are independent travel agents and owner proprietors of hospitality businesses (e.g. bed and breakfast establishments, hotels and fish and chips shops).

ii. Public Limited Company 'plc.'
This is a legal business company structure. A Public company [legally abbreviated plc.] is a type of publicly held company under UK Law. A company which offered shares to the general public and has limited liability. Examples of public limited companies involve in the travel and tourism industry and listed on the Stock Exchange include; Hilton Group, British Airways, Stagecoach, First Choice and others.

All these companies are public limited companies and must include 'plc.' as part of their name. Because the share prices of these companies are 'quoted' and the shares are sold openly on the Stock Exchange, any member of the public can invest in them.

Ownership control is divided between the shareholders who technically own the company (because they have invested the capital) and the controllers who are the board of directors.

iii. Co-operatives
A cooperative in its simplest sense is formed when individuals organize together around a common goal, usually an economic goal and are willingly to work together for a common purpose or benefit. Demonstrating a with willing to cooperate

It is based on shareholders who own the company. The principles involved are more democratic.

iv. Partnerships
A partnership means that the ownership of the business is undertaken by several individuals between two and twenty people. Since a partnership involves more than one person, there is usually more capital available so the business is likely to be larger than for a sole proprietor. Profits have to be shared and so does the decision-making process. All partners of a business are subject to unlimited

liability. The exception to this is a 'sleeping partner' who invests in the partnership but plays no active role in running the business, and whose liability to debt is limited to the amount of capital that person has invested. Each of the partners is bound by the actions of the others, which may cause problems. For example one partner might be unreliable and could bring problems, landing the other partners in debt.

v. Private Limited Companies

Any business organization with the word 'limited' in its name implies that investors in the business are liable only for the company's debts up to the amount they have invested.

Sir Richard Branson's Virgin Atlantic is a private limited company. Another private limited company is Trailfinders. Trailfinders has become one of Britain's most popular independent travel agency. It was founded in 1970 by Mike Gooley.

3.6.2.2 Non-Commercial Organizations

Non-commercial organizations are non-profit organizations that are not intended to make or distribute profits.

i. The Public Sector

The state (central or local government) provides travel and tourism activities and facilities in the public sector. The Public Sector facilities exist to provide a service to the community. A service in this context means something that benefits or is useful to the members of the public in the area.

ii. The Voluntary Sector

The voluntary sector or community sector is also known as the nonprofit sector or 'not for profit sector'. The National Council for Voluntary Organizations [NCVO] is the largest umbrella body. Falling between the public sector and the private sector is the voluntary sector, which embraces all kinds of organizations, such as clubs, societies and charities. These are not controlled by the state nor do they operate solely for profit. They have been formed because of some interest or need in the community.

Chapter Four

PROCEDURE FOR THE ACQUISITION OF A PROPERTY

4.1 PLANNING PERMISSION

4.1.1 Contacting the Relevant Authorities for Planning Permission

After deciding upon a business structure, the would-be proprietor must then consider the acquisition of property. Before he buys a land or property or before he incurs the cost of preparing detailed plans, the businessman may apply for outline planning permission. This will indicate to him whether he is likely to obtain full planning permission or not.

Formal consent of a local planning authority must be sought by one who wishes to develop a land. Permission may be granted unconditionally or subject to such conditions as the authority thinks fit.

The government working with the local authorities controls building development. The legislation controlling planning is in a series of Acts contained in the Town and Country Planning Act. 1971. The businessman must therefore ensure that he has conformed with the requirements of planning law.

The planning law is administered by local planning authorities under the Town and Country Planning Act.1990, which is subject to supervisory powers of the Secretary of State. The authorities include both county and district councils [or unitary authorities] and also, in Greater London, the London Borough Councils and the Court of Common Council of the City.

The background to control is the developing plan. Councils formulate and keep under review structure plans of general policy for their areas, and other authorities maintain local plans of general policy for theirs. The structure plan and the local plan for an area constitute its development plan. The machinery of control is Planning Permission, without which no development of land may take place.

The Secretary of State has granted permission for certain classes of development [permitted development] by a general development order applicable throughout England and Wales; permission may be granted for particular cases by special development orders. In all other cases, permission is a matter for local planning authorities [normally at district or borough level] with a right to appeal to the Secretary of State against its refusal or against conditions attached to it. The implementation of control is by local planning authorities, primarily by serving an enforcement notice.

4.1.2 Construction of a New Building, Enlargement, Renovation or Alteration of an Existing Building

Once the outline planning permission is granted, the local planning authority is then bound to allow the proposed development to go ahead.

Planning permission must be obtained from the appropriate planning authority for the construction of a new building, or the substantial enlargement of existing buildings, as such work constitutes the development of land. Planning permission, however, is not required for the enlargement, improvement or other alteration of a dwelling house, so long as the external cubic content of the original house is not exceeded by more than[49 cubic metres]. This is because such work comes under one of the classes of 'permitted development' in the Town and Country Planning

General Development Order 1973, which is deemed to be sufficient planning authorization.

4.1.3 Changing the Use of the Building

Changing the use of a property is also classified as 'development' and therefore requires planning permission. [Town and Country Planning Act 1971, s.290 and s.22]. The private householder contemplating opening a guesthouse is likely to be caught by this requirement. Permission is required if there is going to be a material change in the use of which the property is put, and this can only be decided in the light of all the circumstances. Obviously, to change a dwelling house into a shop is easily recognizable as a material change of use. However, a householder who takes in paying guests ceases to be a private householder and become the owner of a guesthouse needing planning permission. This will not be that difficult since the change is not so great.

Any householder or businessman who is in doubt on this point is able to have the matter resolved by consulting the local planning authority and the Town and Country Planning. As a general guideline, the majority of householders intending to turn their properties into guesthouses do require planning permission.

A greengrocer who wishes to change to selling clothes or newspapers can do so without acquiring planning permission, as these are all shops within the same class. But he will need planning permission if he wishes to change the premises into a cafe, a restaurant or hotel. The businessman who contemplates changing one trade to another does not need permission if the change is 'permitted development'.

To find an answer or solution to this type of difficulty, the Town and Country Planning classify a group of business which are similar in nature to each other.

No planning permission is needed if the owner wishes to transfer from one business to another, which is within the same class. For the purpose of the Act, a shop includes, amongst others, a travel agency, and a ticket agency, but does not include a hotel, restaurant, snack bar, cafe or premises licensed for the sale of intoxicating liquors for consumption on the premises.

Therefore the owner of an existing guesthouse can change it into a hotel without planning permission, but the private householder wishing to open a guest house or hotel on his premises must seek planning permission. A public house is not within any class and permission is always needed to open such a place.

When planning permission is obtained, it is now possible for the local planning authority to impose a condition, which will prevent the use of the land for which permission is granted from being changed in any way.

If development takes place without permission or without complying with the conditions, the local planning authority may serve an enforcement notice, specifying the breach complained of and requiring the land to be restored or the conditions to be observed. Failure to comply with the notice gives the local planning authority the right either to enter the land and restore it as required by the notice or take proceedings in the Magistrate's Courts where a fine may be imposed.

4.2 PURCHASING/ LEASING A PROPERTY

4.2.1 Entering Into a Written Contract to Buy or Sell a Property

If anyone wants to purchase a house, it would be very important to employ a good estate agent and a solicitor who specialized in the law of conveyance and leave the matter in their hands. A conveyance for the sale of property i. e. land or building is an agreement that must be concluded in writing.

The Law of Property Act, 1925, enacts that, contracts for the sale of land must be in writing signed by the seller or his agent, 'there unto by him lawfully authorized' and the conveyance (i.e. the deed by which the property is passed from the seller to the buyer) must be executed by seller.

A contract of sale sets out:-

- What the vendor is selling
- What title he has
- The purchase price
- When the possession will be given
- The names of the parties, etc.

This transaction is generally referred to as exchanging contracts. Once this document is drawn up and signed, the parties have entered into a legal contract and one side will run the risk of having to pay heavy damages if he tries to back down from the agreement without good cause. It is a false or mistaken view, idea, or belief that, an exchange of oral promises to sell a property is binding agreement.

Once the agreement to sell is completed, and usually when the buyer has paid a deposit of ten percent of the purchase price, the seller will send the document known as 'the abstract of title', which shows the history of the land. It is here that a solicitor's knowledge is necessary to find any flaws in the title, and to send to the seller a list of questions arising out of the abstract of title, known as 'requisitions'. When these requisitions have been answered, the buyer through the 'solicitor' prepares a draft conveyance, which, when approved, is executed by the seller, and forms the title to the property.

LIABILITIES OF THE BUYER AFTER CONTRACT IS SIGNED

As soon as the contract is signed and the buyer becomes an 'equitable' owner of the property, he must pay the purchase money even if the property is destroyed before the conveyance is executed. To counter-balance this seeming hardship, the buyer is entitled to any benefit, which may accrue to the estate between the time of contract and conveyance.

When buying a house you should, immediately, after signing the contract, either arrange with the seller that he shall give you the benefit of any existing insurance on the house, or you should effect a fresh insurance yourself, and thereby afford yourself cover should the house be burned down before the conveyance is executed.

IMPLIED COVENANTS

On a sale of freehold land certain covenants are implied, and these are:

- That the seller has the power to convey
- That the buyer shall have quiet enjoyment
- That the land is free from encumbrances; (something that is difficult to bear)
- And the seller will do everything else required to assure the land to the buyer.

When the property that is being sold is leasehold, then, in addition to the above covenants, there are three further covenants:

- That the lease is valid
- That the rent has been paid and
- That all the covenants in the lease have been observed.

If for any reason either party to a contract fails to complete his part, the remedy of the other party is either:

- By action for damages or
- To compel specific performance.

No relief will be granted if a party was guilty of fraud, misrepresentation or concealment at the time of making the contract.

MISREPRESENTATION AND MISDESCRIPTION

If the conditions of sale or the particulars contain mistakes, inaccuracies, misjudgements and mis-states, then the sale shall not commence. If the particulars are misleading, or contain any gross misrepresentation by the vendor, or any mis-description as to the property, the purchaser is not bound to complete his contract, but may get back his deposit; specific performance of the contract will not be enforced.

When the buyer has been induced to enter into a contract by a material misrepresentation of the seller, he is entitled to have the contract set aside. If the seller makes a statement, which is merely a matter of opinion then, the contract stands.

4.2.2 The Conveyance of Land to the Purchaser
Before drawing up the conveyance, which is the document transferring the legal title from the seller to the purchaser, enquiries known as 'searches' must be made both with the local authorities and with the Land Registry to find out whether or not rights of other persons exist over the land.

In the case of leasehold property restrictive covenants have been placed upon the land by the landlord restricting the use to which the land can be put. It is vital, therefore to discover any such restrictions or a further development by the local authorities, such as road development that may affect the property in future before completing purchase.

Once the conveyance is signed, the title in the property passes to the purchaser. The property may be freehold, which means that the purchaser to all intent and purpose owns the property outright, or it may be leasehold in which case the purchaser acquires the property for a term of ninety nine years.

During this time, he enjoys exclusive possession of the property, but he does not buy the land on which it stands. He as tenant pays the owner of the ground an annual rent known as the ground rent. At the end of the time limit, the property reverts to the ground landlord. Provided that certain conditions are met, he had a choice of buying the freehold or renewing the lease.

4.2.3 Mortgages
Not many of us are fortunate to have sufficient money to pay for property outright. Most people have to borrow money from the

bank and mortgage the property as security for the loan. The mortgage documents are completed along with the conveyance. The mortgagee (the lender) is entitled to place restrictions upon the use of the land whilst it is mortgaged.

The loan is repayable with interest over a period of time, for example twentyfive years. In return for the loan the mortgagee acquires rights over the property, such as right of sale, which can be exercised if the mortgagor defaults with repayment. The mortgagor is entitled to repay the loan with interest at an earlier stage if he so wishes after giving appropriate notice.

4.2.4 Leasing Business Premises

The essence of an agreement to lease business premises is that the landlord grants to the tenant exclusive possession of the property leased, for definite period of time, with the intention of creating the relationship of landlord and tenant.

A lease may be drawn up by deed or made orally but the tenant has more security if the agreement is drawn up formally. The lease can last for a period of time, for example ten years, or it can be a periodic tenancy, a quarterly for yearly tenancy, which can then be determined by either party giving the requisite notice to quit.

The conditions upon which the tenant is entitled to occupy the property are generally within the terms of the lease, but certain conditions are implied into the agreement, even if the document is silent upon the matter. The expectations are such that

- the landlord will not disturb the tenant in his occupation of the premises and
- the tenant will pay his rent.

4.3 THE LANDLORD AND TENANT ACT

4.3.1 The Landlord and Tenant Act

In recent years, Parliament has passed a series of Acts that restrict the freedom of landlord and tenant to make their terms in a lease.

As far as business premises are concerned, the relevant Act is the landlord and Tenant Act 1954, as amended by the law of Property Act 1969.

4.3.2 The object of Part 11 of the Act

The object of Part II of the Act is to give security of tenure to tenants who occupy business premises. If the tenant wishes to remain at the premises, and, if he is presented with a notice to quit, he may apply to the court for the grant of a new lease. If the parties cannot agree to the terms of a new tenancy, the court will make the terms on their behalf. Unless the landlord can establish one of the following grounds, the court will be bound to grant a new tenancy for a period not exceeding fourteen years or on such terms as it thinks fit, including a power to increase the rent.

4.3.3 Grounds for refusing to grant a new tenancy

That the tenant has broken certain of his obligations under the tenancy. For example:

- persistent delay or failure to pay the rent or, failure to carry out repairs and maintenance.
- the tenant's obligations must be broken to such an extent that he ought not to be granted a new tenancy.

If the landlord offered suitable alternative premises, the premises so offered must be comparable with the old.

4.3.4 Grounds for Compensation

- That the tenant has been occupying part only of the premises and the landlord would be able to secure a higher overall rent if he could let the premises as a whole to one tenant.
- That the landlord intends to demolish or reconstruct the premises. Note: The provisions outlined above apply to all business premises except licensed premises whose main function is the sale of intoxicating liquor for consumption on the premises. Thus public houses are not protected by

the Act; but the off licences, hotels and restaurants are so protected.

If a new tenancy is refused on any of the last two grounds mentioned above, the tenant is entitled to compensation. The compensation will be decided by the court. In addition, any outgoing tenant who has used the premises for business purposes is entitled to compensation from the landlord for any structural improvements he, the tenant, has made which have increased the letting value of the premises. If the parties are unable to reach an agreement over the improvements then an application can be made to the court for a settlement. All compensation claims must be made within or before six months after the lease expires.

4.4 LICENSING

4.4.1 What is a licence

A licence is an official document which allows someone to do something. For example; a driving licence is a permit that allows you to drive. A liquor licence is a government document that allows someone to sell alcohol.

In Great Britain an Off licence means, licence to sell alcohol to be consumed away from the place (the shop) where it is bought. The shop has official permission to sell beers, wines and spirits. A licensed hotel or restaurant is a hotel or restaurant which has a licence to sell alcohol.

4.4.2 Premises Licensed for Retail Sale of Intoxicating Liquor

Premises on which the business carried on is the business of selling intoxicating liquor by retailing for consumption either on or off the premises ('the public house')

Premises on which the business carried on is the business of selling intoxicating liquor by retail for consumption off the premises (the off licence).

4.4.3 Points to Consider Before Granting a Liquor Licence

A licence may be granted to an individual or to a partnership. The person to whom a licence is granted, should be the owner of the proposed business to be carried on under the licence. A court must be satisfied with the following before a licence can be granted.

- In considering the fitness of a person to hold a licence for any premises, the court shall have regard to: his character, reputation and financial standing.
- His qualification and experience in respect of managing the business which is proposed to be carried on under the licence.
- If the premises is suitable for that kind of licence.
- The, premises are what was specified in the application.
- The statutory procedures has been carried out.
- Is there not enough existing public house or off-licence shops.

4.4.4 Applying for a Licence

A person intending to make an application for a licence shall:

Display notice of that application on or near the premises for which licence is to be sought during the weeks before that time.

- Not less than three weeks before that time
- The following persons must be notified as to where the premises is situated i.e.
- The police, at the district or area where the premises is situated
- The district council for the district in which the premises is situated. The applications which are served must also have the following attached to them:
- The plan of the premises showing the area to be licensed and a copy of the planning permission.

4.4.5 Objection to the Grant of a Licence.

Persons, such as competitors can object to the grant of a licence or any of the court orders available based on the grounds that the application fails to fulfil the criteria laid down by the statute and the court. Residents nearby could also object to the grant of a licence.

4.4.6 Renewal, Transfer and Altering of a Licence

- The licence, unless suspended, is renewable after five years. After this time an application must be made to the magistrate's court for a renewal.
- Where the owner of the business sells intoxicating liquor by retail in the licensed premises, has, or is about to change, then the new proposed owner must make an application to the magistrates' court for the transfer of the licence.
- Licence holders must apply to the court for consent to certain alterations to the licensed premises. If such alterations are major, then a new application for a licence may have to be made to the county court.

4.4.7 Opening Hours

In the United Kingdom, the general permitted hours for all licensed premises except off-licences and places of public entertainment are:

On week days, other than Christmas Day or other holidays are from 11.30 a.m. to 11.00 p.m. and on Sundays and on Christmas day from 12.30 – 10.00 p.m.

The general permitted hours for an off-licence are:

On weekdays, other than Christmas day, from 8.00 a.m. to 11.00 p.m. and on Sundays from 10.00 a.m. to 10.00 p.m.

4.5 HOLDERS OF A LICENCE FOR THE FOLLOWING ESTABLISHMENTS

The holder of a licence for a public house, a hotel, a restaurant, a conference centre or higher education institution may apply for an order that part of his premises be declared suitable for functions.

Once such an order is in force, the licensee may then apply for an extension licence as and when it is proposed to hold a function in the specified part of the licensed premises. However, such a suitability order would only be granted if the relevant part of the premises is structurally adapted for use, or intended to be used for the purposes of providing persons frequenting the premises with a main table meal. A main table meal is, or includes, a main course, which is eaten by a person seated at a table or a counter. The hours are normally between 11.30 a.m. and 1.00 a.m. into the morning of the next day.

In addition to the above permitted hours, an additional hours order mainly in certain circumstances may be obtained by the licence holder.

For such an application to be successful the court has to be satisfied that the relevant part of the licensed premises is structurally adapted and used, for the purpose of providing:

- musical or other entertainment;
- substantial refreshment; or
- both such entertainment and refreshment.

4.6 PERMITTED HOURS FOR CHILDREN

4.6.1 Children Under the Age of 18

During the permitted hours a person under the age of 18 must not be in:

- any part of any licensed premises which contains a bar; or
- is used exclusively or mainly for the sale and consumption of intoxicating liquor.

The prohibitions in respect of the off-sales part of the public house or the offlicence do not apply if a young person is accompanied by a person who is over the age of 18.

The licence holder of any licensed premises which has either an open bar in a particular part of the licensed premises or which has a part used exclusively or mainly for the sale and consumption of intoxicating liquor may apply for a childrens' certificate. A children's certificate may be operational at any time up to 9.00 p.m. and the licence holder must display the notice.

The court will not make such an order unless it is satisfied:

- The specified part constitutes an environment in which it is suitable for a person under the age of 18 to be present
- Meals and suitable beverages other than intoxicating liquor will be made available for consumption in the specified part when the certificate is operational
- The specified part is equipped and furnished with an adequate number of tables and chairs.
- There has been compliance with the condition prescribed by the regulations.

4.6.2 The Sale of Intoxicating Liquor at Meal Times

Table meals and intoxicating liquor are sold only to persons as an ancillary to their meals. The effect of this provision is that on Sundays, for example, one may designate a bar as a restaurant area, operating it considerably according to restaurant conditions. During that time it will be permissible for children to be present.

It has always been possible in recent years to allocate for the use of children a room, which is clearly not a bar by reason of its layout, location or usage. Such arrangements have however frequently proved unsatisfactory from the point of view of the licensee who may not be able adequately to supervise the area. The licensing justified who might be aware of these practical shortcomings and be willing to permit a more favourable arrangement if they are able also to regulate it by way of conditions. This is the justification for the children's certificate.

4.6.3 Childrens' Certificate

One of the conclusions of the much respected Errol Section 171 Committee Report, published in 1972, was that, the licensing justices should be able to issue a certificate, on application by a personal licensee, to the effect that the premises are licensed and that the public interest and convenience does not require the exclusion of children under 14 years of age from part or parts of the premises."

"The licensing justices should have absolute discretion in deciding whether to grant a certificate and they should be able to attach conditions to it governing the conduct of the premises. Justices should be able to suspend or revoke the certificate on complaint and would be required to have regard to the suitability of the premises for children under 14, and there would be a right of appeal against their decisions." The somewhat belated enactment of this recommendation, almost without qualification, is testimony to the committee's success in achieving its stated goal of anticipating the likely development of leisure patterns and consumer needs.

The Provision finally came into force in England and Wales on 3 January 1995.

4.7 LICENSING MATTERS

Licensing matters are dealt with in the court. The application is usually initially for 'provisional' grant of a licence because the application may be refused. Application for a final grant is made to the court when the shop is furnished and ready for business. At the final stage, no advertisement is required but notice must be served on the same parties as mentioned above.

Licence holders must apply to the court for consent to certain alterations to the licensed premises. If such alterations are major, then a new application for a licence may have to be made to the county court.

4.8 SIGNS AND ADVERTISEMENTS

As a general rule, an advertisement may not be displayed unless consent is given either by the regulations themselves or by the local planning authorities.

The regulations do permit the display of advertisements on business premises relating to the business or to goods sold from the premises. Control is placed upon the size of advertisements and extensive powers are available both to the local planning authority and the Secretary of State, even to the extent of ordering the removal of the signs in the interest of amenity and public safety.

Chapter Five

THE LAW OF CONTRACT

5.1 INTRODUCTION

A contract is a formal agreement between two or more parties. A formal agreement can be made with a person or a company to do or deliver something. When you sign a formal written document or agreement, you are entering into a contract with these people whereby each side acquires legal rights in respect of the promises or actions of the other party.

It is often thought that contracts made orally are not legal contracts, but this is not true. An oral contract may be difficult to prove. This is because the court will have to decide as to whose statement to believe. But such difficulties do not take away the legality of the contract. There are other contracts that have to be done in writing and drawn up under seal, such as a contract for the sale of a house or a land.

We shall be dealing mainly with simple contracts, which means they can be made orally or in writing. Anytime you make a hotel booking, order a meal in a restaurant, shop from a supermarket, employ a person in a company, or buy a ticket for a train, a bus or an aeroplane to travel it means, you are entering into a contract.

All contracts must contain three elements. No contract exists if the elements of a contract are less than three, but only a friendly arrangement, which can be kept or broken at the convenience of the parties.

5.1.1 Definition of a Contract

"A contract may be defined as an agreement, enforceable by the law, between two or more persons to do some act or acts; their intention being to create legal relations and not merely to exchange mutual promises, both having given something or having promised to give something of value as consideration for any benefit derived from the agreement".

[Smith and Keenan – English Law, Eleventh Edition]

5.1.2 The Important Elements of a Valid Contract

The important elements for the formation of a valid and enforceable contract can be summed up as follows:

- An offer and acceptance (which is in effect the agreement)
- Consideration (unless the contract is by deed), an intention to be legally bound (this requirement usually operates to prevent a purely domestic or social agreement from constituting a contract)
- As well as capacity of parties to make a contract.

The agreement must also comply with any formal legal requirements (it may be oral, written, partly oral and partly written or implied from conduct). Finally, the agreement must be legal. There should be written formalities in some cases, the genuineness of the consent by the two parties to the terms of the contract, and the contract must not be in opposition to public policy.

The three Elements of a Contract

[i]   Agreement
[ii] Consideration and intention to be legally bound
[iii] Capacities of parties to make a contract

5.2 THE FORMATION OF A CONTRACT

5.2.1 Agreement –Making a Contract (I)

A contract is a formal agreement between two or more parties. A contract is formed when one party (the offeror) makes an offer, which is accepted by the other party (offeree). The bargaining and negotiation must be concluded and the arrangement must be certain and final. In the business world, very few contracts are to such an extent that one conversation or two letters need to be exchanged before parties reach a bargain. More often than not, agreements take time and bargaining to solve difficulties. It may be necessary to inspect several documents before being able to say that the parties are in agreement or that there is a 'meeting of minds'. When the price, the time or place are still undecided, then the court would not enforce such a bargain because it would be too vague and uncertain. The agreement is arrived at by a process of 'offer and acceptance', made in writing or by word of mouth or even by conduct as in an auction sale.

MAKING A CONTRACT I (AGREEMENT)

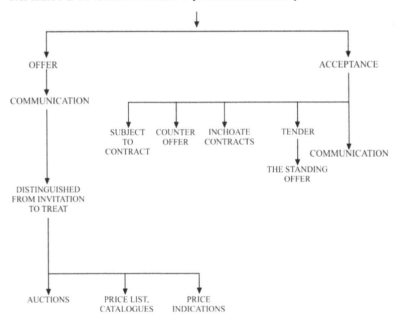

Fig.1.8.1 A diagram of making a Contract (Agreement)

5.2.1.1 Types of Agreement

5.2.1.1.1 Incomplete (or Inchoate) Agreement

A contract will not be enforced unless the parties have expressed themselves with reasonable clarity on the matter of essential terms. A situation may therefore exist in which the parties have gone through a form of offer and acceptance but this has left some terms unclear so that if either party wishes to avoid the contract he may claim to do so on the basis that he does not know precisely what to do in order to perform his part of it. The concept of the inchoate contract normally arises as a defence to an action for breach of contract.

However, it is necessary to distinguish between:

1. a term which has yet to be agreed by the parties; and
2. a term on which they have agreed but is in the event, meaningless or ambiguous.

In the first case, no contract exists unless the deficiency can be made good by the methods outlined above. In the second instance, it may be possible to ignore the term and enforce the contract without it. However, if the term is still being negotiated, the contract will be inchoate and unenforceable. In addition, the term must be clearly severable from the rest of the contract, i.e. it must be possible to enforce the contract without it.

Case Law

a. Scammell v. Ouston, 1941, where the agreement is inchoate
b. Nicholene v. Simmonds, 1953, A meaningless term is ignored.

5.2.1.1.2 The Meaning of the term 'waiver'

At Common Law

Where a party promises to relinquish some or all of his rights under a contract, he sometimes said to have 'waived' those rights. Unfortunately, however, the word 'waiver' covers a variety of situations different in their legal nature.

- **Rescission** – Sometimes waiver means total rescission of the contract; 'The waiver spoken of in the case is an entire abandonment and dissolution of the contract.' This usage assumes that the rescission is supported by consideration. It has been judiciary criticised so far as it refers to a purported release without consideration. 'To say that a claim is to be waived is incorrect. If a right has accrued, it must be released or discharged by deed or upon consideration.'

- **Variation** – Waiver is occasionally used to refer to a variation which, though supported by consideration, is for some other reason not binding contractually. This usage occurs in the context of the rule that a contract which is required to be in, or evidenced in, writing can be rescinded but not varied orally. Here waiver is sometimes used to refer to a variation as opposed to a rescission. For example, in one case a written contract for the sale of iron called for delivery in June; later the delivery date was orally extended at the request of the buyers. In spite of the extension, the buyers failed to take delivery, and the seller recovered damages for breach of the original contract. 'There was no fresh agreement which can be regarded as having been substituted for the original written contract. There was nothing more than a waiver by the defendants of a delivery by the plaintiff in June.'

- **Forbearance** – A variation may not be contractually binding for want of consideration or of contractual intention, or because it fails to comply with a legal requirement that it must be in, or evidenced in, writing. It may nevertheless have certain limited legal effects, which are sometimes said to arise because one party has 'waived' his rights. To distinguish such arrangements from contractually binding variations, they will here be referred to as 'forbearances.'

Their effects are as follows;

- The party requesting the forbearance cannot refuse to accept the varied performance. Thus, if a seller at the request of the buyer delivers late, the buyer cannot refuse to accept on the ground that delivery was made after the time specified in the original contract.

- If the varied performance is actually made and accepted, neither party can claim damages on the ground that performance was not in accordance with the original contract. Thus, in the above example the seller who delivers late, is not liable in damages. But if the contract is not performed at all, the damages are assessed on the footing that the breach took place at the end of the extended period.

- The cases that give rise to the present difficulty are those in which the party granting the forbearance, refuses to perform, or to accept performance, in accordance with it.

- But in many cases the party for whose benefit the forbearance was granted was allowed to enforce the contract in accordance with the new terms. In Hartley versus Hymans a buyer of cotton agreed to allow the seller to make a delivery. It was held that he was liable in damages for peremptorily refusing to take delivery after the original date specified in the contract had expired. Similarly, a party may acquiesce in a method of payment other than that specified in the contract so as to indicate that the new method is to become the 'accepted method.' He cannot then refuse to perform his part simply because the other party has not performed his obligation to pay strictly in accordance with the terms originally agreed; nor can be peremptorily require performance strictly.

- Waiver refers to the act of abandoning or refraining from asserting a legal right. It can be express or implied.

- **Express Waiver** – A voluntary and intentional waiver. An example can be seen in cases of Estoppel.

- **Implied Waiver** – may arise where a person has pursued such a course of conduct as to evidence an intention to waive a right, or where his conduct is inconsistent with any other intention than to waive it. It may be inferred from a conduct or act of putting one off his guard and leading him to believe that a right has been waived. Mere silence however, is no waiver unless there is an obligation to speak.

Definitions by some writers;

"The term waiver is one of those words of indefinite connotation in which our legal literature abounds; like a cloak, it covers a multitude of sins".

–William R. Anson, Principles of the Law of Contract

"Waiver is often asserted as the justification for a decision when it is not appropriate to the circumstances".

– Robert E. Keaton and Alan I. Widiss, Insurance Law.1998

Waiver of Communication

There are some cases in which the offeror is deemed to have waived communication of the acceptance. This occurs in the case of unilateral contracts such as promises to pay money in return for some act to be carried out by the offeree. Performance of the act operates as an acceptance, and no communication is required.

Case Law–(Carlill v. Carbolic Smoke Ball Co., 1893)

5.2.1.2 Types of Offer

An offer can be made either to a particular person, or to a group of persons. For example a proprietor offers accommodation to Mr Thomas, or, e.g. The Hoteliers Association. However, the offer can only be accepted by the person to whom it is made because the proprietor's mind is only directed towards an agreement with that person. So in the above example, an attempt by a third party, Mr White, to take the accommodation offered to Mr Thomas is not an acceptance, but is in truth, a fresh offer from Mr White.

An advertisement giving details of the services of a restaurant is no more than an invitation to treat, i.e. an invitation to persons to visit the hotel or restaurant to do business. Proprietors must not change their prices prior to or on arrival of their guest. There should be no additions to the initial charges, and anything contrary to this will be a criminal offence under the Trade Description Act 1968.

5.2.1.2.1 Communicating Information

A request for information is really one step further back from an offer. It merely leads up to possible agreement but is not part of the agreement itself. A guest who enquires of the proprietor if he has vacancies in his hotel is merely requesting for information. The proprietor's answer may be general in giving the information or it may be more definite and include an offer to supply the accommodation. No liability however is incurred by either party simply by requesting and supplying information.

5.2.1.2.2 Lapse of Time

An offer can be open for a fixed period of time. For example, a proprietor states that he must have a reply to his offer of accommodation within one week. Once the time has expired, the offer lapses automatically. If no fixed period is stated in the offer, it will lapse at the expiration of a reasonable time. What is reasonable depends upon the commodity and the custom in a particular trade. In a contract for the sale of perishable goods, two or three days is a reasonable time. In the hotel trade perhaps, a fortnight would be classified as a reasonable time.

5.2.1.2.3 Invitation to Treat I

Problems relating to contractual offers have arisen in the case of auction sales, but the position is now largely resolved. An advertisement of an auction is not an offer. At the auction, the bid is the offer and the auctioneer's request for bids is merely an invitation to treat. The sale is complete when the hammer falls, and after that time any bid may be withdrawn.

5.2.1.2.4 Invitation to Treat II (price indications/ price lists and catalogues)

According to the ordinary law of contract, articles in a shop window is merely an invitation to treat. It is in no sense an offer for sale .The acceptance of the offer which would constitute a contract

A dress priced £40, in a shop window is not an offer to sell. It is not possible for a person to enter the shop and say, "I accept that offer, here is the £40". It is the would-be buyer who makes the offer when tendering the money. If by chance the dress has been wrongly priced, the shop owner shall be entitled to say: "I am sorry, the price is £80" and refuse to sell. An invitation to treat is often merely a statement of the price and not an offer to sell. The same principles have been applied to price lists, catalogues, circulars, newspapers and magazines.

Case Law

Pharmaceutical Society of Great Britain v Boots Ltd.1953 AllER – price indication.

Partridge v. Crittenden, 1968 –Magazines and Circulars.

5.2.1.2.5 Other Situations

In other cases, such as automatic vending machines, the position is doubtful, and it may be that such machines are an invitation to treat. However, it is more likely that the provision of the machine represents an implied offer, which is accepted when a coin is put into it. However, it seems that if a bus travels along a certain route, there is an *implied offer* on the part of its owners to carry passengers at the published fares for the various stages, and it would appear that when a passenger puts himself inside the bus, he makes an *implied acceptance* of the offer, agreeing to be bound by the Company's conditions and to pay the appropriate fare:

Case law

Wilkie v. London Passenger Transport Board [1947].1 A11 ER 258

5.2.1.3 Types of Acceptance

Once the existence of an offer has been proved, the court must be satisfied that the offeree has accepted the offer, otherwise there is no contract. It should be noted that an acceptance brings the offer to an end because the offer then merges into the contract.

5.2.1.3.1 By Letter or e-mail

To complete the agreement, the offer must be accepted and the acceptance must be communicated to the offeror. It is not enough for a guest to think that the terms offered are suitable, he must communicate his agreement to the proprietor. A letter or an e-mail by a guest stating that he accepts the accommodation offered in the terms quoted means that the parties have reached an agreement. In other words, the contract is concluded even though the time for the guest's visit has not yet arrived.

The booking of a hotel consists really of a mutual exchange of promises, i.e. the proprietor promises to supply the room and board and the guest promises to pay for the services. In agreements such as this, a condition that silence shall amount to acceptance cannot be imposed by the offeror [proprietor], upon the offeree [guest] without the latter's consent. Acceptance of the offer is complete and a contract made as soon as the letter or e-mail is received.

5.2.1.3.2 By Telephone

Where negotiations are being conducted over the telephone, the acceptance must be heard by the offeror [proprietor]. It is up to the person accepting the offer to make a proper communication and to make certain that the other party has heard his acceptance. Suppose, for instance, I made an offer to a man by telephone and in the middle of his reply, the line goes dead so that I do not hear his words of acceptance, there is no contract at that moment.

5.2.1.3.3 Revocation of an Offer

An offer may be revoked at any time before the acceptance has been given. So, the proprietor who writes, offering accommodation to a guest, may withdraw that offer at any time before the guest accepts.

It is not enough for the proprietor to decide in his own mind to withdraw the offer. To be effective, the notice of revocation must reach the guest. It is preferable for the notice to be expressly communicated to him, for example, by a telephone call or letter but this is not essential. It is acceptable for the guest to learn of the revocation indirectly through a reliable third party. If the notice of revocation is in the form of a letter, the revocation is effective only from the moment the letter is received by the guest and not when the proprietor posts it.

5.2.1.4 Termination of an Offer

5.2.1.4.1 By the Refusal of the Offeree

A guest may refuse the offer of accommodation made to him by the hotelier. He incurs no liability by so refusing. Should the guest change his mind after this, and try to claim the booking, then negotiations must start afresh.

5.2.1.4.2 By the Death of Either Party

If the guest dies, then the negotiations are ended. If the proprietor dies and if he is running the business personally, and its reputation depends on the proprietor, the negotiations may cease. But if the hotel is owned by a company, the death of the manager will not usually interfere with the bookings.

5.2.1.4.3 By Qualified Acceptance

This terminates the original offer. A qualified acceptance is a counter offer. For example, the proprietor offers Mr. Thomas accommodation at 20 dollars a week, but only on condition that he is given one of the double bedrooms. This is the original offer. Mr. Thomas reply is not an acceptance on the exact terms the proprietor offered. It cancels the original offer, becomes a counter-offer and the proprietor is free to accept or reject Mr. Thomas' requests. Where the counter-offer introduces a new term, the original offer is cancelled through the counter-offer.

5.2.2 Consideration – Making the Contract II

5.2.2.1 Consideration

Every simple contract, which is not drawn up under seal must be supported by consideration. As very few business arrangements are made through the channel of a document under seal, we can concentrate our attention on the meaning of consideration.

Consideration can best be explained by saying it is the price paid for the bargain. For example, in a restaurant, the owner (promisor) supplies the meal in exchange for the customer (promisee) paying the price. There must always be a benefit accruing to the promisor or a detriment suffered by the promisee (in that he may give value to the contract).

So long as some price is charged, the law does not worry about whether the bargain is good or bad. The parties are free to make whatever bargain they choose. Furthermore, the consideration must move from the promise, which means that, a person can only enforce a promisee if he himself promised to do something in return for the others' promise. To put it in another way, only the two parties to a contract can sue or be sued upon it.

Definition 1

Consideration which is essential to the formation of any contract not made by deed was defined as:

> "Some right, interest, profit accruing to one party, or some forbearance, detriment, loss or responsibility given, suffered or undertaken by the other. Paying (or promising to pay) money in return for the supply of goods or services constitutes the most Common form of consideration.

> "Consideration may be executory, where the parties exchange promises to perform acts in the future, e.g. B promises to deliver goods to C and C promises to pay for the goods; or it may be executed where one party promises to do something in return for the act of another, rather than for mere promise of future performance of an act. Here the performance of the act is required before there is any liability on the promise."

Definition 2

> "An act of forbearance of one party, or the promises of the promise thereof, is the price for which the promise of the other is bought, and the promise thus given for value is enforceable."

SIR FREDERICK POLLOCK

The definition which was adopted by the House of Lords in Dunlop v Selfridge, 1915 fits executory consideration as well as executed. The 'promise for a promise' concept really means that consideration can consist in a promise to act in the future, e.g. to deliver goods or to pay for goods.

Definition 3

> "An exchange of promises by which each party makes a gain and suffers a detriment– the requirements for there to be consideration before there will be a legally binding contract in English law emphasizes the theory held by many legal commentators and theorists that contract is based upon a bargain – something for something else. The consideration must be sufficient but needs not be adequate".

Collins Law Dictionary

5.2.2.2 Consideration In Relation to Formation of a Contract

A number of general rules govern consideration in terms of the formation of a contract. Here, we shall deal with some considerations that concern the hospitality industry.

a. Simple contracts must be supported by consideration

In practical terms, it is the Common Law's way of limiting the number of agreements which can be brought before the courts for enforcement. Other legal systems have required, e.g. part performance by one or other of the parties or that the contract be made in writing and, if so, no consideration is required. The effect of the consideration rule is that in English law, an agreement, even if the parties intend legal relations, is not a contract unless it is supported by consideration or made by deed. *b. Bailment*

Definition of bailment

This is where a person may be held liable for negligence, damage or loss of goods in his care, although he received no money or other consideration for looking after them. However, confusion can best be avoided by regarding bailment as an independent transaction, which has the characteristics of contract and tort but is neither. It seems that when B hands his goods to C under a bailment, C has certain duties in regard to the care of the goods whether the bailment is accompanied by a contract not.

The court may refuse a claim on the contract by a person who has given inadequate consideration. The basis of this doctrine [the doctrine of inequality of bargaining power] which has been applied in particular by Lord Denning, has not, as yet, received much direct judicial support.

Case Law:

Coggs v. Bernard (1703) 2 Ld.Raym.909.

Bacvar v. Jarvis Norfolk Hotel [1999] 10CL

112. c. Consideration must move from the promisee

For example, the person to whom the promise is made (the promisee) must give some consideration for it to the promisor. From this, comes the doctrine of privity of contract, which is as follows; *d. Privity of Contract*

It means that in general, third parties cannot sue for the carrying out of promises made by the parties to a contract. If a contract between Karl and Louis requires Louis to benefit Chris, the privity rule prevents Chris from suing Louis. Karl may sue Louis if Louis breaks the contract, and the court may award Karl damages or grant a decree of specific performance under which Louis must perform the contract to the benefit of Chris.

This view is based on the belief that the 'privity' rule is merely an aspect of the rule that 'consideration must move from the promise'.

The situation is different if Karl, Louis and Chris are all parties to a deed. Chris can then sue Louis for damages if Louis fails to carry out his promises in the deed. There can be no consideration in the case of deeds. *e. Main Exceptions to the Privity Rule*

There are cases in which a person is allowed to sue upon a contract to which he is not a party as follows:-

f. Agency

A principal, even if undisclosed, may sue on a contract made by an agent. This exception is perhaps more apparent than real, because in fact the principal is the contracting party who has merely acted through the agent. *g. Other Main Exceptions to the Privity Rule are*

Bills of Exchange, Price restrictions under the Resale Act 1976, s, 26, Insurance, Section II of the Married Women's Property Act 1882, Bankers' Commercial Credits and Performance Bonds, Assignment and Land Law.

Case Law–Smith and Snipe Hill/Farm Ltd. v. River Douglas Catchment Board, 1949.

5.2.2.3 Intention to Create Legal Relations/ or to be Legally Bound.

The parties must be willing to be legally bound by their agreements. In the event of a disagreement, they must be prepared to allow a court of law to settle their differences. However, if the parties do not wish to be legally bound, the agreement must expressly state.

> "The law will not necessarily recognize the existence of a contract enforceable in a court of law simply because of the presence of mutual promises. It is necessary to establish also that both parties made the agreement with the intention of creating legal relations so that if the agreement was broken the party offended would be able to exercise legally

enforceable remedies. For example, a gentleman's agreement is an agreement between businessmen where they expressly state that there is no legal intent behind their bargain. Generally speaking, domestic agreements made between husband and wife living together are presumed not to be legal contracts, but financial agreements between separated spouses are usually binding contracts."

5.2.2.3.1 Parties Not Expressly Denying Their Intention to be Legally Bound

Advertisements

Some advertisements are statements of opinion and as such are not actionable unless the advertisement makes false statements of specific verifiable facts. The court will not enforce the claims made for the product on a contractual basis.

Family Agreements

Regarding family agreements, the court will not interfere unless it is necessary. The intention to create legal relations arises for consideration here as well but it seems the less close the relationship between the parties the more likely that the court will presume that legal relations were intended. Legal proceedings are an inappropriate way of settling purely domestic disputes.

For example, where a husband and wife are living together in harmony when agreement was made, then the agreement is not enforceable as a contract, but where a husband and wife were living together and not in harmony or were separated altogether when the agreement was made, the court will enforce it.

5.2.2.3.2 Parties Expressly Denying any Intention to be Legally Bound

Agreements of a commercial nature are presumed to be made with contractual intent. A person cannot escape liability simply because he did not have a contractual intention. Where businessmen agree to and if they expressly declare that they do not wish to assume contractual obligations, then the law accepts and implements their decision.

5.2.2.3.3 Statutory Provisions

Some Acts of Parliament render some agreement unenforceable. For example, a contract of engagement, which is an agreement to marry is not enforceable at law since there is no intention to create legal relations. The acceptance of ordinary letters and packets for transmission does not give rise to a contract between the post office and sender. Also, under s.179 of the Trades Union and Labour Relations (Consolidation) Act 1992, collective agreements between Trade Unions and employers (or Employers' Associations) concerning industrial conditions, are considered not to be intended to be legally enforceable unless they are in writing and contain a provision to that effect.

5.2.3 Capacity of Parties to Make a Contract III

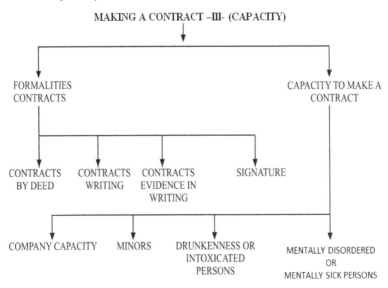

Fig. 1.9.2 A diagram of making a contract (Capacity)

5.2.3.1 Categories of People Who Have the Capacity to Enter into a Contract

We now consider the capacity of persons to make a contract. Adult citizens have full capacity to enter into any kind of contract but certain groups of persons and corporations have certain disabilities in this context. The law divides people other than normal adults into the following categories:

Infants (Minors}
Mentally sick
Drunkards
Married Women
Companies

In addition to the above, there are two other categories of persons to consider, namely managers and agents.

Infants (Minors)

Children of eighteen years and below are considered infants (Minors). Knowledge of the rule is still vital, for example young people starting in fulltime employment or travelling and staying in hotels who could well be under eighteen years of age.

The law aims to protect infants against their own inexperience while realizing that it should not cause unnecessary hardship to adults who deal with infants. Although it is not legal for an infant to make a contract, only certain classes of contracts can be enforced against him; an agreement to supply an infant with 'necessaries' is one of such contracts. Necessaries are goods which he needs because he has not sufficient of them when the contract is made and which are of a type suitable to his way of life.

Hotel accommodation could certainly come within the classification of necessaries for a student who has to live away from home during term time. The infant must pay a reasonable price for the goods received which is not necessarily the contract price. The question is always whether it is reasonable for the infant to buy such an article. It is up to the supplier to prove that the infant needs the goods and that they are suitable to his way of life. Provided he can prove this, then the contract is enforceable against the infant. Contracts for the minor's benefit including contracts of service, apprenticeship and education such as a teaching trade are also enforceable against the infant. Should the infant break the agreement, he may be liable in damages. The infant cannot be forced to repay money he has borrowed or pay for unnecessary goods unless he has entered into the contract fraudulently. Such agreements are classified as void and unenforceable against the infant.

Mentally Sick and intoxicated Persons

A contract made by a person with a mental disorder or a person who is drunk and is incapable of understanding what he is doing is valid unless he can prove that he did not understand the nature of the contract and the other party knew he was not well, and that his disability prevented him from understanding the agreement.

Such a person must pay a reasonable price if he is supplied with necessaries. Necessaries are goods suitable to the condition in life of such a person and to his actual requirements at the time of sale and delivery. The Common Law defines necessary services in the same way. Therefore the principles of 'necessaries' is applied to persons with mental incapacity and drunkards in the same way as to minors.

Married Women

A married woman is free to enter into and be bound by the terms of a contract. Should she book a hotel room but fail to pay, then, the correct course is to sue her for breach of contract. Sometimes, the wife may be acting as her husband's agent. i.e. she may book a room on his behalf and at his request. In this case, the husband is then liable for any expenses incurred: A husband is liable for the debts incurred by his wife, unless he expressly notifies the hotel that he will no longer be liable for her debts. Where a husband and wife or a man and his mistress are living together, there is a presumption that she can pledge his credit for necessaries. However, he can escape liability in several ways– by proving that he had told the tradesman not to give credit to his wife or that she had sufficient goods.

Companies

As so many hotels are owned by companies, it is important to have some knowledge of the ability of a company to enter into a contract. A company, being an artificial person must negotiate through its directors and employees. Acting through such persons, the company may enter into and be bound by contracts in the same way as human beings.

Directors can make contracts on behalf of the company, but they can only make such contracts as they are permitted to make by the documents incorporating the company, i.e. the Articles of Association and the memorandum. Should they go beyond its powers stated therein, we say that the company is acting beyond its powers. Not every employee may bind the company by a contract. It is only those persons who have such authority by the articles of a company. For example, in a hotel, a chef would have authority to purchase food and a booking clerk would have the authority to make accommodation agreements, whereas a room attendant and waiter would have no such authority. If the articles expressly forbid the employee to make the contract, the company is not bound even if that agreement is of a type normally made by such an employee.

Managers and Other Employees

The ability of such persons to enter into contracts on behalf of their employers, acting as their employer's agent must depend initially on the terms of their personal contract of employment. A restaurant owner who expressively authorizes his manager to make a contract on his behalf is bound by the agreement. But the owner may also be bound by those actions, which he has not authorized if those agreements are within the normal scope of a restaurant manager's work. This is so even though he may have expressly forbidden the manager to make such a contract and provided the other party to the contract is not aware of the prohibition.

Travel Agents

It is quite usual for a holidaymaker to book his holiday through a travel agency, especially if he is going abroad. In the legal sense, an agent is a person who makes a contract on behalf of his principal with a third party. Once the contract is made, the agent's role is completed. A travel agent is not always an agent in the legal sense of the word: A travel agent who helps a customer on an individual basis by booking accommodation, obtaining train tickets or excursion tickets is working as a legal agent. Once arrangements are completed, his task is over and any dispute over bills is then a matter between the hotelier and the customer.

The travel agent who arranges package tours may make a contract between himself and the hotel proprietor by which he agrees to take a block-booking of hotel rooms. Any dispute over non-payment of bills is then a matter between the hotelier and travel agent, and the prudent hotelier will obtain a written statement from the agent concerning responsibilities for payment of the bill. Also, he will obtain a separate contract between himself and the customer, on terms usually set out in the standard form of booking.

Exclusive clauses are very common in the booking forms and the holidaymaker is well advised to read the form carefully before signing, as he is taken to have agreed to any conditions on a document to which he has put his signature.

Case Law–Cook v. Spanish Holiday Tours (1960 AC).

Mr. Cook booked a Spanish Holiday through the defendant's company, but when he and his wife arrived in Spain, no room was available for them in the hotel. They were offered a filthy room in an annex where beetles were running around the floor boards. They had to spend the night in the hotel and fly back to England the next day and the remainder of their holiday was spent in Brighton. Damages for breach of contract were awarded to Mr. Cook.

The Appeal court said that the agent could not rely on the argument that his duty was only to book a room and not to provide a room. "It isn't much good booking a room if you can't have a room," said the Judge.

Some protection has been given to holiday makers by two Acts, namely the Misrepresentation Act 1967 and the Trade Descriptions Act 1968, both of which enable civil actions and criminal prosecutions to be started against persons who mislead others by false descriptions. There is also the fact that one false statement in a brochure can give rise to any number of prosecutions.

Travel agents, in October 1974 agreed a voluntary code giving more protection to the customer. At the moment, anyone can set up in business as a travel agent, there being no form of registration. The only control comes under the Civil Aviation Act, whereby from April 1973, some agents who need an air travel organizer's licence will have to prove that they have adequate financial resources.

DISCHARGE OF CONTRACT

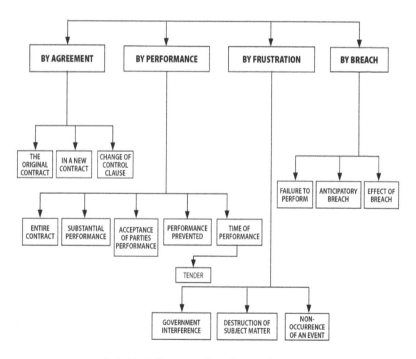

Fig 5.10 A diagram of Discharge of Contract

5.3 DISCHARGE OF CONTRACT

The discharge of a contract means in general that parties are free from their mutual obligations. A contract may be discharged in four ways: lawfully by agreement, by performance or by frustration and unlawfully by breach.

5.3.1 Discharge by Agreement

Normally what has been created by agreement may be ended by agreement.

5.3.2 Discharge by Performance

A contract may be discharged by performance, the discharge taking place when both parties have performed the obligations which the contract placed on them.

5.3.3 Discharge by Frustration

The agreement has been impossible to perform from the beginning.

Frustration:-One party dying or is seriously ill or the building is destroyed. A contract which is initially valid and binding, may later be discharged if it turns out that the contract has become impossible to perform. In this situation, it is said that the contract is frustrated. The parties will not be held to their promises in the light of the altered circumstances. Examples of frustrated contracts: –

- where the government has passed a law or issued an order making the performance of the contract illegal, e.g. an order that hotels and restaurants within a specified area must cease to operate because of bomb threats.
- where the contract depends upon the personal service of one man, his death or illness will frustrate it. For example, a small hotel or restaurant whose business reputation relies on the service of one man, perhaps the chef.
- where the contract depends upon the continuous existence of an object, such as a hotel, Should the hotel be destroyed, the contract itself will be frustrated.

5.3.4 Discharging Unlawfully by Breach

A breach of contract occurs when one party to an agreement tells the other party that he has no intention of performing the contract when the time falls due. When one party refuses to perform his agreement during the time it should be performed, then the other party has a right to sue for breach of contract.

A guest who refuses to pay a bill is breaking the contract and can be sued for damages. A hotelier whose premises or food are of sub-standard is breaking a condition of the contract and can be sued. In the hotel trade, the most common instance of breaking a contract occurs when one of the parties cancels the booking without the consent of the other, or the hotel over-books, thus making it impossible to carry out the agreement.

5.4 REMEDIES FOR BREACH OF CONTRACT

5.4.1 Breaching a Contract and the Consequences

Whenever a term of the contract is broken, whether it be a condition or warranty, the injured party is entitled to claim damages. There is also a contractual duty on the part of the hotel to maintain its facilities in such a manner that its guests should be safe and afforded treatment that corresponds with the quality of the accommodation offered. Another area where the hotel or restaurant proprietor owes a duty to the guest is in the area of retention of employees and this stands on the theory that hotel owners should exercise reasonable care in protecting their customers. Whenever a term of contract is broken, the innocent party is entitled to claim damages. It must be appreciated that damages are intended as compensation and not as punishment.

5.4.2 Cancellation by the Hotelier and the Rights of the Guest

A hotelier who cancels a guest's booking is liable for breach of contract. He must return any deposit paid by the guest. If the cancellation is done well in advance of the booking date, it is unlikely that the guest could recover more in the way of damages. However, if the cancellation occurs when the guest presents himself at the hotel and the hotelier has overbooked and cannot, therefore, accommodate the guest, it is likely that the guest can claim the return of any deposit paid. He can also claim the financial difference, if any, between the cost of the original accommodation and the cost of new accommodation together with any incidental expenses.

5.4.3 Cancellation by the Guest and the Rights of the Hotelier

Once the hotel booking is agreed upon, the contract comes into existence. It follows that if the guest then cancels the booking, when the time is due, he is in effect breaking the agreement. But if a guest cancels the booking well in advance then, it is likely that the hotelier will have enough time to re-let the room. The hotelier is entitled to keep any deposit paid by the guests for late cancellation. In addition, the hotelier may claim damages against the guest. If the hotel room is not re-let, it is the amount which the guest would have paid less a sum for food, heating and lighting. Should he re-let the room, the damages awarded would be minimal, as he has suffered little loss. Should the cancellation be due to the guest's illness or other circumstances, this may amount to frustration.

5.5 REFUSING A GUEST ACCOMMODATION

A hotelier can legitimately refuse a guest lodging for many reasons. It has been the rule that if a hotel has no accommodation, it may refuse persons desiring accommodation. Such a denial is affirmative defence, i.e. the hotelkeeper must prove that no rooms are available. The hotelkeeper can also refuse persons who are intoxicated, disorderly, unclean or suffering from contagious diseases. The law also allows the hotelkeepers to refuse criminals or persons of bad reputation because of the effect such guests can have on the reputation of the hotel. Obviously, a prospective guest who is not able or willing to pay the price for accommodation may be refused. If a guest refuses to pay in advance as required, it can be used as grounds for refusal. In the case where the guest has unusual property such as firearms or explosives that the hotel proprietor does not customarily receive, the hotel has grounds for refusal. The question of refusing guests with pets has been complicated by statutory inhibitions. On the other hand, local laws may prohibit animals in hotels and restaurants. The fact that the hotelkeeper closes at night does not permit him to refuse a guest. A hotel is presumed to be open for the convenience of travellers at all hours.

5.6 THE LAW OF CONTRACT IN RELATION TO A HOTEL RESERVATION

By custom, guests are not permitted to take up residence in their rooms before midday on the day of arrival and are expected to vacate their rooms by noon on the day of departure. However, a guest may arrive or depart from the hotel at any time within the agreed dates. Example, a guest who has booked the room for one week from say Saturday to the next Saturday, may arrive at any time in the Saturday, or even any time during the week. As he has booked the room, he is entitled to have it kept free for him during that time, but must of course pay the contract rate or price. Should the hotelier re-let the room to a third party, he runs the risk of the original guest turning up late and claiming damages for a broken contract. It is therefore advisable to make the date and time of arrival a term of contract.

Chapter Six

THE RESPONSIBILITIES OF THE HOTEL PROPRIETOR

6.1.1 The Historical Background of the Hotel and Catering Industry and the Hotel Proprietors Act 1956

The innkeeper has been held responsible for the safekeeping of his guests' property for many centuries. His liability arose as a safeguard to the guest against the dishonest innkeeper. This rule of law was well formed before the laws of contract came into existence.

The Common Law rules which protected guests during the 14th to 19th century from unscrupulous innkeepers are still part of the current legal system. The rationale in legislature in allowing these archaic rules to remain on the books must be that if modern hotelkeepers are honest and conduct their businesses properly, such old laws will not affect them, but if a hotelkeeper deviates from accepted practice, the ancient law will be there to protect the injured party. The Common Law protected travellers in several ways, e.g. the imposition on innkeepers' absolute liability for all goods of the guests. If a person lost any bag, the innkeeper was liable with certain limited exceptions.

Hotel Proprietors Act 1956
The Innkeepers' Liability Act 1863 which was modified by the Law Reform Committee were incorporated into s.2 of the Hotel Proprietors Act 1956, and which superseded the Innkeepers Liability Act of 1863 states that, the hotel proprietor is strictly liable

for the loss of any property stolen or damaged, but can limit his liability by displaying notices at prominent places. This rule of law only relates to hotel proprietors. It does not apply to owners of private hotels, restaurants or similar establishments, whose liability for loss or damage is based on negligence. The hotel proprietor is made personally liable for any such loss or damage, if the goods are stolen by a burglar, by his employee; other guests or even if the loss cannot be explained. He is not liable if the goods are lost or damaged by the guest himself.

By s.1 [3] of the Hotel Proprietors Act 1956, Parliament first defined the word

'hotel' as follows;

> "an establishment held out by the proprietor as offering food, drink, and if so required, sleeping accommodation, without special contract, to any traveller presenting himself who appears able and willing to pay a reasonable sum for the services and facilities provided and who is in a fit state to be received."

Establishments which are not within the definition of a hotel e.g. guest house, and boarding house etc. are excluded from these special liabilities.

6.1.2 Modification of the Absolute Liability Rule

Since the innkeeper's risk was great, the courts have allowed the innkeeper to exercise more direct and efficient control over a guest's goods. In the case of Fuller v Coasts, the court held, "To enable the innkeeper to discharge his duty and to secure the property of the traveller from loss while in an open house to the public, it may in many instances, become necessary for him to provide special means and to make necessary regulations. He also has to make requirements to be observed by the guests, to secure the safety of their property. When such means and requirements are reasonable and proper for that purpose, and they are brought to the knowledge of the guests with the information that if not observed by him, the innkeeper will not be held responsible for the loss of the guests property. Ordinary prudence, the interest of both parties and public policy would require the guest's compliance therewith and if he should fail to do so and his goods are lost solely for that reason he would justly and properly be chargeable with negligence."

The liability rule modifies the Common Law rule by adding the provision that hotelkeepers are liable only if the loss occurs through their negligence. Therefore, this rule encompasses the general rule that hotelkeepers are the insurers of the goods of their guests unless it is caused by an act of God, the public enemy or the contributory negligence of the guests. Under the Prima Facie rule, hotelkeepers can also exculpate themselves from the loss by proof that the loss did not occur through any neglect on their part and that of their servants for whom they are responsible.

6.1.3 Exceptions to the Rule

There are three exceptions to the rule and these are:

a) A loss attributed to an Act of God:– This is a natural event that results in some casualty thereby exonerating the hotelkeeper from liability for the guest's property. General, events such as earthquakes, lightning, rain, snowstorm, tornadoes and floods are considered acts of God.

b) A loss attributed to an Act of the Public Enemy (The adversary of the government at war).

c) Contributory negligence of the guest: – If a guest is negligent in taking normal precautions to safeguard his own goods, he is not normally allowed to recover damages. If for instance, a guest leaves his suitcase in a hotel area that is not customarily used for such purposes, he cannot recover. In the case of Cohen v Jan Lee, the court held that, the guest did not take the normal precautions of locking the door to her room before going to bed, knowing very well that she had a valuable coat in her room which facilitated the theft and therefore was to be considered guilty of contributory negligence.

6.1.4 The Liability is Strict

The legal meaning of this is that the proprietor is liable for goods lost within the hotel even though he or his servants have not been negligent. Furthermore, illness or insanity does not relieve him of responsibility. Neither is it of any effect for him to warn guest that there may be people of dubious character staying in the hotel.

6.1.5 Premises Covered by the Liability

The goods must be lost or damaged within the premises of the inn (hotel). This includes not only the hotel itself but also any outbuildings such as garages, etc. which are regarded as forming part of the hotel premises.

Case Law – McLenan v. Segar (1917)

The plaintiff (guest) sued for personal injuries sustained in jumping from a second-floor window of the defendant's (hotel) building during a fire outbreak. The guest who had arrived late and who had been taken immediately to her bedroom had no knowledge of the emergency procedure to be followed and was injured when she tried to escape from the premises through a second floor window. The court found that the defendant (hotel) was negligent in failing to warn the guest of the fire safety requirements. It had been discovered that, this failure to warn, was negligent and this resulted in causing the injuries. It was held that the proprietor was liable.

In one case, the infant, son of a hotel guest, heard the sound of music, and went to the room where a porter was playing the harmonica and was shot by the porter. The porter argued that he was only trying to frighten the boy by waving the revolver.

The court held the hotel owner liable on the grounds that it is tantamount to a breach of the implied contract that requires a hotelkeeper to treat guests with due consideration for their safety and comfort. This rule was not limited to the employer but applied to the employee as well.

There is also a contractual duty on the part of the hotel to maintain its facilities in such a manner that its guests should be safe and afforded treatment that corresponds with the quality of the accommodation offered.

Another area where the hotel or restaurant proprietor owes a duty to the guests is the selection and retention of employees. This stands on the theory that owners should exercise reasonable care in protecting their customers. Therefore, hotel and restaurant proprietors must use due care to avoid the selection and retention of employees whom they know or should know are undesirable because of their habits, temperaments or nature.

Case Law – Bennet v. Mellor (1793)
The plaintiff put his possessions on the floor behind his chair whilst he took some refreshment in an inn. When he was ready to leave, he found that the goods had been stolen. The hotel owner was held liable for the loss. The liability owed by the proprietor for his guests' property covers most types of property.

Practically, all moveable goods are caught by the rule not merely items such as luggage, clothing and sporting equipment but also business and legal documents and even money.

The guest need not own the goods himself, it is sufficient that he has the right to carry them.

This second point is particularly useful for guests who may have to vacate their rooms early in the day but who wish to leave their luggage in the hotel until later. If the guest has lost his status of traveller and becomes a boarder, the proprietor's strict liability towards his property ceases. Liability, however, may still exist under negligence. Strict liability is not owed to a friend staying at the hotel at the invitation of the proprietor. It is not necessary for the guest to be within the hotel when the goods are damaged or stolen. What happens if the guest leaves the hotel for few days but leaves some goods with the hotel proprietor? It is submitted that if he is paying for the room, then the liability is still owed to the hotel proprietor.

6.1.6 When can a Hotel Proprietor Escape Liability?

Although the proprietor is generally responsible for the safety of his guest's property, there are some exceptions to the rule.

The proprietor escapes liability if the goods are stolen or damaged by the guest's own servant or companion.

Also a hotel proprietor is not liable if the loss is caused by the misconduct or negligence of the guest who actually suffers the loss. The term negligence covers a wide range of actions and behaviour. If a guest deliberately leaves his bedroom door unlocked, the court will ask if the guest has taken care towards his possession. If the answer is 'no', the proprietor is relieved of his liability and the responsibility is put upon the guest.

So the guest who leaves his money lying around in the open where other people could not fail to see it was acting carelessly. The above two examples are contributory negligence.

The hotel proprietor is not liable if a guest has assumed exclusive control over a room or his goods in order to safeguard his possession, thus indicating to the proprietor that he is relieved from the responsibility. Evidence that a guest has told the proprietor to stay out of his room, or not to clean it, will be one guideline to determine whether or not the guest has assumed exclusive control.

6.1.7 Eviction of a Guest

Eviction for failing to pay hotel bills is ordinarily carried out by asking the guest for the amount due and requesting him to leave by a certain hour if the bill is not paid. If the guest fails or refuses to pay after such demand, the hotel may evict him.

6.1.8 Overstaying

Occupying a room beyond the agreed time can also become a reason for eviction. The contract for a room is for a definite time, be it one day or a year. When this period is over, the contract has been satisfied and the guest may leave.

6.2 DUTIES AND LIABILITIES OF THE HOTEL PROPRIETOR

After identifying a hotel, it is now possible to examine the duties of the proprietor. The hotel proprietor, in the case of a company-owned hotel run by a manager, the company is the proprietor. The proprietor must accept as guests all people who are travellers and entertain them at a reasonable price without any special or previous contract, unless he has some special grounds for refusal.

6.2.1 Must Entertain all Travellers

All travellers are entitled to be entertained irrespective of sex, creed or colour. It is submitted that if a proprietor refuses children as such, then his establishment cannot be classified as a hotel. The proprietor may not pick and choose his guests. He holds himself out as being willing to receive all comers.

Case law

In Constantine v. Imperial Hotels (1944) Mr. Learie Constantine, the West Indian cricketer was awarded damages by the court after being refused a hotel room without a good reason. The fact that he was able to check into another hotel belonging to the same company was said to be no excuse for its behaviour.

The Common Law rule is now strengthened by S2 of Race Relations Act 1968 which makes it unlawful for a person to discriminate on the ground of colour, race or ethnic or national origins, in the provision of accommodation in a hotel, boarding house or other similar establishment and in the provision of facilities for refreshment.

A traveller is entitled to walk into a hotel and make use of the amenities offered without having come to an arrangement with the proprietor beforehand. The proprietor only discharges his liability if he has reasonable grounds for refusal. Failure to pay a bill in advance is not sufficient justification to refuse service to the traveller. This is one distinguishing feature of a 'hotel' private and residential hotels differ in that they enter into a contract with their guests to accommodate them, the condition under which the guest stays in such a hotel being governed by the terms of contract.

The duty of the proprietor is to charge his guest reasonable prices, little if any guidance can be gained from old case law on what is reasonable except that he is entitled to charge such rates as will give him a reasonable gain or profit: but obviously size, locality and amenities offered by a hotel are all factors to be taken into account.

It must not be thought that the Common Law rules were devised solely for the benefit of the traveller. The Innkeeper was given protection against the dishonest travellers. He did not have to trust them and was entitled to demand a reasonable sum, in advance as payment. This undoubtedly was the forerunner of the present day deposit. In fact, some hotels now go as far as to ask their guests to pay the bill in full in advance.

Common Law remedies were and still are available to the innkeeper against the guest who refuses to pay his bill.

6.2.2 Provide Sleeping Accommodation to all Travellers

A traveller who is offered accommodation is entitled to be provided with such reasonable and proper accommodation as the proprietor in fact possesses. The standard must be that which it would be reasonable to expect in that particular establishment.

A traveller arriving at a small village inn cannot complain that he is not supplied with all the amenities to be found in large modern hotels. Regardless of where a hotel is situated and whatever class it belongs, either upper, middle or lower end of the market, there should be no excuse for that establishment being unclean or untidy. So a guest who finds his room dirty or bed linen soiled is justified in bringing an action against the proprietor for failing in his duty to provide reasonable accommodation. The guest is not to insist upon a particular room but of course, if, when booking accommodation in advance, the proprietor expressively agrees to provide a particular room, it would then be a breach of contract entitling the guest to damages, if he fails to carry out that promise.

6.2.3 Accept Luggage and Goods

Once the hotel proprietor accepts guests, it is his duty to accept his luggage along with goods that do not personally belong to him.

Case law

In Robins v. Gray (1895) .A commercial traveller staying at a hotel was sent some samples of sewing machines which belonged to his employers. It was held that the innkeeper was bound to take in the machines; he could not accept the guest and refuse the luggage. It may seem that such a rule is harsh, especially if the guest brings into the hotel goods which do not belong to him. However, the rule is not as one-sided as it may appear to be at first sight.

- An innkeeper (hotelier) has a right to seize goods belonging to his guest should the guest fail to pay his bill and this right (a lien) can be enforced not only against the person who brings in the goods, but also against the true owner.
- Moreover, the hotel proprietor can refuse to accept goods which are of an exceptional nature. Explosive could certainly be refused. The proprietor is not obliged to take in a person's luggage if he seeks neither refreshment nor accommodation. However, should the parties come into an arrangement for the luggage to be left in the hotel, then the proprietor acts as a bailee of the goods which means that he will be liable for their loss or damage only if he acts negligently.

The Hotel proprietor can place a lien on the guest's belongings for unpaid bills. A possessory or statutory lien allows an innkeeper (proprietor) to hold the guest's belongings as security for payment of personal property that a guest brought into the hotel – also termed innkeeper's lien.

6.2.4 Supply Travellers with Food and Drink

The Hotel Proprietor must also provide food and drink. The food need not be given to only those staying in the hotel but also those who he knows will be coming to the hotel.

6.2.5 Provide Refreshment

The duty to provide refreshment to a traveller is one which the proprietor must fulfil unless he has a reasonable excuse. There is no definition of refreshments. Perhaps, the offer of a simple meal and a drink will be adequate.

A hotel proprietor has the right to refuse to serve a customer who is drunk, or is under the influence of drugs, or is behaving improperly and is not in a fit condition to be received. What is meant by the term 'fit condition' can include the state of a traveller's dress and even lack of it. A street sweeper appearing in his working clothes can be refused refreshment in an inn.

So the rule revolves around acting reasonably. Also, the class of the hotel account in question must be a factor to be taken into account. The hotel proprietor is entitled to maintain the standards of dressing he desires within his property.

The duties discussed in this chapter relate especially to hotels within the meaning of the Hotel Proprietors Act 1956 which is a guideline to assist owners of hotels and similar establishments.

6.2.6 Provide Car Parking Accommodation

The innkeeper is bound to supply only such garage accommodation for his guest's car as he in fact possesses, and the test for reasonableness is again applied. The traveller arriving at a small hotel cannot complain that his motor car is not placed in a garage of quality to be found in the most modern and luxurious establishments or even that he is not provided with any accommodation at all for his motor car. If garage accommodation is offered, then it must be reasonable. A car parking area that has large holes could be a danger and may incur the proprietor's liability.

6.2.7 Ensure Guests' Safety

A duty is owed to persons using the premises of a hotel, motel, restaurant, bar, club or a similar facility by its owners. The owners must maintain the safety of his guests.

No reliable number of accidents that occur each year in hotels and restaurants are available, although many do occur.

Generally, civil action may be brought in the civil courts against restaurants or hotels in which such accidents occur under the broad category of law called 'Tort'. The simplest definition of a tort is that it is a private or civil wrong caused by the act or failure to act on another person, i.e. a 'tort' is an offence against an individual. A duty of ordinary law is owed by a hotel to its guests and an innkeeper can be held liable for the manner in which he responds to guests' problems.

6.3 REGISTRATION OF GUESTS

6.3.1 Duty to Register Guests

Under the Common Law, a hotel proprietor must accommodate a guest even if he refuses to reveal his identity and address. However, this rule has been replaced by the statutory duty of a hotel proprietor to keep a register. All guests must supply their names and nationality and aliens must provide additional details. A proprietor is therefore justified in refusing accommodation to a person who fails to provide these particulars.

It is the responsibility of the hotel proprietor to obtain certain information from all persons over the age of eighteen years. Visitors or would-be guests must supply information about themselves either in writing, or by completing a registration form verbally or by a third person. No matter which way the information is given, the burden is on the hotel keeper to obtain it and record it in writing. The information that must be recorded are as follows:-

- Date of arrival
- Full name
- Nationality
- Name and Address of next of kin.

If the person is an alien, the following additional information must be obtained:

- The number and place of issue of a passport or registration certificate, or other document confirming his identity and nationality.
- Date of departure
- Next destination, if known to him, and his address there.

These records are to be retained for the next twelve months, and they must be available for inspection by the police or any person authorized by the Minister of State for the Home Office.

6.3.2 Duty to Request for Valuables for Safe-keeping

The hotel proprietor must accept for safe custody any valuables offered by the guest for safe-keeping. He has the right, however, to insist that they be placed in a container and sealed by the guest before being accepted by the hotel. Only if the guest refuses to do this will the hotel proprietor have no obligation to accept the valuables. These valuables should be kept in a safe. Guests must be given receipts for money and valuables deposited. Receipts must be made out in duplicate and, the original receipt that is given to the guest must have all relevant details recorded on it. It is very important to attach the exact description of the article deposited. Jewellery can cause difficulties unless the cashier is fully conversant with all precious stones.

To prevent theft or loss, all deposits must immediately be locked away in the safe. The number of the receipt is written on the article deposited or attached to it and the articles are kept in a safe in numerical order to help identify the article easily when demanded by the guest. The duplicate receipts are retained in the Deposit Receipt Book in numerical order.

When the guest wishes to withdraw his deposit, he must produce the original receipt. Until this is done, the cashier must not hand over the article. If it happens that a guest's original receipt is missing, then a positive identification of the guest must be made before handing over the deposit. When the guest withdraws his valuables, the guest must be asked to put his signature on the duplicate receipt as proof that he has received them. The original and duplicate receipts are then stapled together and completed

Front office work requires responsible staff who must therefore be intelligent and trustworthy since they take care of guests' precious articles of considerable value. As can be seen, the front office staff must be people of good character which will in turn, give the hotel a good reputation.

We now live in a world of technology where there are various sophisticated methods of making payments. For example, card transactions like MasterCard and other credit cards etc., and so guests may not carry large sums of money but they may still carry some sort of valuables with them. As a result of this, safekeeping will still be in great demand. There should be no room for carelessness and mistakes. Staff must be trained very well in order to gain confidence in discharging their duties.

A SAMPLE OF A SAFE DEPOSIT RECEIPT

HOTEL LAPALOMA NO. 24 – 25

NAME:...

DATE:...................................

ROOM NO.:...

DESCRIPTION:..

....

....

RECEIVED BY:...

DATE WITHDRAWN:...

GUEST'S SIGNATURE:...

RETURNED BY:..

Monies or valuables must be requested for safekeeping immediately after registration of guest. There must also be a notice conspicuously written just behind the reception desk alerting guests of the importance of declaring their valuables and the consequences for refusing to declare.

6.3.3 Contract of Bailment

This section refers to both private hotels (guest houses, hostels, boarding houses etc). and hotels. When an hotelier assumes control over a guest's property, he is in effect, entering into a contract of bailment. Bailment can take many forms. In the hotel trade, a common example of bailment is handing over keys to a porter to park or move a car. A contract of bailment occurs when one person (hotelier or bailee) comes into possession of goods belonging to another (the guest or bailor). It is essential that the guest hands over possession of his property. The hotelier implies promises to return the goods as soon as requested. He also implies promises to take reasonable care of the goods. If they are damaged or lost, the hotelier is liable to pay damages for them unless he can show that he or his servants have taken all reasonable care of them. The burden is upon the hotelier to prove that he has acted carefully. It is advisable that the package is in a sealed container and the contents are documented and receipted in the presence of the guest.

In the contract of bailment, the bailee can contract out of his duty of care by displaying a notice exempting him from liability for negligence. Once again, the notice must be displayed in a prominent position and be brought to the bailor's attention at the time the contract was made. Furthermore, it must be clearly worded; any ambiguity will be interpreted in the bailor's favour. It could be said that the courts are willing to distinguish between goods left out of doors and those deposited within a building. In any event the hotelier can help himself by displaying an exemption notice.

6.3.4 Possession

Bailments are concerned with pure personalty and not with real property. The bailment may or may not originate in a contract.

An essential feature of a bailment is the transfer of, possession to the bailee.

An employee who receives goods from his employer to take to a third party has mere custody: Possession remains with the employer and the employee is not a bailee. If a third party hands goods to an employee for his employer, the employee obtains possession and he is the bailee.

Case Law – **South Staffordshire Water Co v. Sharmon1896**
The plaintiffs sued the defendant claiming possession of two gold rings found by the defendant in the pool. The plaintiffs were owners of the pool and the defendant was a labourer employed by them to clean it. Whiles the defendant was cleaning the pool he came across the rings. He refused to hand them to his employers but gave them to the police for enquiries to be made to find out the true owner. No owner was found and the police returned the rings to the defendant who retained them.

HELD – The rings must be given over to the plaintiffs. The plaintiffs were freeholders of the pool, and had the right to refuse anyone coming on the land; and also had a right to clean the pool out in any way they choose. They possessed and exercised a practical control over the pool and they had a right to its contents.

6.3.5 Conspicuously Displayed Notice Limiting Liabilities

Assuming that the hotel proprietor is liable for stolen or damaged property, he may limit his liability by displaying a statutory notice. The proprietor can claim this limited liability protection except:

- Where the property has been lost, stolen or damaged through his own default, neglect or wilful act,

- Where his servants' default, neglect or wilful act,
- Where although the guest has asked to deposit his property, the proprietor or his servant has refused or where the guest wanted to offer the property for deposit but has .been unable to do so through the default of the proprietor or his servant. It is important for the guest to make it quite clear to the proprietor that he wishes to deposit his property for safe custody. The guest has to prove that the loss or injury is the fault of the proprietor.

In these three cases, as the goods have been lost or damaged through the proprietor's own fault, he remains liable for their full value.

The notice, which must be boldly printed or written and be conspicuously displayed at a place where it can be conveniently read by the guest. For example, in front or behind the reception desk, where the guest can read whiles checking in.

The notice may also be displayed at the main entrance to the reception. This notice must also be communicated to the guest. The reason being that, some people may have problems with their eyes and may not be able to read.

Staff must be polite and helpful as much as possible so as to create a good name for their establishments and above all a repeated custom.

This liability however:

- Extends to the property of guests, who have engaged in sleeping accommodation at the hotel.
- This liability does not cover motor cars or other vehicles of any kind or any property left in them, or live animals, but it will be to the hotel's reputation to provide tight security at the car park to prevent break-ins. Car should be covered by insurance by the owner. The hotel proprietor is therefore not liable for cars left on his premises. It is enough if he provides car parking accommodation with a notice saying

"CARS PARKED AT OWNER'S RISK", which should be prominently placed.

The notice at the reception may read as follows:

MAY WE RESPECTFULLY REMIND OUR CHERISHED GUESTS TO DEPOSIT MONIES OR VALUABLES FOR SAFEKEEPING. MANAGEMENT CANNOT BE HELD RESPONSIBLE FOR LOSS OF ITEMS NOT DEPOSITED FOR SAFEKEEPING.

THANK YOU BY MANAGEMENT.

Again, such notices must not be hidden behind the bedroom doors, otherwise, guests will claim they did not see it and the proprietor may be liable.

6.3.6 Duty to Search When Necessary to Ensure Safe Premises

From previous horrible occurrences, some proprietors of hotels have experienced some unacceptable behaviour by guests, which has helped them to design their own rules and regulations. Guests must conform to these rules for the safety and comfort of everyone in order to assist staff to run their establishments safely and efficiently.

Now, the court will not intervene if the rules are not that harsh. These are rules and not laws. There is a case study in the later pages in this book where a guest who was being hunted by police for murdering a policewoman went to lodge in a hotel and still had the gun with him when he checked into the hotel. Had it not been the intelligent and observant receptionist who realized that the photo-fit on the television and in the newspapers resembled the descriptions of the guest who was then lodging in the hotel and informed his proprietor, who then reported it to the police, this lodger might have caused havoc in the hotel. When the police arrived, they found the guest in his bedroom. When the police were searching his bedroom, his mattress was lifted and the police discovered a gun under his mattress. The police then took him away to the police station for questioning.

In order not to go too far and take the law into your own hands by dealing inappropriately with your guests, it is important for hotel staff to know the nearest police station and the phone numbers, e-mail address etc. so that they can easily be contacted in case of emergency.

Security staff in hotels must be trained to know how and when to search a suspect (a guest). Now the question is– Is it important to search or not to search for illegal drugs and arms? If you do not search a suspect, it can cost you a fortune and the hotel's reputation will be tarnished. The hotel would also then lose custom and eventually go out of business. Everyone wants to lodge at a safe hotel. If you do not want to search because you may lose your reputation or custom, just simply refuse the guest a room by politely saying 'the hotel is full'.

The hotelier is always made a suspect and sent straight away for questioning if a guest dies in his hotel, until he can prove his innocence. So it pays if the front office staff and other staff in the hotel are vigilant. If staff are efficient, they can reduce incidents.

When one thinks about a hotelier's liability for the safety of his guest, it reminds one of the book, *Macbeth* by William Shakespeare. A guest in your hotel is under your protection.

For example, – As a sign of honour for his good work done, when Macbeth returned from the battlefield, Duncan the King of Scotland paid him a visit. Duncan was found dead the next day. Whether Macbeth did it or not, he was made a suspect.

In addition to this, if a couple are living together and one of them is found dead overnight, the other is suspected and sent to the police station for questioning. In recent times, such case in hotels has been on the increase in hotels all over the world.

6.3.7 Hotel Information and Regulations / House Rules

It is customary for hotels to display notices to explain the way in which that particular hotel operates, e.g. meal times, use of public rooms, etc. Such regulations are not regarded as terms of a contract but internal domestic arrangements. For any other information, please contact the reception.

Valuables

Guests are advised to deposit any valuables and large amount of monies at the reception for safekeeping. Management cannot be held responsible for such items left in the rooms.

Key and Key Cards

All doors must be securely fastened and keys or key cards left at the reception when leaving the hotel premises. Keys or key cards may also be left at the reception when outside your room while you are in the hotel.

Restaurant

The hotel has an excellent restaurant service and stock of assorted drinks. Please notify the restaurant staff of your intention to take lunch or supper.

Laundry Service

Please leave a list of clothing intended for laundry in a bag provided in your room. If only ironing is required, please contact the reception.

First Aid Box

The management maintains a reasonable supply of first aid drugs. Guests are kindly advised to contact the reception if their condition necessitates first aid.

Medical

There is a doctor on call if your condition requires one. This must be paid for by the guest, or at the discretion of the proprietor.

Settlement of Account

Guests are requested to make part payment as deposit for accommodation and other charges. If accounts are sponsored by a reputable organization, a letter of confirmation is required.

Departure

Please inform the receptionist of your intention to depart. Guests departing are expected to vacate their rooms before noon or twelve mid-day.

Complaints

Every effort is made by the management to ensure maximum satisfaction.

Please bring complaints to the notice of management.

Disorderly Behaviour

Guests who misbehave to the discomfort of other guests (noisy or quarrelsome) would be asked to vacate their rooms and leave the premises.

6.4 GROUNDS FOR REFUSING A GUEST ACCOMMODATION

A hotel must be opened to all callers. The proprietor may only refuse to entertain or receive a guest if he has reasonable grounds for so doing. What are the reasonable grounds?

6.4.1 Refusing to Disclose Identity

This means the refusal to show a passport, driving licence or any relevant document confirming your true identity.

6.4.2 The Hotel is Full

If all its bedrooms are occupied then it is a good ground for refusing to accommodate guests. In Browne v. Brandt (1902) a guest, when told that all the bedrooms were full, asked if he could sleep downstairs in the lounge. The court agreed that, the proprietor was justified in refusing this request. To allow a guest to sleep in the public area would constitute both a health and a fire hazards.

6.4.3 Drunkenness and Behaving Disorderly or Being Improperly Dressed

A guest who is behaving in a noisy and quarrelsome manner, disturbing other guests, under the influence of drugs, being violent and aggressive and using the hotel for immoral practices and thereby making the hotel an unsafe place for staff and guests must be ask to leave. If he chooses to be unmanageable then the necessary force must be used to evict him. A guest who dresses inappropriately or fails to dress at all must also be evicted.

In addition, a traveller who is suffering from an easily visible or detected disease which other guests may be affected by, can certainly be refused a room, for example, chicken pox. Under the Public health Act 1875, the proprietor may pay a penalty for letting an infected room.

If the guest suffers an infectious disease while staying in your establishment, the proprietor must assist in calling the doctor to examine the guest and to send him to the hospital.

Before re-letting the room, the proprietor must disinfect the room and its contents. A guest carrying drugs, explosives, and unusual goods must certainly be refused a room.

6.4.4 Other Grounds

There are no other grounds justifying the proprietor in refusing a guest accommodation. A traveller is entitled to be accommodated anytime he arrives in a hotel, even if he arrives in the middle of the night.

6.5 WHAT IS A LIEN?

A lien is a right over the property of another which arises by operation of law and independently of any agreement. It gives a creditor the right:

(a) To retain possession of the debtor's property until he has paid or settled the debt; or

(b) To sell the property in satisfaction of the debt in those cases where the lien is not possessory. Where the parties agree that a lien shall be created, each agreement will effectively create one.

6.5.1 Possessory or Common-Law Lien

To exercise this type of lien the creditor must have actual possession of the debtor's property, in which case he can retain it until the debt is paid or settled. It should be noted that the creditor must ask for possession of the debtor's goods in order to exercise a lien. A Common Law lien may be particular or general.

(i) **Particular Lien**: This gives the possessors the right to retain goods until a debt arising in connection with those goods is paid

(ii) **General Lien**: This gives the possessor the right to retain goods not only for debts specifically connected with them, but also for all debts due from the owner of the goods however arising. A general lien may arise out of a contract or custom, and the following classes of persons have a general lien over the property of the customers or clients – i.e. factors, bankers, and in some cases insurance brokers. The law favour particular rather than general liens.

The following are cases of particular lien:

1. A carrier can retain goods entrusted to him for carriage until his charges are paid
2. An innkeeper has a lien over the property brought into the inn by a guest and also over property sent to him while there, even if it does not belong to him. The lien does not extend to motor cars or vehicles, or to horses, or other animals
3. A ship owner has a lien on the cargo for freight due
4. In a sale of goods, the unpaid seller has a lien on the goods, if still in his possession to recover the price.

6.5.2 The Hotel Proprietors' Lien

It is a possessory or statutory lien allowing an innkeeper (proprietor) to hold, as security for payment, personal property that a guest brought into the hotel – also termed innkeeper's lien.

This area of the hotelkeeper's law that concerns his lien has been the subject of much litigation. The early Common Law placed many duties and liabilities on hotelkeepers, but it also protected them from dishonest guests who would leave with their accounts unpaid. The strategy used for that protection was the hotelkeeper's lien that extended to all property that the guest brought to the hotel. A hotelkeeper is under the duty to investigate the ownership of the baggage that the guest brings in with him. The hotelkeeper's lien extends therefore to chattels (personal property or animals) brought on the premises irrespective of ownership.

6.5.3 Exceptions

Hotelkeepers cannot place a lien on property brought to their hotel by a guest if they are aware that a third party owns it or if they are aware that the property is stolen. However, the lien on such goods is valid if the hotelkeeper was unaware of such third party ownership. The lien is terminated when the bills are paid. The hotelkeeper must then return the guests' property.

An American Court enforced the rule that a wife may not be held under the hotelkeepers' lien when it appears her husband contracted the indebtedness. If a third person contracts to pay the bill of a guest, then the hotelkeepers have a lien on the personal baggage of their guests, and if the guest attempts to take it away, he can be held for theft.

6.5.4 Enforcement of Lien – Power of Sale

Unfortunately, the lien is of little value to the hotelkeeper because he must retain the property at his own expense and takes as much care of it as though it was his own property. Should the bill be paid, he must repair any damage done to the property through insufficient care before returning it. However, the Innkeepers Act 1878 gives the proprietor a special right to sell by public auction any property over which he has a lien. At least, one month before the sale, an advertisement must be inserted in the daily newspapers setting out:

- Details of the sale
- A short description of the goods

- The name, if known, of the owner or person who deposited or left it there
- The amount of the unpaid bill
- Any necessary repairs prior to sale
- Expenses of the sale.
- **The hotelkeeper must hand any surplus money to the guest.**

6.5.5 Right Under the Lien

The hotelkeeper may prevent the guest from removing property from the premises and take possession of it himself. The lien is so powerful that it has few limitations. When goods are stolen, the general rule is that no person has a better title to them than the true owner. But when hotel owners are unaware they are dealing with stolen property and attach a lien to such goods, they have better title to these goods than their original owner. Liens have been held valid on such diverse objects as pianos, valuables in safe-deposit boxes, stolen property and automobiles.

Liens cannot be used on debts incurred during previous visits by a guest. Generally, a hotelkeeper is under a duty to investigate the ownership of the baggage that a guest brings with him. The hotel proprietor can seize the guest's property but cannot seize the person or what he is wearing i.e. clothes, personal jewellery such as wedding rings and articles necessary for travel, i.e. passport etc. Neither can he seize goods when the guest is out of his premises because goods cannot be seized when the guest is out of his premises. He must therefore act quickly before the guest leaves his premises. The innkeeper cannot sell the goods held under the lien until after six weeks. However, the property should not remain on the premises for a long time, so long as the proprietor has control over it.

Case Law – **In Chesham Automobile Supply Limited v. Beresford (Birchington) Ltd. (1913) the proprietor kept control over a car because, of the lien. He sent the car for repairs within six weeks but arranged for the sale to take place at the expiry of the six** weeks. He was held to be still in control of the vehicle at the time of repairs.

Case Law –In Robins v. Gray (1895)

A plaintiff dealing in sewing machines employed a traveller to sell machines on commission. The plaintiff's traveller checked in at the defendant's inn in April 1894, and stayed there until the end of July. During this time the plaintiff sent machines to the traveller to sell in the neighbourhood. At the end of July, the traveller owed the defendant some money for board and lodgings, and he failed to pay. The defendant placed a lien on some of the goods sent by the plaintiff to the traveller, claiming he had a lien on the goods for the amount of debt due to him even though the defendant knew that the goods were the property of the plaintiff.

Held – The defendant has a right of lien on the plaintiff's property for the traveller's debt.

6.6 VICARIOUS LIABILITY

6.6.1 What is the Meaning of Vicarious Liability?

The doctrine of respondeat superior 'Let the principal or the master answer', recognizes that the 'master' is civilly liable to persons for the tort of his employees. This doctrine is founded on the theory of agency or representation that the employer is constructively present.

Although the person who is actually responsible for the act of a tort is always liable, sometimes another person may be liable even though, he has not actually committed it. In such a case, both are liable as joint tortfeasors. A tortfeasor is one who commits a tort, which is a civil wrong independent of contract. Liability in tort arises from breach of a duty primarily fixed by law, which is repressible by an action for unliquidated damages affording some measure of compensation. This is the doctrine of vicarious liability, and the greatest area of this type of liability is that of master and servant.

A master (employer) is liable for the tort of his servant (employee) committed in the course of his employment and so wide is the risk that it is commonly insured against. Under the employers' Liability (compulsory Insurance) Act 1969, an employer must insure himself in respect of vicarious liability for injuries caused by his employees to their colleagues.

There is a comparison to be made with contract because whether the employer is bound as a party to a contract made by the employee depends upon whether the employee has the authority to make the contract on behalf of the employer and not simply whether the employee was acting within the course of employment which is the basic tort test.

Case Law –Director General of Fair Trading v. Smiths concrete, (1991).

Who is a Servant or Employee?

According to Salmond on Torts, a servant may be defined as "any person employed by another to do work for him on the terms that he, the servant, is to be subject to the control and direction of his employer in respect of the manner in which his work is to be done."

This definition was approved by the court in Hewitt v. Bonvin (1940). In most cases the relationship is established by the existence of a contract of service, which may be express or implied and is usually evidenced by such matters as, for example, the power to appoint, the power of dismissal, the method of payment, the payment of National Insurance by the employer, the deduction of tax under PAYE, and membership of pension schemes (if any).

However, in deciding whether the relationship of employer/ employee exists, the courts have not restricted themselves to cases in which there is an ordinary contract of service but have often stated that the right of control is the ultimate test.

Case Law – In Performing Right Society Ltd. v. Mitchel and Booker (Palais de Dance) Ltd (1924).

6.6.2 Nature of Vicarious Liability

The doctrine seems at first sight unfair because it runs contrary to two major principles of liability in tort,

(a) That a person should be liable only for loss or damage caused by his own acts or omissions; and

(b) That a person should only be liable where he was at fault.

The doctrine of vicarious liability is a convenient one in the sense that employers are, generally speaking, wealthier than their employees and are better able to pay damages, though the doctrine is often justified on the grounds that an employer controls his employee.

However, it should be noted that control is not in itself a ground for imposing vicarious liability, e.g. parents are not vicariously liable for the torts of their children. It is also said that vicarious liability is a just concept because the employer profits from the employees work and should therefore bear losses caused by the employee's torts. Again the employer chooses his employee and there are those who say that, if he chooses a careless employee, he ought to compensate the victims of the careless employee's torts.

Further, employer and employee are often identified in the sense that, the act of the employee is regarded as the act of his employer and there is this theory that an employer and his employee are part of a group in much the same way as other associations of persons, e.g. companies which is expressed in the often quoted maxim "he who does a thing through another does it himself." However in practice, the employer does not really suffer loss because he commonly insures against the possibility of vicarious liability and usually the cost of this insurance is put on to the goods or services that he sells.

6.6.3 Course of Employment

In order to establish vicarious liability, it is necessary to show that the relationship between the defendant and the wrongdoer is that of employer and employee, and that when the employee committed the wrong, he was in the course of his employment.

It is sometimes difficult to decide whether a particular act was done during the course of employment, but the following matters are relevant.

6.6.4 Emergencies

Where the employee takes emergency measures with the intention of benefiting his employer in cases where the employer's property appears in danger, the employer will tend to be liable even though the acts of the employee are excessive.

Case law –Poland v. John Parr and Sons (1927)
A boy was injured by a carter who knocked the boy off the back of his cart to protect his employer's property from theft.

Held; The carter's action was within his implied authority and his employers are liable.

6.6.5 Acts Personal to the Employee

Some acts done by an employee while at work are so personal to him that they cannot be regarded as being within the scope of employment. Employees do not generally have authority to use violence against third parties, and the use of such violence will usually be beyond the scope of employment and the employer will not be liable.

Case Law–Warren v. Henlys Ltd (1948)
The employer of a petrol pump attendant was held not liable for the employees assault on a customer committed as a result of an argument over payment for petrol.

However, where such authority exists, e.g. in the case of door-keepers at dance halls, the employer will be liable if the employee ejects a troublemaker but uses excessive force.

6.6.6 Management Principles

The innkeeper or restaurant owner is in the best position to prevent accidents and injuries to guests. In general, employers are held responsible for the actions of their employees when they are acting within the scope of their employment. The relevance of the initial selection of staff in your establishment is very necessary so as to create a safe environment; otherwise the law will deal with you as an employer.

Take note of the following procedures:-

- check a new employee's background.
- Assess and evaluate new personnel for a period of at least, six months.
- Train personnel to recognize aggressive or warlike behaviours of customers.
- Train your security staff how to deal with guests who should be asked to leave and what to do if they won't leave in order not to break the law.

6.7 BASIC INSURANCE POLICIES REQUIRED BY THE HOTEL AND CATERING PROPRIETOR

Insurance plays an important role in our everyday lives; we need to insure our homes, our property, our lives and businesses against a variety of risks.

There are different types of insurance policies that the hotel and catering manager may require to ensure that he obtains full insurance cover for all his operations. Insurance Companies issue all these to customers. These include:

- Products Liability Policy
- Public Liability Policy
- Burglary Policy
- Workmen Compensation
- Group Personal Accident
- Fidelity Guarantee
- Policy Fire Insurance
- Group Life Insurance.

6.7.1 Products Liability Policy

The Products Liability Policy is useful to restaurants and hotels, public houses etc. The policy covers the owners or proprietors for their liability in connection with products supplied to them. That is, contaminated food or drink etc.

6.7.2 Public Liability Policy

The Public Liability Insurance Policy is specifically designed to insure property owners, businesses and establishments against their liability in respect of death, body injury and damage to property or any financial loss caused by them or their representatives to third parties. This policy is particularly useful where the business premises are used by the general public. Examples are hotels, night clubs, and restaurants etc. It also covers various responsibilities.

6.7.3 Burglary Policy

The Burglary Policy covers property stolen from one's premises through violent and forcible entry. It also covers damage to property or the premises as a result of burglary.

6.7.4 Workmen Compensation

The Workmen Compensation Act makes it mandatory for all employers to compensate their employees for occupation injuries and death. The act also fixes minimum rate of compensation to any victim. Several employers find it prudent to pass this risk to an insurance company. The insurance company pays for all their liabilities as and when they occur. The policy covers employees during working hours only.

6.7.5 Group Personal Accident

The Group Personal Accident insurance policy gives compensation for accidental death or body injury to a group of people that are workers and members of associations or clubs. It is a very important policy considering the various types of risks which we are exposed to daily, especially as workers. This is a 24-hour cover, compared to the Workmen's Compensation Policy which ends at the close of work.

6.7.6 Fidelity Guarantee

This is a type of insurance policy against the loss arising out of acts of dishonesty or disloyalty of an employee to an employer. The policy compensates the employer against direct financial loss, and also loss of stock which might result from dishonesty, fraud, misappropriation, or embezzlement by an employee in the course of his employment. Commercial and business outfit require this guarantee not only for their cashiers and other employees handling money in the normal course of their work, but also for commercial travellers and others who may handle money.

6.7.7 Policy Fire Insurance

The Fire Policy offers protection to the insured in respect of domestic as well as commercial property (including industrial properties) against the risk of material damage and business interruption, which arises out of fire outbreak.

6.7.7.1 Material Damage Policy

The Fire Policy covers the properties of the insured against loss or damage to buildings, plant and machinery, stocks, fixtures etc. and other domestic items that may be destroyed by fire. In the event of loss or damage, the insured is restored to his position before the loss by monetary compensation, repair, or replacement of item destroyed.

6.7.7.2 Consequential Loss/Business Interruption Policy

A Consequential Loss/Business Interruption Policy essentially follows the material damage policy, in that, in the event of loss or damage by fire, the results of a business may be affected if production ceases. It is designed to make up for the loss of profit, which as a result of a fire outbreak, reduce or brings production to a standstill.

6.7.7.3 Additional Perils

There are a number of additional perils which may be covered under the Fire Policy if the insured so desires. These are:

a. Impact – This extension covers destruction or damage caused by contact with a vehicle, animal or any moving object

b. Explosion –This extension covers destruction or damage to property resulting from explosion. For example, a boiler

c. Flood – This is an extension which covers damage to property resulting from overflowing of natural waters or rainwater

d. Bursting and overflow of water pipes apparatus and the like – This is an extension which covers destruction of or damage to property resulting from bursting of overflowing water pipes, apparatus and the like

e. Hurricane, Cyclone, Tornado and/or Windstorm –This is an extension which covers destruction of or damage to property resulting from hurricane, cyclone, tornado, and/or windstorm

f. Earthquake and Volcanic Eruption (Fire and Shock) –This is an extension which covers destruction of or damage to property resulting from Earthquake and Volcanic Eruption (Fire and shock).

When any of the above perils causes damage to property, the insurance will offer monetary compensation to the insured.

6.7.8 Group Policy

6.7.8.1 Group Life (Term Assurance) Policy

The Group Life (Term Assurance) Policy provides protection for employees of a company or members of a society at a premium lower than what they would have paid if the policies had been purchased individually. The policy is renewable annually. If the employee/member should die, in active service, the sum assured goes to his nominated beneficiaries or next-of-kin.

6.7.8.2 Group Life Endowment Policy

The Group Life Endowment Policy provides for a sum assured to be paid either at the death or retirement of the employees, whichever comes first. This Policy, therefore, provides both death-in-services and retirement benefit for employees of a company or a firm.

It is expected that if a hotelier takes all the above-mentioned policies, he would have obtained the fullest cover both for his business and himself. One has to choose which policy is relevant to his or her circumstances.

Chapter Seven

FOOD REGULATIONS AND THE CONSUMER

7.1 SAFETY OF THE CONSUMER

7.1.1 Introduction

Food safety is about protecting consumers from harm. When working with food, you must make sure that nothing in the food you prepare, serve or sell to consumers can cause harm. If you get it wrong, customers may complain or become ill and the business may get a bad reputation and have to close down. Legal claim may be made against the food business. If you get it right, customers are happy; and the food business has a good reputation and a secure future.

It was not until the nineteenth century that general legislation was put into place. Two statutes enacted in the same year established a food safety and consumer protection framework still recognisable in current British law. The Sale of Food and Drugs Act 1875 laid the foundations of modern provisions controlling the composition of food. Added to an existing ban on injurious ingredients was the key prohibition on selling food not of the nature, substance and quality demanded by the purchaser together with the important supplemental procedures relating to sampling analysis and legal proceedings. The main protection against chemical contamination of food was thus established. Basic control on biological (bacterial) contamination began with the Public Health Act 1875, which provides that it is an offence to sell unfit food for consumption and provides powers for its inspection, seizure and condemnation.

The offence of rendering food injurious to health is now provided for in Section 7 of the Food Safety Act 1990 (FSA 1990). The offence of selling food not of the nature, substance or quality demanded can now be found in section 14 of the same Act. There is a substantial body of case law relevant in section 14 of FSA1990. It is important to note however that the FSA 1990 modified the previous structure of the legislation. On the face of things at least, the chemical and biological control provisions have been separated.

The FSA 1990 acknowledged and integrated what had in practice taken place over the years. In particular, it classified the prohibition on rendering food injurious to health provision under a food safety heading, together with key provisions aimed at the biological control of food, which has been codified in the Public Health Acts. These biological control provisions are the powers for the inspection and seizure of suspected food which are now respectively contained in sections 8 and 9 of the FSA 1990 .The modification was not a mere formal change.

The prohibition on selling, offering or exposing food intended to be sold which was considered injurious to health was incorporated into section 8. In addition to that, there has been the incorporation of a new wider concept of food safety requirement with the prohibition of the sale of unfit food.

Food failing to comply with the food safety requirements was likewise subjected to section 9, which gives the powers to inspect and seize unwholesome food. The prohibition in section 14 of the Act on selling food not of the nature, substance or quality demanded was classified under a 'consumer protection' heading. This prohibition does not cover only selling food that threatens the purchaser's pocket. It most certainly also continues to extend to the selling of food unfit for consumption which threatens the purchaser's health.

7.1.2 Rendering Food Unfit For Human Consumption

Whether or not food is unfit for human consumption is a question of fact.

The following points should be noted:

- Food which is of poor quality or decomposed is within the definition.
- Where a wholesome article of food contains a single extraneous body, not itself toxic, although not to be eaten, then that food does not become unfit for human consumption
- In the case of J. Miller Ltd. v Battersea Borough Council (1955), a child bit into a piece of metal while eating a chocolate bun.
- In Turner and Sons Ltd. v. Owen (1955), a loaf of bread contained a piece of string. In both cases, the court did not find that the food was unfit for human consumption

(In both these cases there would be an infringement of s.2 of the Act.)

- But if a single extraneous article, which finds its way into food is toxic, then the food will be unfit for human consumption.
- In Chibnall's Bakeries v. Cope-Brown (1956), it was held that a loaf of bread containing part of a used and dirty bandage was unfit for human consumption.
- Where an article of food is going mouldy, prima facie, it is 'unfit for human consumption' and it matters not whether there would be injury to health if it were eaten. It is a matter of degree in each case. It is an offence for a person to sell or offer for sale food unfit for human consumption. It is an offence to deposit or consign food unfit for human consumption to any person for the purpose of selling it or preparing it for sale.

This section aims to protect a customer from purchasing contaminated food. It is an offence and it is also difficult for the accused to evade liability. The accused cannot plead that he did not know the food was bad.

An employer can be charged for an offence under the Act committed by his employee, even if he had no knowledge of the employee's wrong-doing and even though he had taken steps to prevent a breach of the law, provided that the employee was acting in the normal course of his employment.

Case Law

In Hobbs v. Winchester Corporation, a butcher sold meat unfit for human consumption and was prosecuted under the Public Health Act 1875. He was found guilty of the offence even though the contamination could not have been discovered until it had been professionally analysed.

7.1.3 Rendering Food Injurious to Health

Food Law owes its origins to the bad practice of adding substances to food to make it go further or the abstraction of substances which may have an alternative use. The addition of water to milk and other drinks, sawdust to bread, sand to pepper, and many similar practices were common in the midnineteenth century. The abstractions of fat from milk, lean from meat and similar practices, although perhaps not as frequent because they involved more effort, were also practised. In recent times, the use of harmful additives in food has posed a danger to the public.

The Modern Food Law

Modern law prohibiting the sale of adulterated food, in fact dates back to the Adulteration of Food and Drink Act 1860 and by the time of the Sale of Food and Drugs Act 1875, the prohibition on rendering food injurious to health by adulteration becomes recognisably like section 7 of the FSA 1990.

Section 7 FSA 1990 makes it an offence for any person to render food injurious to health by means of the addition of any article or substance to food, or the use of any article or substance as an ingredient in the preparation of food, or abstracting any constituent from food and subjecting food to any other process or treatment, with intent that it shall be sold for human consumption. In requiring proof on intent, section 7 is exceptional. In the 1990 Act, offences are generally strict liability.

In determining whether food is injurious to health, a court is required to regard not only the probable effect of the food on the health of a person consuming it, but also the probable cumulative effect of food of substantially the same composition on the health of a person consuming it in ordinary quantities. The food in question must be injurious to a substantial portion of the community, such as invalids and children. However, the prohibition was extended by the inclusion in the FSA 1990 of the section 7(3). This provides that 'injury', in relation to health, includes any impairment, whether permanent or temporary.

The section does not, therefore, apply to food which has become injurious to health by reason of decomposition. Moreover, illegal residues of pesticides and veterinary medicines are not, it is submitted, caught by these provision, because the substances in question are added not to 'food', but to 'food sources'. In food, such residues are properly to be regarded as contaminants, rather than additives.

Deliberate contamination and illegal use of food additives are practices covered by more specific offences. Adulteration by producers has not been entirely eradicated and section 7 remains a threat to anyone who contemplates committing this grave form of dishonest practice.

7.1.4 Food not of the Nature, Quality or Substance Demanded

What is now section 14 of the FSA 1990 has been the principal protection for the consumer from unsatisfactory food since 1875. There was much judicial consideration of the sufficiency or otherwise of notices given to purchasers. Although the FSA 1990 dropped specific provision of this kind in favour of a general due diligence defence, it evidently remains the case that a person cannot be prejudiced if given positive information as to the true nature, substance and quality of the food. However, such information, no matter how accurate, is no defence where a compositional standard has been laid down by law for the food. Thus, a purchaser would be prejudiced by the sale to him of pork sausages containing only 50% of meat in spite of a notice to that effect; because such products are required by regulations to contain not less than 65% of meat. In such a case, there would be an offence of 'quality' under this section and one of deficiency of meat content under the Regulations.

Nature

The term is obviously appropriate where a different sort of food is sold from that demanded by the purchaser. Thus, fruit or fish not of the variety of species asked for would not be of the 'nature' demanded. It has, for example, been held to cover savin sold for saffron, reformed white fish sold as scampi, minced beef containing quantities of pork and lamb meat, and in one case, caustic soda mistakenly sold as lemonade.

It should also be noted that where the food is different from that described, there might also be contraventions of regulation 5(a) of the Food Labelling Regulations 1996, Section15 of the FSA 1990 or Section 1 of the TDA (Trade Description Act 1968).

Case Law

- Savin sold for Saffron– Knight v. Bowers
- Reformed white fish sold as scampi – Preston v Greenclose Ltd. (1975)
- Minced beef containing quantities of pork and lamb meat. Shearer v. Roule
- Caustic soda mistakenly sold as lemonade (1978).

Quality

Where there is no statute that makes provision for the standards of food or special demands by the purchaser, the courts must decide what quality of food an ordinary purchaser would expect to receive. Other instances of food quality which have been considered by the courts have concerned defiant extract of meat and malt-wine, alleged sugar deficiency in orange, citric flavoured cordial, excess fat in minced beef and excess sugar in diet cola. Additionally, actions under quality have been against mouldy, bad and decomposed food.

Substance

This term is usually applied to circumstances in which the composition of the food is incompatible with what was demanded, as in cases where the food contains improper ingredients or adulterants. Until the 1990 Act, it would also have been the most obvious heading for dealing with foreign bodies and contaminants in food, but section 8(2) of the Act now afford a more specific basis. Even though a foreign body is not of the substance demanded, an offence may not necessarily be committed. A distinction was drawn in two milk cases. There was a good defence where the foreign body was a sterile and harmless milk cap, but the action failed where the foreign body was a dangerous sliver of glass. In more recent cases however, a bottle of milk containing a green straw was held not to be of the quality demanded. Mould has also been regarded as contamination of food and a matter affecting its substance.

The Nature, Quality and Substance

The nature, quality and substance of the food for the purposes of section 14 is defined in terms of the purchaser's demand. Where there is a Statutory Standard as indicated, the purchaser will be deemed to have demanded a food for which there is a statutory standard but receives an inferior products, he is prejudiced under the offence committed. "A purchaser who insisted on a product inferior to the statutory standard would evidently be guilty of a secondary party offence such as procuring the illegal sale."

Where there is no statutory standard, the justices must determine the nature, quality and substance of the food demanded by the purchaser as a question of fact on the basis of evidence. The public analyst's option about the normal standard for food has always been an important contribution to the magistrates' consideration.

7.1.5 The Food Safety Requirements

It is unlawful to sell for human consumption, or offer, expose or advertise for sale for such consumption, or have in possession for the purpose of such sale, or preparation for such sale, or to deposit with, or consign to any other person for the purpose of such sale any food which fails to comply with the food safety requirements. An offence under section 8 may arise at any point of manufacture and distribution.

Food fails to comply with the food safety requirements if it has been rendered injurious to health by means of;

a. adding any article or substance to the food;
b. using any article or substance as an ingredient in the preparation of the food;
c. abstracting any constituent from food; or
d. subjecting the food to any other process or treatment with the intention that it shall be sold for human consumption.
e. If it is unfit for human consumption; or
f. if it is so contaminated (whether by extraneous matter or otherwise) that it would not be reasonable to expect it to be used for human consumption in that state.

As explained above in the food safety requirement that, the food shall not be unfit for human consumption, long predated the FSA 1990 and is, therefore, by no means unfamiliar to the courts. But they have not always found it easy to state what is meant by the expression 'unfit for human consumption'. In 1961, in upholding a conviction for sale of a pork pie bearing mould of the penicillin type, Lord Parker CJ said the phrase meant more than unsuitable.

A stale loaf would be unsuitable but not unfit. He was not prepared to say that in all cases the prosecution must prove the food injurious or dangerous. The phrase must be looked at in a broad sense. When an article of food is admittedly going mouldy, it is prima facie (accepted as correct until proved otherwise) unfit for human consumption whether or not there is evidence as to whether there would be any injury to health if it were eaten. It is a matter of degree in every case.

Extraneous objects, which have often formed the subject of proceedings, do not necessarily render food unfit for human consumption. Offences were found to have been committed where there was potential toxicity such as from a dirty bandage in a loaf of bread, or a dead mouse in a bottle of milk. However, cases in which a piece of metal was found in a cream bun and a piece of string in a loaf of bread did not cause the food to be unfit.

Mould spots found on crumpets at 2.30 p.m. were held to be sufficient evidence that they must have been so contaminated at 9.30 a.m. (the time of purchase) and that it would not be reasonable to expect them to be used for human consumption in that state.

*Case Law_* In Kwik Save Group PK v Blaenau Gwent (1995) Unreported (ref. Co/2246/95), DC. It is to be hoped that the use in section 8(2)(c) of the words 'whether by extraneous matter or otherwise' when read with 'would not be reasonable to expect it to be used for human consumption in that state' will catch most occurrences which might deter the ordinary consumer from eating a food. Due regard must be given to the words 'in that state' because there would appear to be no offence if the food is to be subjected to further processing or treatment.

7.2 INSPECTION AND SEIZURE OF SUSPECTED FOOD

7.2.1 Powers of the Officer

An authorized officer of a food authority may at all reasonable times inspect any food intended for human consumption which has been sold or is offered or exposed for sale or is in possession of, or has been deposited with or consigned to, any person for the purpose of sale or preparation for sale.

Where it appears to the officer on such an inspection that the food fails to comply with the food safety requirements, or in other circumstances that food is likely to cause food poisoning or any disease communicable to human beings, he may either give notice to the person in charge of the food that, until the notice is withdrawn, the food or any specified portion of it is not to be used for human consumption. He may seize the food and remove it in order to have it dealt with by a Justice of the Peace.

The form of notice is prescribed and it is an offence knowingly to contravene the requirements of a notice. The inclusion of the word 'knowingly' in this offence requires proof by the prosecution of criminal intention; that is, that the defendant knew of the existence of the notice and its contents. Since the notice must be given to the person in charge of the food, it is submitted that proof of service of the notice in accordance with the FSA 1990 should normally be sufficient in the case of an inspection, since the recipient would find it difficult to claim ignorance of its contents.

Normally, 'reasonable times' for inspection will be when premises are open for business purposes. However, in the case of a serious danger to public health, it may be reasonable to inspect such food businesses regularly.

Both the Public Health Officers and the Weights and Measures Inspectors have power to make regular inspections and to take samples for examination.

The authorized officer has power to enter the following: –

A dwelling house and other premises at all reasonable times. If admission is refused, a magistrate may issue a warrant authorising the officer to enter, by force if necessary.

7.2.2 Referral to a Justice of the Peace

Where the authorized officer exercises his powers to refer the matter to a Justice of the Peace, he must inform the person in charge of the food of his intention to do so. A person who might be liable for prosecution in respect of the food concerned must be given an opportunity to attend before the Justice of the Peace, to give evidence and, to call witnesses.

If it appears to the Justice of the Peace, on the basis of such evidence and he considers it appropriate in the circumstances that, the food fails to comply with the food safety requirements, he must condemn the food and order the food to be destroyed or, to be so disposed off as to prevent it from being used for human consumption; and any expenses reasonably incurred in connection with the destruction or disposal must be defrayed by the owner of the food.

Referral to a Justice of the Peace should be within two days of seizure and in the case of perishable food such referral should be as soon as possible.

7.2.3 Compensation

If a notice issued by an authorized officer is withdrawn or if a Justice of the Peace refuses to condemn the food, the food authority must compensate the owner of the food for any depreciation in its value resulting from the action taken by the authorized officer. Any dispute as to the amount of compensation must be settled by arbitration.

7.2.4 Action to be Taken by the Authorised Officer in Case of Food Poisoning

In the event of a food poisoning outbreak, the authorized officer should seek expert advice from the Consultant in Communicable Disease Control (CCDC) and may also need to contact the local Public Health Laboratory Service (PHLS) or the public analyst. Whenever possible and appropriate, there should be full and open discussions with the owner or person in charge of the food and with the manufacturer.

Where destruction or disposal of food is necessary the food authority is responsible for the necessary arrangements. The food should be fully supervised until it can be dealt with in the appropriate manner. If there is likely to be considerable delay before destruction, the food should be disfigured in some way to prevent any possibility of it being returned to the market place illegally or accidentally.

If food is to be destroyed, the food authority should arrange for total destruction and incineration of the food. If this is not possible, the authority should arrange for a complete destruction to the extent that, the food could never again enter the food chain again.

An example is by flattening tin cans for disposal in a suitably licensed site.

7.3 FOOD AND DRUGS ACT

The aim of the Food and Drugs Act, 1955 is to protect the public against adulterated food and to impose penalties against persons who contravene its regulations. It is an offence to treat or add a substance to food intended for human consumption so as to render it injurious to health or to sell such food or to even possess such food for sale. Mistake is no excuse to a charge of adulterating food or selling it. The seller cannot plead that he made a mistake. However, if he has a good defence he can plead it:

- If he can prove that he is actually ignorant of the fact that the article is not of the nature, substance or quality demanded
- Or if he can prove that he did not act fraudulently and that the article carried a notice clearly stating the contents, or was sold in a wrapper clearly displaying such a notice. However, this defence is not available if the food has been rendered dangerous to health
- Or if he can prove that where the food contains some extraneous matter and got into the food as an unavoidable consequence in the process of collection and preparation
- It is an offence to sell food which is not of the nature, substance or quality demanded, if the purchaser is prejudiced by the sale.

This section affords general protection to purchasers of food. How does the court decide whether a foodstuff is of "the quality demanded?" The person who sells margarine as butter is obviously guilty of an offence.

Case Law

The licensee of a public house was convicted for selling spirits below the minimum strength required by law. He claimed that he did display a notice informing the purchaser of this fact, but his plea was dismissed by the court on the grounds that the notice was insufficient. The purchaser must be told in substance that the thing which he is getting is not the thing he asked for. Furthermore, in this case, the notice was ambiguous and misleading.

Note: An employer can be charged under this section of the Act with an offence committed by his employee, even if he has no knowledge of the employee's wrong-doing and he has taken steps to prevent a breach of the law.

Case Law

Smedleys Ltd was fined for contravening the Food and Drugs Act in respect of a sale of a tin of peas containing a caterpillar to a housewife. It was conceded that the caterpillar was harmless. This was so because the caterpillar was dead and was incapable of causing harm. There was no suggestion of negligence either on the part of the manufacturer or on the part of the seller.

The court was told that in one year, a total of three and a half million tons of peas had been manufactured by Smedleys Ltd. and out of this number; only four complaints had been received. Smedleys Ltd had a screening process which eliminated waste matter of a markedly higher or lower specific gravity than peas, and a system of supervised visual inspection. Unfortunately, the caterpillar was of the same or similar density, diameter and weight as the peas, and so had escaped the screening process; being of green colour similar to the peas, it appeared to have been missed by the visual inspectors.

Smedleys Ltd. was found guilty because the firm could have avoided it. In fairness to Smedleys Ltd, the court did comment that they could see little useful purpose in prosecuting the firm; but no further suggestions were put forward as to how Smedleys Ltd. could avoid such an event happening again, the chances of which are a million to one. However, technically, the firm was guilty of an offence.

7.4 TRADE DESCRIPTIONS ACT

Completing the protection of food is the Trade Description Act 1968. The Act prohibits wrong description of foods, accommodation and facilities in the course of the trade. It covers false description of price lists on menus or false description of food.

It is an offence for anybody in the course of trade or business to:

- Apply a false trade description to goods
- Supply or offer goods to which a false trade description is applied.

The term "trade description", relates to all manner of things including quality, composition and fitness for purpose. It is an offence to give any false or misleading statement concerning the price of goods. This is why it is so important for hotel and catering proprietors to set out their prices in full. Many prosecutions have been successful against hoteliers who impose a service charge upon their customers without prior warning.

7.5 FOOD HYGIENE REGULATIONS 1970

In accordance with the Community Food Directive 93/43/EEC, the proprietors of food businesses are subject to specified obligations. They must ensure that the preparation, processing, manufacturing, packaging, storing, transportation, distribution, handling and offering for sale or supply of food is carried out in a hygienic way and complies with detailed requirements in respect of food businesses.

Individual food businesses bear the principal responsibility for ensuring consumer safety. There is now a clear emphasis on identifying risks and the control of practices and procedures. The food industry itself is strongly urging people to develop voluntary guides to good food hygiene practice. Since there can be no absolute standards of cleanliness, hygiene regulations are necessarily broadly done leaving a great deal to the common sense of enforcement officers and the courts. In the past, this resulted in widely differing interpretations between food authorities. However, the evenness of enforcement has been improved through better coordination and the issue of guidance in the form of statutory codes of practice under the FSA 1990. Hygiene regulations have also acquired a new significance with the enactment of the FSA 1990.

The Provisions

To ensure that the preparation, processing, manufacturing, packaging, storing, transportation, distribution, handling and offering for sale or supply of food is carried out in a hygienic way, the food business proprietors must comply with the following detailed requirements:

- The cleanliness of premises and equipment including toilets and washing facilities
- The cleanliness, adequacy and location of washbasins, ventilation and temperature of rooms, lighting, drainage and changing facilities at food premises
- The cleanliness and avoidance of risk of contamination in moveable and/or temporary premises (such as marquees, market stalls, mobile sales, vehicles), used occasionally for catering purposes and also, vending machines
- The cleaning and avoidance of contamination as regards transport, equipment, food waste, water supply, personal hygiene, storage and other operations regarding foodstuffs and other substances and the training of food handlers
- The cleanliness of rooms where food is prepared, treated or processed, and served
- Personal cleanliness of the employees and their clothing
- First aid facilities.

The regulations are made for the purpose of protecting public health in all catering establishments. Within the Food and Hygiene Regulations, it is stated, "No persons shall expose food to the risk of contamination."

The definition 'contamination' is by water, dust, disease, insects and animals. Food business proprietors are also subject to further essential requirements of the Community Food Hygiene Directives.

They must identify steps in the activities of the business which are critical to ensuring food safety and ensure that adequate safety procedures are identified, implemented, maintained and reviewed on the basis of the principles used to develop the Hazard Analysis and Critical Control Points system, commonly referred to as 'HACCP'. This is an internationally recognised structured approach to assessing the potential hazards in an operation and deciding which are critical to the safety of the consumer. These Critical Control Points (CCPs) are then monitored in the appropriate position and specified remedial action is taken if any CCPs, deviate from their safe limits.

To assist the local authority environmental health officers in explaining these hazard analysis requirements to small businesses, the Department of Health produced a presentation pack on *Controlling Food Hazards*.

The 1995 regulations also require persons working in food handling areas to notify the proprietor of the food business if they are suffering from specified medical conditions and there is any likelihood that they will directly or indirectly contaminate food with pathogenic micro-organisms.

Food authorities must inspect food premises with a frequency which has regard to the risk and must assess the potential food safety hazards associated with those premises. And they must give due consideration to whether the food business proprietor has acted in accordance with any relevant guide to good hygiene practice developed by a national food industry sector, and is complying with Article 3 of the Food Hygiene Directive.

The Food Hygiene Regulations have also recently been amended to provide for the annual licensing in England of retail butcher's shops, mobile shops and market stalls handling both unwrapped raw meat together with other ready to eat foods from the same premises. Certain large mixed business premises selling a range of goods, such as supermarkets, which have butchery service outlet, are also required to have a licence. The licensing conditions apply only to those parts of the premises engaged in the butchery service. In order to be licensed, premises will have to satisfy a range of conditions. These include:

- Compliance with existing food hygiene legislation;
- Enhanced staff training; and
- Payment of an annual licence charge.

It should be noted that offences under Food Hygiene Regulations are not being complied with, this is due to the fact that, there are continuing offences being committed each day.

7.6 STAFF TRAINING REGARDING FOOD HANDLING

Provision is made in the Food Safety (General Food Hygiene) Regulations 1995, requiring food business proprietors to ensure that food handlers engaged in the food business are supervised, instructed and trained in food hygiene matters to correspond with their work activities. Guides to good hygiene practice include advice on the training of food handlers. Food authorities are empowered to provide training courses in food hygiene, whether within or outside their area for persons who are or intend to become involved in food businesses whether as proprietor or otherwise. A food authority may contribute towards the expenses incurred by any other person in providing such courses.

7.7 FOOD LABELLING AND ADVERTISING

An offence is committed, when food is sold or exposed for sale with a label or in a container which falsely describes the article, or is calculated to mislead as to the nature or substance or quality of the food. Pre-packed foods must be labelled with the common or usual name of the food, or the description of the food must be clear enough to indicate its true nature. Unless the quality or proportion of each ingredient is specified, they must be listed in order of importance, according to weight, with the greatest first.

With the main exceptions of bread, pastries and sweets, if goods are sold without being pre-packed, then, a ticket must be displayed near them, clearly visible to customers, stating the name or description of the food. In particular, the name and list of ingredients are compulsory in the labelling of foodstuffs.

Deceptive or Misleading Labels and Advertisements
According to the Food Safety Act 1990, (FSA 1990), Section 15(1) states that it is an offence to give with any food sold, or to display with any food offered or exposed for sale, or in possession for sale, a label, whether or not attached to or printed on the wrapper or container, which falsely described the food or which is likely to mislead as to the nature or substance or quality of the food.

Labelling must not mislead to a material degree as to the characteristics of the foodstuffs and, in particular, as to its nature, identity, properties, composition, quantity, durability, origin or method of manufacture or production.

A Label or Advertisement

These offences are basic to the prevention of false or misleading labels and advertisements and are very wide in their application. Labelling is defined by article 1(3)(a) of Directive 79/112/EEC as "any words, particulars, trademarks, brand name, or symbol relating to a foodstuffs and placed on any packaging, documents, notice, label, ring or collar accompanying or referring to such foodstuffs".

That definition is not reproduced in the Food and Drugs Act 1990, but the use of the words "whether or not attached to or printed on the wrapper or container" suggest that information given visually by words or illustrations could give rise to an offence. A label would not include a verbal statement but the definition of 'advertisement' in the Act includes any notice, circular, label, wrapper, invoice or other document, and any public announcement made orally or by any means of producing or transmitting light or sound. It should also be borne in mind that a verbal statement can be a false trade description under the TDA 1968 which, in appropriate cases is often employed by enforcement authorities instead of or in addition to proceedings under the FSA1990. For all practical purposes it may be assumed that any false or misleading statement as to food for human consumption, however given, is an offence.

The Food Labelling Regulations 1996 generally

The Food Labelling Regulations 1996 are arranged into the following five parts:

Part I Preliminary.

Part II Food to be delivered as such to the ultimate consumer or to caterers.

Part III claims, nutrition labelling and misleading descriptions.

Part IV offences and legal proceedings.

Part V Revocation, amendments and transitional provisions.

Of particular interest to us is Part II of the Food Labelling Regulations 1996.

The Food Labelling Regulations 1996 Part II

Part II of the Food Labelling Regulations 1996 generally implements food labelling Directives 79/112/EEC and applies to food which is ready for delivery to the ultimate consumer or to a catering establishment. However, for some foods, specific labelling provision is made.

Part II does not apply to the following products so far as their labelling is controlled by other Regulations: –

- Specified sugar products
- Cocoa and chocolate products; honey; condensed milk products and dried milk products; coffee; coffee mixture; coffee extract product, chicory extract product or other such designated product which is ready for delivery to a catering establishment; hen eggs; spreadable fats; wine and grape

musts; sparkling wines and aerated semisparkling wines; spirit drinks; fresh fruit and vegetables; preserved sardines; preserved tuna.

General Labelling Requirement

Subject to the provisions of Part II of the Food Labelling Regulations 1996, all non-exempted food must be marked or labelled with:-

- the name of the food;
- a list of ingredients; and (added in 1998 to implement Directive 97/4/ EC) the quantities of certain ingredients or categories of ingredients;
- the appropriate storage conditions or conditions of use;
- the name or business name and address or registered office of the manufacturer or packer, or of a seller established within the European Community;
- particulars of the place of origin of the food, if, failure to give such particulars might mislead a purchaser to a material degree as to the true origin of the food; and
- Instructions for use if it would be difficult to make appropriate use of the food in the absence of such instructions.

7.8 WHAT IS PRESENTATION?

Presentation is defined to include the shape, appearance and packaging of food. It also comprises of the way in which food is arranged when it is exposed for sale and the setting in which the food is displayed with a view to sale, but does not include any form of labelling or advertising.

Examples of food presentation

Prosecutions for misleading presentation have included cases on fatty mince displayed under red lighting to give a misleading impression as to its fat content, meat containing novel protein displayed together with whole meat, and artificially flavoured fruit products being packed on fruit-shaped containers.

7.9 NAMES OF FOOD

A food must be labelled or marked with:

- a name prescribed by law, or if there is none;
- a customary name; or
- a name which indicates the true nature of the food.

Names prescribed by law

Where there is a name prescribed by law, that name must be used as the name of the food. Such a name may be qualified by other words, which make it more precise unless such qualification is prohibited.

Foods for which names have been prescribed by the Schedule to the 1996 Regulations are; fish, melons (the species must be given), potatoes (the variety must be given) and vitamins. With regard to the prescribed fish names, the Council Regulation 104/2000/EC (on the common organization of the markets in fishery and aquaculture products), will as from 1st January, 2002 require member states to draw up and publish a list of the commercial designations of specified fish, crustaceans, and molasses accepted within their territory for the purpose of retail labelling.

Many other names are prescribed by legislation on specific product. Names are prescribed in implementation of community directives for sugar products, cocoa and chocolate products, coffee products, honey, fruit juices and fruit nectars, condensed milk and dried milk jam and similar products, natural and mineral waters and caseins and caseinates (the main protein present in milk and cheese). Names are also prescribed by Community Common Agricultural Policy Regulations for drinking milk, spreadable fats, poultry meat, still wine, sparkling wine, aromatised wine, spirit drinks and olive oil.

Customary Names

Where there is no name prescribed by law, a customary name may be used. A customary name is one which has come to be accepted in the United Kingdom or in the area where the food is sold. Examples are 'fish fingers', 'Bakewell Tart', 'Cornish Pasty', 'Welsh rarebit', 'Lancashire Hot Pot', 'Chicken Maryland'. In Ghana, 'Red Red', is an accepted customary name for fried ripe plantain and beans. Some food names of foreign origin have become common in the United Kingdom over the years and may qualify as customary names. Examples are 'lasagne', 'macroni' and 'petit fours'.

Some food manufacturers are tempted to apply geographical words to a common product or to search out old-fashioned and seldom used names which have a marketing appeal in the belief that, they will qualify as customary names. And a name which is customary in a particular area may not be understood on its own when sold outside that area. In such cases, it will be wise to add an accompanying description satisfying the requirements as to the indication of the true nature.

The Food Advisory Committee has recommended that the option to use a customary name should be abolished.

Indication of the true nature of the food
If there is no name prescribed by law and if there is no customary name used, the name used for the food must be sufficiently precise to inform the purchaser of the true name of the food and to enable the food to be distinguished from products with which it could be confused and, if necessary, must include a description of its use. 'True nature' means a clear and accurate description of the characteristics of the food but it does not require a detailed description including all the main ingredients. The name should be easy to understand and should not be confusing.

A trade mark, brand name or fancy name may not be used as a substitute for a name satisfying the requirement of this regulation. However, it is acceptable to print a trade mark, brand name or fancy name in large type followed by a name which meets these requirements, provided always that the provisions as to intangibility in Regulation 38 are met.

Ingredients

Food must be labelled with a list of ingredients, which is headed by the word "ingredients" and sets out all the ingredients in descending order and by weight as determined at the time of use in the preparation of the food. Enforcement officers have the power to examine recipes to verify the correctness of lists of ingredients.

Chapter Eight

NEGLIGENCE

8.1 THE MEANING OF NEGLIGENCE

Negligence means not done intentionally. During the first half of the nineteenth century, negligence began to gain recognition as a separate and independent basis of tort liability. This was the period of the industrial revolution and there appeared to be an increase in the number of accidents caused by industrial machinery and in particular by the invention of railways.

Everyone owes to another who might be affected by his actions, a duty to take reasonable care. Negligence is the breach of this duty, which is measured by the standard of a reasonable man.

For example, whether the pedestrian who is injured in a road accident can claim damages against a motorist depends on whether the motorist was careful as a reasonable person would have been in the circumstances. This duty to use reasonable care must be complied with by everybody in every aspect of life. The pedestrian may be liable to the motorist if it was he who failed to take reasonable care likewise the motorist.

The duty of taking reasonable care extends to the manufacturer of goods. He must use reasonable care in making sure all the articles sold to the consumer are safe.

The motorist ought to be able to foresee that if he drives carelessly, someone might be injured. Likewise, the manufacturer ought to be able to foresee that if he is careless in manufacturing an article, someone might be injured. The carelessness of the manufacturer includes, of course, the carelessness of his employees, because he is generally responsible for what his employees do in the course of their work.

We shall be looking at definitions by some prominent authors as follows:

"The failure to exercise the standard of care that a reasonably prudent person would have exercised in a similar situation, any conduct that falls below the legal standard established to protect others against unreasonable risk or harm except for conduct that is intentionally, wantonly, or wilfully disregard of others' rights. This denotes culpable carelessness which is negligent conduct that while not intentional, involves a disregard of the consequences likely to result from one's action".

"A tort grounded in this failure is usually expressed in terms of the following elements: duty, breach of duty, causation and damages."

"Negligence in law ranges from inadvertence that is hardly more than accidental to sinful disregard of the safety of others". **Devlin, P.** _The Enforcement of Morals **36 (1968)**

"The tort of negligence has three ingredients, and to succeed in an action the plaintiff must now show:

- 'The existence of a duty to take care which was owed to him by the defendant.'
- 'Breach of such duty by the defendant,' and
- 'Resulting damage to the plaintiff.' "

Smith and Keenan – _English Law_

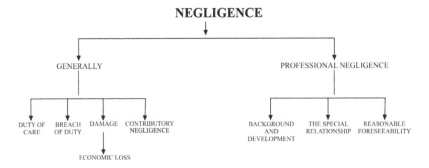

Fig 8.1 A diagram of Negligence

8.2 CATEGORIES OF NEGLIGENCE

8.2.1 Contributory Negligence

It refers to a plaintiff's own negligence that played a part in causing the plaintiff's injury and is significant enough to bar the plaintiff from recovering damages.

"The contributory negligence of a third party is no excuse for the negligence of the defendant".

Thomas E. Holland, The Elements of Jurisprudence 154(13th ed. 1924)

Even though the plaintiff has managed to prove negligence of the manufacturer, the manufacturer may still be able to obtain a reduction in the damages or even defeat the claim by proving that the plaintiff was guilty of contributory negligence because he contributed to the damage or was even entirely responsible for it. For example, failure to observe operating instructions or using the product after knowledge that it is defective.

The Law Reform (Contributory Negligence) Act applies. Under it the court may, for example, assess damages at $10,000 but decides that the plaintiff is 50% to blame and reduce the damages to $5,000. In an extreme case the court may decide that the plaintiff is 100% to blame so that he recovers nothing.

8.2.2 Criminal Negligence

Criminal negligence is gross negligence, so extreme that it is punishable as a crime. For example, involuntary manslaughter or other negligent homicide can be based on criminal negligence and also when an extremely careless automobile driver kills someone.

8.2.3 Culpable Negligence

Negligence, while not intentional, involves a disregard of the consequences likely to result from one's action.

8.2.4 Gross Negligence

A lack of slight diligence or care; a conscious, voluntary act or omission in reckless disregard of a legal duty and of the consequences to another party who may typically recover exemplary damages. It is also termed reckless negligence; wilful negligence or hazardous negligence.

8.2.5 Negligence – Professional Liability

The law of negligence also applies to the provision of services. It mainly applies to those who provide professional business advice, i.e. against accountants, lawyers, surveyors, valuers and consultants.

Liability for negligent statements is also of great significance to the law and a highly effective cause of action at law concerning negligent acts. Some companies have been sued for damages for making negligent statements.

Case Law – Donoghue v Stevenson 1932 is related to negligent actions for physical injury arising from negligent acts, i.e. liability for a negligently manufactured product, which causes physical injury to a customer. Liability under that test extended to anyone who might, reasonably be foreseen to suffer such injury.

The most practical suggestion that can be made in terms of avoiding liability is for professionals to follow strictly the recommendations of their professional bodies, e.g. the many financial reporting standards and other published material.

Professional indemnity policies are available for a whole range of professional persons and experts, e.g. accountants, solicitors, company directors, insurance brokers and other professionals.

8.2.6 Negligence of Employers

An injured employee will have to prove that his injury was the result of the employer's breach of a duty of care. The employee is assisted in such incidents because certain specific duties of an employer were laid down by Parliament in the leading case of Wilsons and Clyde Coal Co. v. English A.C. 57. An employer must therefore take reasonable care to provide;

    I. proper and safe plant and appliances for the work
    II. A safe system of work with adequate supervision and instructions,
    III. Safe premises; and
    IV. A competent staff of fellow employees.

Case Law – Millard v Search Tubes Ltd 1969 (A Statutory duty of care)

8.3 FURTHER ASPECTS OF NEGLIGENCE

8.3.1 Occupiers' Liability

The Occupiers' liability Act should be of particular interest to hotel proprietors and other sleeping establishments etc. The occupier is a person who has control of premises or possession of them. An employer may be vicariously liable for the torts of an employee who is acting within the scope of his employment.

Case Law– **Stone v Taffe (1974)**
The owner of a hotel was held liable when the manager failed to ensure that there was adequate lighting on the hotel premises. A guest fell as a result and was killed.

8.3.2 The Occupiers' Liability Act 1957

A common duty of care is owed to all lawful visitors to premises.

'Visitors' being a term includes anyone to whom the occupier has given, or is deemed to have given an invitation or permission to use the premises by right of law, such as inspectors, but not those who cross land in pursuance of a public or private right of way. These are governed by the Occupiers' Liability Act 1984 which now governs the position of trespassers and other non-visitors.

Implied permission to enter premises is a matter of fact to be decided in the circumstances of each case, and the burden of proof is upon the person who claims implied permission. However, persons who enter upon premises for the purposes of business which they believe will be of interest to the occupier, as where they wish to sell him a product, have implied permission to enter even though the occupier is not expecting them.

Under the Act, an occupier of premises owes to all visitors the duty of care depending on the circumstances of the case. It is necessary to see that the visitor will be reasonably safe in using the premises for the purpose for which he is invited or permitted to be there. If the visitor uses the premises for some other purpose, the occupier does not owe him the same duty; such a person is in effect a trespasser, and liability will be decided on that basis.

Under 2(1) of the 1957 Act, the occupier may restrict or exclude his liability, by giving adequate warning. However, the Unfair Contract Terms Act 1977 states that, the Common Law duty of care in regard to liability for death or personal injury cannot be excluded in relation to business premises. In addition, liability for other losses or damages occurring on such premises can only be excluded where it is reasonable to do so.

Where the accident has arisen through the defective work of an independent contractor, the occupier can avoid liability by showing that he carefully selected the contractor.

However, this defence (to one who is willing, no harm is done) is available to the occupier, though he must show that the entrant consented to the risk, not that he merely knew of it. Therefore, the entrant's knowledge is no longer a defence.

There are two main aspects of this defence; they are deliberate harm and accidental harm. The plaintiff's assent may prevent him from complaining of some deliberate conduct of the defendant, which would normally be actionable. The following are some examples;

- Deliberate harm – To stick a knife into a person would normally be actionable, but if a surgeon does it with the consent of the patient it is not so.
- Accidental harm – There are occasions where the defence of inevitable accidents can be raised. Such an accident is one which is not avoidable by any precautions a reasonable man would have been expected to take. It should be noted that, most accidents have a cause and this defence is comparatively rare occurrence.
- An Act of God – This is something which occurs in the course of nature and is beyond human foresight. It is so unexpected in its consequences that the damage caused must be regarded as too remote to form a basis for legal liability. It arises always from the course of nature and has no human causation.

Case Law – Nichols v. Marsland, (1876) Act of God

8.3.3 Trespassers / Invitees
Duty of Care
An occupier of premises owes a duty of care to all persons who come on to his premises. Such persons can be divided into two classes – trespassers and invitees

Trespassers
The general rule is that he who comes unlawfully on to land enters at his own risk in all respects. To a trespasser you owe no duty either to see that your premises is safe, or give warning of their danger. But to this general rule, there are qualifications – the first is that if you intentionally harm a trespasser by creating on your premises a source of danger for that purpose, you will be liable for the harm done. Unless, the danger so created by you can be shown to be

nothing more than a reasonable and therefore, a lawful measure of selfdefence.

You must not throw stones at a man because he crosses your land without permission and for the same reason you must not intentionally lay a trap for him so that he may, when trespassing, injure himself. You are quite at liberty to protect your property by means of spikes or broken glass upon the top of your wall or by a barbed wire fence, or by a dog accustomed to bite mankind, unless the dog is so savage and so powerful as to be likely to cause serious bodily harm.

Secondly, you may be liable even to a trespasser for positive negligent acts done with knowledge of his presence. If you shoot unto your own land, you owe a duty of care not only to persons lawfully there, but to any trespasser known to be there.

It is sometimes difficult to know who trespassers are, and to discover into which class such persons as hawkers, beggars, canvassers, etc. are to fall into. The right conclusion seems to be that no person is a trespasser who enters upon your land in order to communicate with you or any other person on the premises, unless he knows or ought to know that his entry is prohibited.

Invitees

An invitee is a person who receives permission as a matter of lawful business, and not a matter of grace, to enter upon your premises. An example is the carpenter whom you invite into your premises to fix a door. If he uses reasonable care on his part for his own safety, he is entitled to expect that you on your part will use reasonable care to prevent damage to him from unusual danger, which you know about or ought to know about. If he suffers injury because of your negligence, you may have to answer questions as to whether you took reasonable care by telling him of the danger, whether the lighting in your premises was sufficient to enable him to avoid danger, whether you placed a guard round a dangerous part of your premises, or whether the carpenter himself contributed towards the negligence.

The main case on an occupier's liability to a trespasser was British Railways Board v Herrington (1972) AC 877 in which the House of Lords unanimously decided that there could be liability to a trespasser. The five judges concerned reached that decision in different ways and the matter was referred to the Law Commission. Parliament later passed the Occupiers' Liability Act 1984 which now governs the position of trespassers and certain other non-visitors.

The duty is to take such care as is reasonable in all the circumstances of the case to see that the non-visitor does not suffer injury because of the danger concerned. The duty may be discharged by giving warning of the danger or taking steps to discourage a person from incurring risk. Thus the defence of "to one who is willing no harm is done) is prevented".

8.3.4 Legal Responsibilities Towards Children on Premises

The duty of care towards children on premises requires much more care than the duty towards adults. If the occupier of a premises knows that children are likely to be trespassers on his premises, it is advisable for him to keep his premises safe as much as possible, so that children will not be injured on his land. The occupier can be sued for negligence if the occupier does not make provision for the safety of children on his premises, e.g. exposure of broken electrical sockets, dangerous or broken fence, a playground with broken bottles The occupier in general will be liable, even though the child was supposed to be a trespasser. Warnings to children must be more conspicuous as compared to adults, because warnings to adults might not be appropriate for children.

Case Law – Yachuk v. Olive Blais and Co. Ltd. 1949 – Negligence liability and children.

Case Law – Mourton v Poulter 1930 – Warning Children.

Case Law – A.J. Contractors v T. Smith.

A warehouse was being demolished by contractors near a park where children played, the children were warned to keep away from the area. The men working on the building piled up rubbish from the premises and set fire to the rubbish. The men were also warned to be extra vigilant and look out for the children so that no child comes to the premises. The children came nearer and were chased away from the fire. Whiles the men were away, one of the children by name T. Smith, got in the fire and was seriously injured by the fire.

The contractors contested that T. Smith was a trespasser and, above all, the children were warned and that they were not negligent.

Held – The contractors were in breach of the duty of care owed to the child. Their workmen should have stayed around until the fire went out completely before leaving the area.

8.3.5 The Landlord's Duty of Care Towards His Tenant and the Tenant's Visitor

Under the 1957 Act, the landlord was only liable to his tenants' visitors if he had been notified of the defect by the tenant. Duty is owed where the landlord knew or ought to have known of the relevant defect, so notice given by the tenant will not be necessary. Where the lease of tenancy expects the tenant to make it a duty to inform the lessor of defects but the tenant fails to do so and a third party sustains an injury, the landlord can still be sued provided it can be shown that he ought to have known of the defect but in this case, the lessor may be able to recover contribution from the tenant who will be a joint tortfeasor.

If the tenant himself sustains an injury, the 1972 Act allows the tenant to sue his landlord for breach of his statutory duty, but the lessor would be able to allege contributory negligence in that the tenant failed to notify him of the defect. However, where the defect was due to a tenant failing to carry out an obligation expressly imposed on him by the lease or tenancy; the landlord does not owe the tenant any duty although he still owes a duty to third parties if they were injured, Section 6(3) of the 1972 Act renders void any exclusion clause in a lease or tenancy agreement. There is little a landlord can do to avoid liability.

8.3.6 Defective Premises Act 1972

The Act brought about three major changes:

- Landlord's liability for defects in leased premises was increased
- Much of the Common-law requirements of a vendor or landlord for negligence was abolished
- There is a statutory duty on those concerned with providing dwellings to do the work properly.

A duty is placed on builders, developers, sub-contractors, architects and local authorities to see that building contracts are carried out in a professional way, with proper materials so that the building is fit to live in.

8.4 THE DUTY OF CARE

8.4.1 The Duty of Care in General

It is the duty of everyone to take reasonable care to avoid acts or omission which one can foresee would be likely to injure his neighbour. A neighbour is anyone who is so closely and directly affected by the act that you ought reasonably to have them in mind as being affected when you are directing your mind to the acts or omissions, is a matter to be decided upon.

Either a duty of care exists or not is a question of law for the judge to decide. The judges influenced by the doctrine of privity of contract, used it to establish that the existence of the duty of care in negligence in those cases where a contract existed by laying down the principle that, if A is contractually liable to B, he cannot at the same time be liable to C, in tort for the same act or omission.

The House of Lords in Donoghue v. Stevenson, 1932 AC 562 dispelled the confusion caused by the application of the doctrine of privity of contract where physical injury is caused to the plaintiff by the defendant's negligent act.

From Donoghue's case, the fact that the maker of the ginger beer was liable for its defects in contract to the café owner did not prevent him from being liable to Donoghue also in the tort of negligence. In this case, Lord Atkin formulated what has now become the classic test for establishing a duty of care when he said: "You must take reasonable care to avoid acts or omissions which you can reasonably foresee would be likely to injure your neighbour. Who then is your neighbour? The answer seems to be persons who are so closely and directly affected by my act that I ought reasonably to have them in contemplation as being affected when I am directing my mind to the acts or omissions which are called in question."

Case Law

Donoghue v. Stevenson (1932) AC 562

The appellant's friend purchased a bottle of ginger beer from a retailer in Paisley and gave it to her. The respondents were the manufacturers of the ginger beer. The appellant consumed some of the ginger beer and her friend was replenishing the glass, when, according to the appellant, the decomposed remains of a snail came out of the bottle. The bottle was made of dark glass so that the snail could not be seen until most of the contents had been consumed. The appellant became ill and served a writ on the manufacturers claiming damages. The question before the House of Lords was whether the facts outlined above constituted a cause of action in negligence. The House of Lords held by a majority of three to two said that they did. It was stated that a manufacturer of products, which are sold in such a form that they are likely to reach the ultimate consumer in the form in which they left the manufacturer with no possibility of intermediate examination owes a duty to the consumer to take reasonable care to prevent injury. This rule has been broadened in subsequent cases so that the manufacturer is liable more often where defective chattels cause injury. The following important points also arise out of the case:

(a) It was in this case that the House of Lords formulated the test that the duty of care in negligence is based on the foresight of the reasonable man. As Lord Atkin said: "The liability for negligence, whether you style it such or treat it as in other systems is no doubt based upon a general public sentiment of moral wrongdoing for which the offender must pay. But acts or omissions which any moral code would censure cannot in a practical world be treated so as to give a right to every person injured by them to demand relief. In this way, rules of law arise which limit the range of complainants and the extent of their remedy. The rule that you are to love your neighbour becomes in law, you must not injure your neighbour, and the lawyer's question, who is my neighbour receives a restricted reply? You must take reasonable care to avoid acts or omissions which you can reasonably foresee would be likely to injure your neighbour. Who, then in law is my neighbour? The answer seems to be persons who are so closely and directly affected by my act that I ought reasonably to have them in contemplation as being so affected when I am directing my mind to the acts or omissions which act called in question."

(b) Lord MacMillan's remarks in his judgement that the categories of negligence are never closed suggest that the tort of negligence is capable of further expansion.

(c) The duty of care with regard to chattels as laid down in the case relates to chattels not dangerous in themselves. E.g. explosives, is much higher.

(d) The appellant had no course of action against the retailer in contract because her friend bought the bottle, so that there was no privity of contract between the retailer and the appellant. Therefore, terms relating to fitness for purpose and merchantable quality, now implied into such contracts by the Sale of Goods Act 1979, did not apply here.

A remedy under the Sale of Goods Act

Case Law – Tucker J. Lockett V. Charles Ltd.1938

In this case, a husband and wife went into a hotel for lunch. The wife ordered whitebait which was not fit for human consumption. She only ate a small amount of the whitebait and was then taken ill. In the subsequent action against the hotel, Tucker, J. held that although the husband ordered the meal, there was an assumption in these cases that, each party would be, if necessary, personally liable for what he or she consumed. There was therefore a contract between the hotel and the wife into which Sale of Goods Act terms could be implied and she was awarded damages because the whitebait was not fit for the purpose or of merchantable quality. This approach is still modern in spite of the fact that the case was decided in 1938.

> The general statement of principles in this case is at the root of negligence. However, it should be noted that The Consumer Protection Act 1987 provides a statutory basis for claims against a manufacturer for product liability and without the need to prove negligence.

> The duty of care therefore is established by putting in the defendant's place a 'reasonable man' and deciding whether the reasonable man would have foreseen the likelihood of injuring, not its mere possibility. The test is objective not subjective, and the effect of its application is that a person is not liable for every injury which results from his carelessness. There must be a duty of 'care.' Nevertheless, new duties are established from time to time by case law.

> Lord Macmillan stated in Donoghue v. Stevenson, 1932 that; "the categories of negligence are never closed."

> However, there is always a requirement of foresight i.e. the plaintiff must be within the area of foreseeable danger.

8.4.2 Economic and Physical Damage

There has been much development, in the field of economic loss which is an area of difficulty. Is there a duty to avoid causing foreseeable economic loss?

Careless misstatements

A person who makes a careless statement which causes economic loss to a plaintiff within the area of his foresight may be liable to compensate that plaintiff for economic loss.

Physical injury – Damages for economic loss may be awarded if there is foreseeable physical injury to the plaintiff or his property, though issues of public policy still govern where the line is to be drawn.

Case Law – Spartan Steel and Alloys Ltd. v. Martin And Co. Ltd. 1972.
(Economic loss following physical damage_

The defendant's employees damaged a cable which supplied electricity to the plaitiffs factory whiles digging the road. The factory was left without electricity and therefore could not function

The cable was the property of the local electricity board. Since there was no electricity the temperature of the furnace dropped and the metal that was being melted had to be thrown away. Whilst the cable was being repaired, the factory was unable to function for hours.

The Court of Appeal, however, allowed the plaintiff only damages for the spoilt metal and the loss of profit, which resulted from the factory being unable to function during the period when there was no electricity.

Lord Denning chose to base his decision on remoteness of damage rather than absence of any duty of care causing economic loss.

However, he made it clear that public policy was involved. In the course of his judgement he said:

"At the bottom, I think the question of recovering economic loss is one of policy. Whenever the courts draw a line to mark out the bounds of duty, they do so as a matter of policy so as to limit the responsibility of the defendant. Whenever the courts set bounds to the damages recoverable– saying that they are, or are not too remote, they do it as a matter of policy so as to limit the liability of the defendant."

8.5 BREACH DUE TO NEGLIGENCE

8.5.1 Breach of Duty

If a duty of care is established as a matter of law, whether or not the defendant is in breach of that duty is a matter to be decided by the judge on the facts of the case. Though the standard required is that of a reasonable man.

Here we are concerned with how much care the defendant must take. It is obvious that if motorists did not take out their cars many lives would be saved, and yet it is not negligent to drive a car. Once again, the test is to place the 'reasonable man' in the defendant's position.

8.5.2 Statutory Duties

Numerous statutes were laid down by Parliament to protect and provide for the health, welfare and safety of employees. Such statutes are high and often very absolute. Though the employer can plead contributory negligence as a defence, where a breach of a statutory duty occurs, e.g. failure to fence a dangerous machine has caused injury to an employee, the employee may be able to sue his employer for damages by using the breach of statutory duty to establish the duty of care under this rule of law.

8.5.3 The Liability of a Manufacturer for Defective Goods

Here we shall consider the liability of a manufacturer for defective goods, in the absence of a contract between the parties liability. This is based on the Common Law of negligence and to some extent now on statute law.

Where goods are purchased from a retailer, the action can be brought under the Sale of Goods Act by the purchaser against the manufacturer in respect of physical injuries caused by defects in the goods. (Case Donoghue v. Stevenson 1932)

The rule arrived at in Donoghue v. Stevenson has been widened since 1932, and now applies to defective chattels generally which cause injuries to purchasers (Grant v. Australian Knitting Mills 1936).

However, although the Donoghue case shows that the manufacturer has a duty to take care, evidence may show that he was not in breach of that duty because he took proper precautions.

In addition, liability in negligence is not strict as it is under the Sale of Goods Act. The plaintiff must prove negligence in the process of manufacturing. However, assistance is given by the plea of 'res ipsa loquitur' (the thing speaks for itself). If this plea is accepted by the court the defendant must show he was not negligent or explain how the matter could have come about without his negligence. If he fails to do so, the plaintiff wins the case.

8.6 DAMAGES FOR BREACH

8.6.1 What is Meant by Damages?

Damages in law refer to a sum of money claimed or awarded in compensation for a loss or for an injury.

The damages awarded are designed to put the plaintiff in the position he would have been in if he had not suffered the wrong. In the case of personal injuries, e.g. loss of a limb, damages obviously cannot restore the plaintiff to his previous position. However, damages for personal injuries may be awarded under the following headings:

a. Pain and suffering
b. Loss of enjoyment of life, or of amenity, e.g. when brain damage causes permanent unconsciousness
c. Loss of earnings, both actual and prospective.

8.6.2 Types of Damages

Damages can be classified under a number of headings, and this classification applies to both contract and tort.

a. Ordinary damages are assessed by the court for losses arising naturally from the breach of contract, and in tort for losses which cannot be positively proved or ascertained, and depend upon the courts view of the nature of the plaintiff's injury. For example, the court may have to decide what to award for the loss of an eye, there being no scale of payment.

b. Special damages are awarded in tort for losses which can be positively proved or ascertained, e.g. damage to clothing. However, where it is difficult to determine the exact proportions of a claim for special damages, e.g., loss of profit not supported by accurate figures, the court must do its best to arrive at a fair valuation. Dixons Ltd. v. J.L. Cooper Ltd. 1970.

8.6.3 The Consumers' Legal Rights

The manufacturer's liability in negligence is not confined to compensation, loss or damage to health or property. He is liable also for the cost of remedying the defect in the goods in the same way as the seller. The negligent manufacturer must also pay any other expenses, which directly and normally arise from the defect. This would include, for instance, the cost of having to hire a substitute while the article is being repaired.

Any manufacturer of goods can be liable for negligence. For example, a person who falls ill as a result of eating poisonous tinned food can claim damages against the negligent manufacturer, irrespective of whether he was the buyer or not. If the person who falls ill is the one who bought the tinned food in the shop, he can claim against the manufacturer under the law of negligence, and also under an implied term in his contract of purchase. He cannot be compensated twice, however, for the same thing. The tinned food itself which turned out to be no good, must always be replaced, or the price refunded by the shop which sold it. <u>If, as a result of eating bad food, or of biting some foreign body in food, you suffer real pain and anguish, or are seriously ill, you should be compensated.</u> How much you get depends on the circumstances. In a serious case, especially one involving a child, a legal representation is necessary. But in a single case where great harm did not result, a person can handle the claim himself. For a cut lip from a sliver of glass in a pot of marmalade, you ought to have more compensation, which includes something for the nasty experience.

8.6.4 Proven Negligence Against the Seller or Manufacturer

The burden of proving negligence both in and out of court is almost always on the consumer. This can make a tremendous difference in practice, when you are claiming for negligence against a manufacturer's part and nothing else. This can go a long way beyond that the article went wrong, except in a case where the fact of negligence speaks for itself. If, on the other hand, you had adopted the guarantee, and asked for defects to be put right under it, you are not called upon to prove the cause of the defect, if it is put right, as a rule with no questions asked.

It is not only the manufacturer who can be made liable under the law of negligence. It is possible that the seller may also be liable if he was negligent. But generally, a shopkeeper like the consumer is entitled to assume that a new article which he has bought is free from dangerous defects, and he is not liable in negligence just because an article which passed through his hands turned out to have a dangerous defect in it. This does not mean that a person has no redress against the shopkeeper. He is still liable to you under The Sale of Goods Act 1893, no matter whose fault the defect originated.

Section 55 of The Sale of Goods Act makes void any attempt by the seller to exclude himself from the contract. This is an example of the increased protection afforded to consumers by the government in recent years.

The injured consumer has a heavy responsibility to prove that the seller was negligent. It is hardly surprising therefore that he is reluctant to start legal proceedings, especially as it may be expensive and long drawn out.

Negligence of an employee in the hotel and catering establishments are in many cases easy to prove, for example, if a guest's bed is unstable and in the course of getting into bed, the bed collapses and the guest sustains a broken leg, this could mean that the room attendant who cleaned the room did not report to the housekeeper for the bed to be put right. This is the negligence of an employee. Also a broken socket in the bedroom, which was not reported to be fixed which electrocutes a guest also amounts to negligence.

Chapter Nine

MISREPRESENTATION

9.1 WHAT IS MEANT BY MISREPRESENTATION

9.1.1 Misrepresentation

Misrepresentation means to represent wrongly or inaccurately; an untrue statement of fact, made by one party to the other in the course of negotiating a contract that induces the other party to enter into the contract. The person making the misrepresentation is called the representor, and the person to whom it is made is the representee. Any behaviour, by words or conduct is sufficient to be a misrepresentation if it is such as to mislead the other party. If it conveys a false impression, that is enough.

Misrepresentation can also be described as an expression used to describe a situation in which there is no genuineness of consent to a contract by one of the parties. The party misled can ask the Court to rescind (to put the parties back into the positions they held before the contract was made) the contract. For example, in a contract for the sale of goods, the goods would be returned to the seller and the money to the buyer.

The remedies for misrepresentation vary according to the degree of culpability of the presenter. If he is guilty of fraudulent misrepresentation, the representee may be, subject to certain limitations, set the contract aside by rescission and may also sue for damages.

- Concealment or (non-disclosure)(in contract law).The failure by one party, during negotiations for a contract, to disclose to the other a fact known to him that would influence the other in deciding whether or not to enter into the contract. A full duty of disclosure exists only in the case of contracts uberrimae fidel, which are usually useful contracts of insurance. If the person to be insured gives any untrue information, the contract will (like any other) be voidable for misrepresentation. If the person also suppresses a material fact, it will be voidable for nondisclosure. In the case of other contracts, there is no general duty to volunteer information and mere silence cannot constitute misrepresentation. There is, however, a very limited duty of disclosure. A person who does volunteer information must not only tell a partial truth and must correct any statement that subsequently becomes to his knowledge untrue. Breach of this duty will render the contract voidable for misrepresentation. Also, failure of a party to include a document that should have been disclosed in his list of documents for discovery and inspection will render the contract voidable for misrepresentation. The other party may seek an order for specific discovery of the document or an order requiring the party making discovery to verify his list of documents by affidavit.

- A statement intended to be truthful may be a misrepresentation because of ignorance or carelessness, as when the word "not" is unintentionally omitted or when inaccurate language is used. But a misrepresentation that is not fraudulent has no consequence unless it is material.

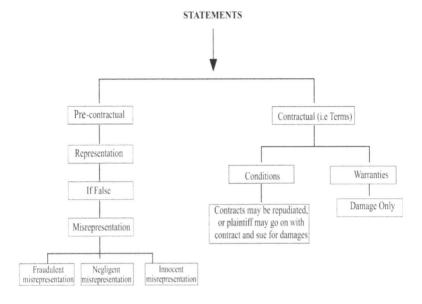

Fig 9.1 A diagram of a Statements

- MISREPRESENTATION ACT 1967

  Under The Misrepresentation Act.1967 Section 2 [1]

  I. This Act creates statutory liability for misrepresentation unless the person making the misrepresentation had reasonable grounds to believe, and did believe up to the moment of making the contract, that the facts represented were true.

  II. The Act also states that, where a person has entered into a contract after a misrepresentation has been made to him by another party, and as a result he has suffered loss, then the person making the misrepresentation would be liable to damages if the misrepresentation has been made fraudulently. Unless he proves that he had reasonable grounds to believe and did believe up to the time the contract was made that the facts represented were true.

9.1.2 Representation

- A representation is a statement made by one party to another relating to some past event or existing fact, which induces a course of action, e.g signing of a contract. It may be inferred from conduct. Under CCA (Consumer Credit Act. 1974, s 189(1)), a representation includes any condition or warranty or any other statement or undertaking, whether oral or in writing.

- A representation can also be described as a way of persuading or influencing the other party to enter into a contract; a statement made by way of allegation or to convey opinion. It becomes a misrepresentation when it is false. However, a statement which is not completely or totally true may be a misrepresentation. A representation must be a statement of some specific existing and variable fact or past event.

9.2 TYPES OF ACTIONABLE MISREPRESENTATION

9.2.1 Innocent Misrepresentation

An innocent misrepresentation is a statement made innocently in which there is no element of fault, i.e. fraud or negligence. A false statement that the speaker or the writer does not know is false; a misrepresentation that, though is false, was not made fraudulently.

A purely innocent misrepresentation is a false statement made by a person who had reasonable grounds to believe that the statement was true, not only when he made it, but also at the time the contract was entered into. As regards reasonable grounds, the representor's best hope of proving this will be in showing that he himself had been induced to buy the goods by some statement, particularly where he is not technically qualified to verify it further. The party misled can ask the court to rescind the contract but has no right to ask for damages provided the remedy of rescission is still available and has not been lost e.g. by delay. (Misrepresentation Act 1967, s. 2 (2). Rescission in effect cancels the contract. The court may in some cases regard this as a drastic remedy, particularly where there has been misrepresentation on a critical matter, such as the quality of tyres on a car. Suppose the seller of a private sale says: "the previous owner fitted new tyres at 26,000 miles". If that statement is false but the seller was told this by the previous owner, then the court could award damages instead of rescission, thus leaving the contract intact but giving the party monetary compensation. Statement by dealers, however, are often taken to be terms of the contract.

Note – Remedies include avoidance and action for indemnity against any obligation created by the contract.

Case Law – Innocent misrepresentation. Hummings Bird Motors v. Hobbs (1986)

"H" was a young man whom the judge found to be an amateur doing some sort of trading in the motor trade. 'H' bought a car from a dealer who told him that the mileage recorded, 35,000 miles, was correct. 'H' sold the car to the plaintiffs making the same statement, i.e. that the recorded mileage, was, to the best of his knowledge and belief correct. The plaintiffs discovered that the vehicle had done 70,000 miles and tried to claim damages for innocent misrepresentation. The Court of Appeal decided it was innocent. He was an amateur and was merely repeating what he himself believed.

9.2.2 Negligent Misrepresentation

A negligent misrepresentation is a false statement made by a person who had no reasonable grounds for believing the statement to be true. The party misled may sue for rescission and or damages. The representor is required to prove that the statement was not made negligently but there were reasonable grounds for believing it to be true. Misrepresentation Act 1967.S 2(1)

Note –Remedies include avoidance, damages and rescission

Case Law – Negligent Misinterpretation. Mapes v. Jones (1974)

A property dealer contracted to lease a grocer's shop to the plaintiff for 21 years but in fact did not have sufficient interest in the property himself to grant such a lease, the maximum period available to him being 18 years. Despite constant requests no lease was supplied as originally promised and the plaintiff was entitled to rescission for misrepresentation.

Under s.2(1) of the 1967 Act. He also found that the defendant's delay in completion was a breach of a condition which also allowed the plaintiff to repudiate the contract.

9.2.3 Fraudulent Misrepresentation

A statement that is known to be false or is made recklessly without knowing or caring whether it is true or false, and that it is intended to induce a party to detrimentally rely on it. It is also termed deceit. A fraud is the most difficult of all the forms of misrepresentation to prove. It must be proved beyond reasonable doubt, which is the criminal standard. The civil standard is proof on balance of probabilities (that an event or version of facts is more likely to be true than not). An element of dishonesty is required, mere negligence is not enough. The party misled may sue for rescission and or damages. As regards action for damages, the claimant sues not on the contract but on the tort of deceit.

Note – Remedies include rescission, and/or damages.

Case Law – **Fraudulent Misrepresentation. Bannerman v. White (1861)**

The defendant wanted to buy hops from the plaintiff and asked the plaintiff if sulphur had been used in making the hops, adding that if sulphur had been used, he would not even ask for the price, meaning, he would not even enter into a contract. The plaintiff knowing very well sulphur had been used, said that no sulphur was used.

Held – Since the plaintiff assured the defendant that sulphur had not been used, it was a term of the contract and the defendant was right in raising the matter as successful defence to an action for the price.

9.2.4 Material Misrepresentation

In Contract –A false statement that is likely to induce a reasonable person to assent and that the maker knows is likely to induce the recipient to assent.

In Tort –A false statement to which a reasonable person would attach importance in deciding how to act in the transaction in question, or to which the maker knows or has reason to know that the recipient attaches some importance.

The question of whether an untrue representation or a concealment makes voidable a contract to the subject matter of which it relates, or whether an erasure or alteration avoids a written instrument, depends in general upon whether misrepresentation, concealment, erasure or alteration is material depends partly on the facts of the case and partly on the nature of the transaction. Thus, altering the date of a cheque is a material alteration. So during negotiation of a marine insurance, a statement is made which has no real bearing on the risk, but nevertheless, influences the mind of the underwriter, as for instance, an assertion that previous insurances have been obtained on the same ship at a low premium, the misrepresentation will entitle the insurer to avoid the policy.

In deciding whether a person has relied on a misrepresentation, one examines the actual state of the representee's mind with regard to the false statement at the time he enters into the contract. Materiality, on the other hand, rests on the importance of untrue statement to the reasonable man of business when he is deciding whether or not to enter into a contract.

Nevertheless, the requirement of materiality has more recently been called into question in the case of Museprime Properties Ltd. v. Adhill Properties Ltd. (1990) where there was a sale by auction of three properties. During the auction certain representations were made to the effect that a rent review was outstanding and that it was still possible for the purchaser to negotiate higher rents. In fact, new rents had already been fixed for the next review period.

The plaintiffs sued to have the contract rescinded on the grounds of misrepresentation. The defendants argued (inter alia), that they could not do so because the misrepresentation was not material since no reasonable bidder would have allowed such a misrepresentation to affect his bid. The court held that the materiality was not determined objectively on the basis of whether a reasonable person would have been induced to enter into the contract. It was sufficient if the purchaser could show that he was actually affected by the representation.

It is considered that the test of reasonableness in relation to materiality was only important in relation to the representee proving to the court that he had in fact been induced by the misrepresentation. In other words, the more unreasonable the misrepresentation, the more difficult it will be for him to prove that, he was actually induced by the statement. Thus, if the representor had made the statement in good faith and the representation would not have influenced a reasonable person, then the representee may find it exceeding difficult to prove that the statement was in fact material to him.

9.3 PERSUADING A PARTY TO MAKE AN AGREEMENT

9.3.1 What is a Brochure

A brochure is a pamphlet, which gives detailed information of an establishment or a hotel. Brochure information includes: Room-rate, Special rates for offseason, children and others. Location – setting, accessibility of road, ship and air; amenities – golf, beach, swimming pool in or near the hotel and, whether free or charged and entertainment – In the hotel or nearby.

The brochure must be given to an expert designer to do. It is necessary for the proprietor to ensure that his brochure carries the right messages. A good design and style can help sell your operation. Also a successful press advertising itself will lead to demand for brochures from the hotel. Examine your brochure well to ensure there is no misrepresentation. Let a good picture or illustration, 'speak for you'. Pictures should attract attention but make sure the picture is an accurate depiction of what is in your establishment.

9.3.2 'MENU' as an 'Advertising Media'

A menu is a list of dishes available in a restaurant. It is in fact an advertising media for the restaurant. It is very necessary that all information on the menu is correct. The date, times of opening and closing, etc. The list of items to be served, written on the menu board or in the menu card must be available. If a particular dish runs out, it should immediately be erased or customers must be informed of a non-availability of a particular dish on the menu and a good reason and apology given. Otherwise it could be misrepresentation if a client requests for the dish and is not available.

9.3.3 The Importance of Giving the Right Information When Advertising

The purpose of advertising, whether in a newspaper, magazine or even on the television is to inform the public of a product with the view to persuading them to buy it. The same is true of advertising accommodation and issuing hotel brochures. The aim is to inform prospective guests of the facilities available and to "sell" the hotel.

Any statement which is made orally or in writing or through the medium of a picture, and which persuades a person to enter into a contract is known as a representation. A hotel brochure informing persons of the facilities available at the hotel or a statement in an advertisement that the hotel is situated on the sea-front, or a television picture showing the lounge of a hotel are all examples of representations. Should any such statement be untrue, then it is termed in law as a misrepresentation and is either an innocent misrepresentation, or a negligent one, depending upon the intent behind it.

The misrepresentation must be a statement of fact, e.g. the hotel overlooks the sea, when in fact, it is hemmed in on all sides by other buildings, or, that every room has its own en-suite when in fact two bedrooms use one toilet and the toilet is outside their rooms. However, it is not necessary to disclose everything. Silence is permissible so long as it does not amount to half-truth. So, if the hotel is in a quiet area, which is not within easy reach to town, the proprietor need not mention such as fact unless he is asked specifically by the guest. Statements of opinion are not misrepresentation, e.g. 'This hotel is the best in town'.

The misrepresentation must have caused the other party to enter into the contract and to have suffered damage as a result.

9.4 REMEDIES FOR MISREPRESENTATION

The remedy of rescission is available to a party misled by innocent, negligent or fraudulent misrepresentation. It puts parties back to the position they were before the contract was made. However, the remedy may be lost by affirmation. If the injured party affirms the contract, he cannot rescind. He will affirm if with full knowledge of the misinterpretation, he expressly accepts the contract by stating he intends to go on with it.

1. *By lapse of time:* This is a form of implied affirmation and applies as follows. In innocent and negligent misrepresentation, the position is governed by equity. The passage of a reasonable time, even without knowledge of the misrepresentation may prevent the court from granting rescission.

2. *In fraudulent misrepresentation:* the position is governed by s.32 of the Limitation Act 1980. Lapse of time has no effect on rescission where fraud is alleged as long as the action is brought within six years of the time when the fraud was, or with reasonable diligence could have been discovered

3. *Where the status quo cannot be restored.* Rescission is impossible if the parties cannot be restored to their original positions as where goods sold under a contract of sale have been consumed.

It is possible for damages to be given as an alternative remedy to withdraw in cases of misrepresentation, if the court feels that it would be a fairer solution. He may claim damages for fraudulent misrepresentation.

He may also claim damages for careless misrepresentation, but the hotelier who draws up the brochure containing the misrepresentation, might successfully plead that he reasonably believed the statements to be true. Damages would include reasonable expenses incurred in finding suitable alternative accommodation and the difference between the costs of the two places. Any statement in a brochure or similar documents purporting to exclude the hotelier or travel agent from liability for misrepresentation within that document is only to be effective if it is considered to be fair and reasonable in the circumstances. The remedies available to any person injured as a result of misrepresentation are civil remedies; however, it can be expensive as well as worrying to persons who are not used to pursuing legal claims. Of far more benefit to the injured person in such cases is the Trades Description Act, which makes false descriptions a criminal offence. It is enforced by the consumer protection officers or inspectors of weights and measures at no personal expense to the aggrieved party. If the prosecution is successful, not only may the accused person be fined but he may also have to pay the aggrieved party a sum of money as compensation.

By the Trade Descriptions Act 1968: It is a criminal offence to make a false description in a reckless manner, knowing it to be false about the nature of any service, accommodation or facility provided in the course of trade or business. This section is very wide, including services set out in the hotel or holiday brochure, travel agent's brochures, advertisements in newspapers, magazines or on television. It is not an offence under the Act to make a reckless promise that certain facilities will be provided in the future, or that work will be done within a period of time.

A person can be acting recklessly, even though he is not acting dishonestly. In fact, a heavy responsibility is placed upon the advertiser to see that the statement is true.

DEFENCES

A person may be found guilty of an offence under the Act without proving that he acted dishonestly. The only proof required is that the statement was false or misleading. However, the accused may defend himself proving the following:

- That he did not apply false description and that he did not know and could not with reasonable diligence have found out either that the description was false or that it has been applied to the goods
- That the offence was due to a mistake or to reliance on information supplied by someone else, or to some other cause beyond the control of the person accused, provided he shows that he took all reasonable precaution and exercised all due diligence to avoid commission of the offence.

A person found guilty of an offence under the Act shall be liable to a fine or an imprisonment for a term not exceeding two years or both. However, a hotel which advertises itself with a star rating but fails to maintain that standard, might well be liable to a guest on the grounds of misrepresentation, e.g. a guest, on learning that a hotel has a star rating perhaps by seeing a sign or headed notepaper, may book a room there. On arrival, he finds that there is no running water in the bedroom and no lounge facilities. It is submitted that he would be entitled to claim that the booking had been entered into on the grounds of misrepresentation, and would be entitled to withdraw from the contract or claim damages.

A hotel must maintain its standard. Falling short of the required standard, it can be liable on the grounds of misrepresentation. For example, lack of facilities, décor, efficiency of staff, cleanliness, etc., can be an offence.

9.5 FURTHER ASPECTS OF REPRESENTATION

As stated above, a representation is an inducement only and its effect is to lead the other party merely to make the contract. It is extremely important to distinguish between statements that are statements of fact and those which are merely statements of law, opinion or intention. A representation must be a statement, of some specific existing and verifiable fact or past event, and in consequence the following are excluded.

9.5.1 Statement of Law

Everyone has the right to know the law which is accessible to both parties and on which they should seek the advice of their legal advisor and not rely on the statements of the other party.

9.5.2 Statement as to Future Conduct or Intention

These are not actionable (giving cause for legal action). If a person who makes the statement has no intention of carrying it out, it may be regarded as a representation of fact, i.e. a misrepresentation of what is really in the mind of the maker of the statement. Often a promise to do something in the future may not only amount to consideration in a contract but also comprise a term of the contract. Failure to carry out the promise in such circumstances will amount to a breach of contract. A mere representation as to future conduct is not actionable either as a breach of contract or as a misrepresentation since such statements do not amount to statements of fact. A statement of intention that induces a person to enter into a contract is, however, actionable as a misrepresentation of fact where it can be shown that the maker knew that his promise would not be carried out.

9.5.3 Statement of Opinion

These are not normally actionable unless it can be shown that the person making the statement held no such opinion whereupon the statement may be considered in law to be a misstatement of an existing fact as to what was in the mind of the maker of the statement at the time.

The rule that a statement of opinion cannot form the basis of an action in misrepresentation may nevertheless be overturned if it can be shown that a reasonable man in possession of the knowledge as the representor could not have honestly held such an opinion. In such a circumstance the statement will be regarded as one of fact rather than one of opinion.

CHESHIRE, FIFOOT AND FURMSTON [2001] define a statement of opinion as a statement of a belief based on grounds incapable of actual proof. The point is easily illustrated by the case of Bisset v. Wilkinson (1927) AC 177.

The vendor of a land in New Zealand, when asked about the number of sheep the land could sustain, declared that, in his judgement it would hold 2,000 sheep. He had no personal knowledge of the facts because the land had never been used for sheep farming. The buyer knew this was so, he understood that the seller could only be stating his opinion

Decision Held – The vendor of the land was not liable for stating that the land would hold 2,000 sheep. In fact the farm had never held sheep and thus it was held that the statement could amount to nothing more than an honest statement of opinion and not a statement of fact. The action for misrepresentation thus failed.

9.5.4 Sales Talk, Advertising

Some statements in this area amount to representations. The law permits businesses i.e. seller of goods or services to make some statements about their businesses in the course of dealing without necessarily being bound by everything he says. For example, statements of opinion such as "This is the most comfortable hotel in the country" there is no misrepresentation. A statement such as "This chicken dish is the chef's choice of the day" and in fact, it happened to be a duck dish, may well amount to a misrepresentation.

A statement will amount to a misrepresentation if the statement is not true.

9.6 A MERE INDUCEMENT OR TERMS OF THE CONTRACT

In order to decide upon the terms of the contract it is necessary to find out what was said or written by the parties. Furthermore, having ascertained what the parties said or wrote, it is necessary to decide whether the statements were mere inducement, (representations) or terms of the contract.

Before the Misrepresentation Act 1967 became law, there was often no remedy for a misrepresentation which was not fraudulent, and in such a case, the plaintiff's only hope of obtaining a remedy was to convince the court that the defendant's statement was not a mere inducement but a term of the contract of which the defendant was in breach and for which damages might be obtained:

Under the Misrepresentation Act 1967 the new form of negligent misrepresentation which did not exist before will now give rise in many cases to an action for damages even in respect of mere misrepresentation or inducement.

- An inducement can be defined as persuasion by promise or threat to a cause of action. Inducement or procuration leading to a breach of contract involves persuading employee procurement is practically impossible in a court of justice. In Lumley v. Gye (1853) 2 E and B 216
- A term can be defined as a condition, provision or limitation. A substantive part of a contract, creating a contractual obligation for whose breach action lies.

When a decision has been taken as to what a particular statement is a term of the contract and not a mere inducement, the court then consider the importance of that statement in the context of the contract as a whole. The following are the major guidelines that are applied:

9.6.1 The Statement and Intentions of the Parties

The court will always be interested in implementing the intentions of the parties as they appear from statements made. However, the court will not follow the parties statements. Where the parties appear to have regarded a little matter as a valid term of agreement, the court may still take the view that it is not.

Where a written contract is concerned, the court may disregard a statement by the parties that a particular agreement is a condition and says it is a warranty.

Where oral contracts are concerned, the court may ignore the statements of the parties and decide that a particular undertaking is a condition, a warranty, or a mere inducement.

9.6.2 The Nature of the Statement

A statement is likely to be an inducement rather than a term if the person making the statement asks the other party to check or verify it, e.g. 'The house appears good, but I should get a surveyor's report on it'.

Also, a statement is likely to be a term, instead of a mere inducement if it is made with the intention of preventing the other party from looking for defects and succeeds in doing this, e.g. 'The house is in good condition, you need not check it over again'.

9.6.3 The Importance of the Statement

A statement is considered to be a term of the contract and not a mere inducement, if the statement is such that the plaintiff would not have made the contract without it.

The effect on timing of a statement

A statement made during the first phase of negotiations tends to be an inducement. If the interval between the making of the statement and the making of the contract is clear and definite then, the statement is almost certain to be an inducement. However, the interval is not always so well marked and in such cases there is a difficulty in deciding whether the statement is an inducement or term.

9.6.4 Modification of Oral Statement

If the statement was oral and the contract was later put in to writing, then the terms of the contract tend to be contained in the written document and all oral statements tend to be pre-contractual inducements. Even so the court may still consider the apparent intentions of the parties and decide that they had made a contract which was part oral and part written.

9.6.5 Conditions and Warranties

The law has applied special terminology to contractual terms in order to distinguish the vital or fundamental obligations from the less vital. The expression condition being applied to the vital and the expression warranty to the less vital. A condition is a fundamental obligation, which goes to the root of the contract.

The distinction is important in terms of remedies. A breach of condition is called a repudiatory breach and the injured party may decide either to repudiate the contract or claim damages and go on with the contract. A warranty on the other hand, is a subsidiary obligation, which is not so vital that a failure to perform it goes to the root of the contract.

Whether a term is a condition or warranty is basically a matter for the court which will be decided on the basis of the commercial importance of the term. It should be noted that, the word warranty is sometimes used in a different way e.g. by a manufacturer of goods who gives a warranty against faulty workmanship offering to replace parts free. The term warranty is used by the manufacturer as equivalent to a guarantee.

9.7 ESSENTIAL POINTS OF A STATEMENT

Silence or non-disclosure has no effect except in the following:

9.7.1 Failure to Disclose a Change in Circumstances

Here, a statement was true when made but becomes false before the contract was made. There is a duty on the party making the statement to disclose the change, and if he does not do so, his silence can amount to an actionable misrepresentation.

9.7.2 Where the Contract is of Utmost Good Faith

Where the contract is uberrimae fidei – (of utmost good faith), it applies to a contract in which the promise must inform the promissor of all those facts and surrounding circumstances which could influence the promissor in deciding whether or not to enter the contract, such as a contract of insurance. Silence does not normally amount to misrepresentation. However, an important exception to the rule, the law requires him to show utmost good faith. He must make full disclosure of all the material facts known to him otherwise the contract may be rescinded. e.g. Insurance Companies and their clients.

At Commercial Law

Contracts of insurance provide the only true example of a contract uberrimae fidei (utmost good faith). There is a duty of the person taking up the insurance to disclose to the insurance company all facts of which he is aware which might affect the premium or acceptance of the risk. Failure to do so renders the contract voidable at the option of the insurance company. This could happen, for example, where a person seeking insurance did not disclose that he had been refused insurance by another company. Where there is a failure to disclose, the insurance company is not required by law to meet the claim but must return the premiums. In other words the contract is rescinded. . **Case Law** –Ullmann SA v. Skandia (UK) Insurance Co. (1989) 3 W.L.R. 25 In addition, most proposals for insurance require the proposer to sign a declaration in which he warrants that the statements he has made are true and agrees that they be incorporated into the contract as terms. Where this is so, any false statement which the proposer makes will be grounds for avoidance of the contract by the insurance company, even though the statement was not material in terms of the premium.

9.7.3 Where the Statute Requires Disclosure

A party to whom a document has been disclosed has a right to inspect it except where it is no longer under the control of the party who disclosed it, or the party disclosing it has a right or a duty to withhold inspection, or where a party considers that it would be proportionate to the issues in the case to permit inspection of documents.

Under the Financial Services Act 1986, a number of specified particulars must be disclosed in an advertisement and a prospectus issued by a company to invite the public to subscribe for shares or debentures. The particulars must give all such information as investors and their professional advisers would reasonably require, and also expect to find in the prospectus and advertisement for the purpose of making a proper examination as to whether an investor should purchase the securities. These provisions, and those in earlier statutes which preceded them, had to be put into law by Parliament because the judiciary had always refused to regard the sale of securities by a company as a contract is uberrimae fidei (utmost good faith). They did not, therefore, require the advertisement or prospectus under which the shares were issued necessarily to disclose all the true material facts.

9.7.4 Concealed Fraud

Silence can amount to misrepresentation in the case of concealed fraud.

- Concealment can be defined as suppression of or neglect to communicate a material fact. If fraudulent, it may provide grounds for rescission of contract.
- Concealment of a valuable security dishonestly and with a view to gain or with intent to cause loss to another, is an offence.
- The deliberate destruction of another's title deeds is an example. In such a case, time does not run until the plaintiff has discovered, or could with reasonable diligence have discovered the fraud.

Case Law – **Gordon v. Selico Co. Ltd**. *The Times*, **26 February 1986**

A flat in a block of flats which was converted by a developer was taken by the plaintiff on a 99-year lease. Soon after moving in, he discovered dry rot.

Held – The Court of Appeal, decided that deliberate concealment of the rot by the developer could amount to fraudulent misrepresentation where upon damages were awarded to the plaintiff. Silence can, therefore, amount to misrepresentation in the case of concealed fraud.

9.7.5 Confidentiality or Fiduciary Relationship Between Parties

Confidential communication which is privileged as being protected from disclosure in evidence given in proceedings, e.g, a communication between a party and a solicitor made during those proceedings.

Even though, this branch of law is close to undue influence, there is a difference in the sense that, in undue influence, the person with special influence, such as a solicitor over his client, is often the prime mover in seeking the contract. Constructive fraud, however, could apply where the client was the prime mover in seeking a contract with his solicitor. If the solicitor remains silent as regards facts within his knowledge material, say, to the contract price, then the client could rescind the contract for constructive fraud.

Fiduciary relationship involves trust or confidence e.g. as describing the relationship between a trustee and beneficiary. 'The distinguishing obligation of a fiduciary is the obligation of loyalty.'

In contracts between members of a family, partners, principal and agent, solicitor and client, guardian and ward, and trustee and beneficiary, the relationship of the parties requires that more disclosure should be added. The duties of disclosure arising from the above judiciary relations recognized by equity are not situations of uberrimae fidei. It is the nature of the contract, i.e. insurance, which requires disclosure regardless of the relationship of parties and not the particular contract which gives rise to the need to disclose.

Chapter Ten

EMPLOYMENT OF STAFF

10.1 EMPLOYMENT LAW

This chapter deals with employment law and the relationship between the employer and employee. An employer is the person or company who engages another (the employee) to work under his direction and control in return for a wage or salary.

The relationship between the parties to a contract of employment was formerly known as master and servant. The relationship is governed by express and implied terms of the contract and by statutory rules that the contract cannot exclude. These relate, for example to unfair dismissal, redundancy, maternity rights, trade union membership and activity, and the health and safety at work.

On the principle of vicarious liability, a third party may hold an employer responsible for certain wrongs committed by his employee in the course of his employment. It is important to know how this relationship comes into being and to distinguish it from the relationship between a person who buys the services of someone who is self-employed (often called an independent contractor).

Employment law is made up of Common Law and of statute law passed by Parliament. An employer is liable to pay damages to those injured by his employee if those injuries took place during the course of the employee's work. An employer was not vicariously liable for injury caused to others by a self-employed or independent contractor who was doing work for him. In the contract of employment, the ordinary principles of the law of contract apply.

There must be an offer and an acceptance, which is in effect, the agreement. There must also be an intention to create legal relations, consideration and capacity, together with proper consent by the parties. There must be no mistake, misrepresentation, duress or undue influence. Most importantly, the contract must not be illegal.

Since we have already looked at these general principles of the law of contract, it is only necessary to highlight certain matters which are of importance in the context of employment law.

10.2 CONTRACT OF SERVICE (CONTRACT OF EMPLOYMENT)

The agreement which results in the relationship of the employer and employee is a contract which is known as the 'contract of service.' It is a contract by which a person agrees to undertake certain duties under the direction and control of the employer in return for a specified wage or salary. The contract need not be in writing, but under the Employment Rights Act 1996, the employee must be given a written statement of terms of employment. Implied in every contract of employment are a duty of mutual confidence and trust, the employer's duty to protect the employee from danger and risks to his health, and the employees duty to do the work to the best of his ability. Employees who have been continuously employed in the same business for certain minimum periods have statutory rights, relating for example to unfair dismissal and redundancy that do not apply to the self-employed. A self-employed person is engaged under a contract for services and owes his employer or customer no other duty than to complete the work in accordance with the terms of the individual contract; he is not otherwise under the direction or control of the employer as to how or when he works.

Termination of a contract of employment in breach of the terms of contract is wrongful dismissal and may be remedied in the County Court or the High Court. In such action the court is not concerned with fairness but purely with compensating for breach of the contract.

Several important consequences follow from the recognition of the employeremployee relationship:

- An employer in certain circumstances is vicariously liable to the third party for the wrongful acts of his employee, performed during the course of his employer's business.
- An employer has a duty to provide a safe "system of work" for his employees, involving a higher duty of care than that which he owes to other persons.
- An employer is required to pay national insurance contribution in respect of an employee and to deduct his income tax through the Pay As You Earn [PAYE] Scheme.
- The conditions of the Redundancy Payment.
- The provisions of a Contract of Employment.

Certain particulars can be given by reference to a document e.g. a collective agreement with a trade union, but any such document must be readily accessible to the employee. Other particulars are pension arrangements, sickness, provisions, entitlement and details of disciplinary matters and grievance procedures.

Disciplinary procedures: This deals with the number of warnings – oral or written which will be given before suspension or dismissal. Normally, there shall be two verbal warnings when the employee misbehaves or does not abide by the contract. If the employee's conduct is still not satisfactory, then a written warning will be given. What follows next is dismissal. Going through the necessary procedure gives the employer grounds to dismiss an employee.

Grievance Procedures: This relates to complaints in regard to any aspect of the employment with which the employee is not satisfied. All employers must inform their employees regarding disciplinary and grievance procedures. Changes must be given to the employee in writing as soon as possible and in any case not later than one month. In other cases, the terms the employment cannot be changed unless the employee has agreed, and if the employer introduces a variation in the contract, e.g. by lowering pay, then the employer is in breach of the contract. An employee can sue successfully for damages from his employer where he has suffered a cut pay to which neither he nor his union has agreed.

Section 11 of the 1996 Act provides that if an employer fails to give written particulars in the time scale required, or fails to notify changes in the terms of the contract, the employee can go to an employment tribunal. If a statement is given, but the employee thinks it is not complete, it is up to the tribunal to see which of them is right. The statement as approved by the tribunal is then assumed in law to have been given by the employer to the employee and forms the basis of the contract of employment. Failure to give written particulars does not make the contract of employment unenforceable by the parties. Written particulars are a right of the employee, not a mere entitlement. Therefore, they must be given whether the employee asks for them or not.

Under the Employment Act 2002, monetary compensation can be awarded e.g. for unfair dismissal, and where the written particulars are incomplete, inaccurate or non-existent.

Health and Safety – The Health and Safety at Work Act. 1974, states that an employer must prepare a statement of policy in regard to the health and safety at work of employees. This must be contained in a separate document but it is often given out with the written particulars. The employee should be required to sign the employer's copy. That is the written particulars of the terms of employment.

10.2.1 Terms of the Contract of Employment

It has already been stated that the contract of service, in general, follows the same rules as those which apply to other forms of contract. For example there must be consideration, thus the employer pays remuneration to the employee in return for agreed services. However, the contract will only come into existence when there has been an offer and acceptance. The purpose of the agreement is legal and conforms to public policy.

Initially, a contract of service can be made in any form, that is, it can be an oral or written agreement. It is usual in the employment of permanent staff that the contract is in writing. The employer presents the intending employee with a form containing as far as possible, all the conditions and benefits attached to the employment. His agreement and signature with that of the employer or his representative will complete the contract. All permanent employees must have a written confirmation of their contract of employment from their employers.

10.2.2 Contract of Employment Act 1996

This section provides that an employer must give 'written particulars' of the terms of the employment to the employee within thirteen weeks of the employee commencing work. The particulars must include the following:

- The names or identities of the parties.
- The date when employment begins.
- The scale or rate of pay or the method of calculating it.
- The hours of work.
- Any terms or condition respecting.
  - Holiday entitlement
  - Sickness or injury arrangement must be set out
  - Whether or not there is a pension
  - Length of notice required to terminate the employment
  - Work location or locations
  - Job title or description, which is important in dealing with redundancy cases to justify that a dismissal is because of redundancy and is not an unfair dismissal. The employer may show that there has been a reduction in 'work of a particular type'. The job title indicates what type of work the employee does. Under the ERA 1996 Amendments, the employer can give a brief job description instead of job title.

If there is any change in the conditions outlined above, the employer must inform the employee in writing of that change within a month of the change taking effect. It is not necessary for the employer to give a detailed account of the particulars. It is sufficient, if in the written notice, he draws the employee's attention to the existence of the document which contains the necessary information.

The provision of the Contract of Employment Act does not apply to the following employees:

- Those who normally work less than 21 hours weekly
- Those who are employed for less than 13 weeks
- Those who are related to the employer e.g. father, mother, wife, son or daughter.

Employment in the hotel and catering trade is greatly affected by one of the above exceptions. The owners in this trade usually start business with their relatives because they are often smaller units.

Certain particulars can be given by reference to documents. e.g. a collective agreement with a Trade Union. However, any such document must readily be accessible to the employee. The particulars, pension arrangements, sickness provision, entitlement and details of disciplinary matters and grievance procedures, and a sample of written particulars of terms of employment.

10.2.3 A Sample Statement of Written Particulars of Terms of Employment

To Miss Lillian James
26 Adare Walk,
Ashford Kent

The following particulars are given to you, pursuant to the Employment Act 1966 (as amended):

1. The parties are as follows –
   Name and address of Employer –Rhema-Christa Company Ltd.,
   5 Ashford High Road,
   Ashford, Kent
   UK
   Name and address of Employee – Lillian James
   26 Adare Walk,

Ashford, Kent,

UK

The date when your employment commenced was 9th December 2005 with Rhema Christa Company Ltd.

The following are the particulars of the terms of your employment as at 9th December2005:

You are employed at Rhema – Christa Company Ltd., 5 Ashford High Road, Ashford, Kent, as a Public Relations Officer.

Your rate of remuneration is five hundred pounds per week. Your remuneration is paid at weekly intervals in arrears.

Your normal working hours are from 8.30 a.m. to 5 p.m., Monday to Friday.

You are entitled to 20 days paid holidays per year, plus authorized bank holidays. The holiday year runs from 1st January to 31st December. All holiday entitlements shall be taken at our discretion, but we will not unreasonably refuse your requests for a holiday.

Regulations as to payment while absent during sickness or injury are available for inspection during normal working hours in the office of the Personnel Manager.

There is no private pension scheme applicable to you. The length of notice which you are obliged to give to end your contract of employment is one week and the length of notice you are entitled to receive unless your conduct is such that you may be summarily dismissed is as follows:

- One week if your period of continuous employment is less than two years.
- One week for each year of continuous employment if your period of continuous employment is two or more but less than 12 years.
- Twelve weeks if your period of continuous employment is twelve years or more.

There is no requirement for work outside the country.

There are no collective agreements which affect the terms and conditions of the employment. ***Disciplinary Procedures***

The employer must set out in writing the alleged conduct or characteristics or other circumstances which led him to contemplate dismissing or taking disciplinary action against the employee.

The employer must send the statement or copy of it to the employee and invite the employee to attend a meeting to discuss the matter.

Meeting

The meeting will take place before the disciplinary action is taken. The disciplinary action can be in the form of suspension or dismissal. The meeting must not take place unless:

1) The employer has informed the employee what the basis is for disciplinary action
2) The employee has had a reasonable opportunity to consider his response to that information
3) The employee must take all steps to attend the meeting
4) After meeting, the employer must inform the employee of his decision and notification of the right to appeal against the decision if he is not satisfied with it.

Appeal

- If the employee does not wish to appeal, he must inform the employer.
- If the employee informs the employer of his wish to appeal, the employer must invite him to attend a further meeting.
- The employee must take all reasonable steps to attend the meeting.
- After the appeal meeting, the employer must inform the employee of his final decision.

It should be noted that, certain of the former exceptions, e.g. that there was no need for particulars here if the employee was the husband or wife of the employer have been repealed.

It is not necessary to give an employee written particulars if he/or she is employed for a specific job, e.g. to clear a backlog of office work, which is not expected to last more than one month. If it does last for more than one month, the worker is entitled to written particulars.

10.3 DUTIES ARISING FROM THE CONTRACT

A contract of service added to written particulars required by the contracts of Employment Act should make provision for all the agreed rights and obligations that pass between an employer and an employee. So far as the hotel and catering industry is concerned, the relevant duties can be summarized as follows:

10.3.1 Duties Owed to the Employer by the Employee

- *To give personal service:*
  The contract cannot be assigned to a third party without the consent of the party who would be affected by the assignment. Therefore, theoretically, the employee should give personal service. This duty obviously applies to the services of a highly qualified chef.

- *To obey lawful orders:*
  The employee must obey lawful orders and reasonable instructions of his employer. However, an employee is not bound to carry out illegal acts. An employee can refuse to drive a vehicle that was not insured so as to satisfy the law set out in road traffic legislation. If the employee does refuse, he is not in breach of his contract.

- *To be loyal to his employer (or the duty of fidelity):*
  Certain activities of employees are regarded by the law as a breach of his duty to give faithful service. An employee who while employed, copies the names and addresses of his employer's customers for use after leaving the employment can be prevented from using the information. A former employee can however, be prevented by the court from using his former employer's trade secrets or confidential information. Therefore, a chef whose reputation is an attraction offered by a hotel or restaurant, would be in breach of his duty of loyalty if, he worked in his off duty time

for a competing establishment. The employee could also be in breach of his duty of loyalty over recipes which had been used by him in his part-time employment and which are recognized as a proprietary right by his true employer and consequently attracts customers away from his true employer's hotel/restaurant. Loyalty also involves giving the best personal service of which the employee is capable. He must therefore be diligent and not idle, and must work the agreed number of hours, not being guilty of persistent lateness or leaving his employment without permission before the end of his agreed period of work. It must be appreciated that, the delinquent employee could be sued as an individual, and beside his liability to contribute, for not giving careful service.

- *To use reasonable skills and care in the work:*
  An employee who claims to have a particular skill or skills, but shows himself to be incompetent may be dismissed without notice. His employer can also raise the matter of the incompetence of the employee if he is sued under statute law, i.e. The ERA (Employment Rights Act), for unfair dismissal. The Common Law also requires unskilled employees to take reasonable care in carrying out their jobs. However, they may be dismissed only if there is a serious breach of this implied term of the contract.

- *To account to his employer for any secret profit to himself or loss caused to his employer by his negligence:*
  The duty of loyalty to an employer implies that, the employee will not make any profits out of his employment without the permission of his employer; nor will he take other employment which will conflict with his employer's interest. In the hotel and catering trade, it is recognized by tradition that, staff can accept tips for service rendered to customers. So this in no way infringes the duty of loyalty. But if a bar attendant, for example, consistently makes a profit for herself by manipulation of the drinks which she serves, the duty of loyalty is breached, and besides the criminal liability which

she has incurred, she can be called upon to account to her employer for the profits she has made. In the industry with which we are concerned, a conflict of this nature would only involve staff who provides special expertise or who carry special responsibility.

- *Duty not to disclose confidential information:*
  It is an implied term of a contract of service that the employee must not disclose trade secrets or confidential information during employment. However, the use by an employee of knowledge of trade secrets and information cannot be prevented if it is used as part of the total job experience, if he could not help but learn from doing the job. While it is normal for employers to bring claims against employees to prevent them from using confidential information obtained in the employment, confidentiality works both ways.

Case Law – In Dagleish v. Lothian Council and Borders Police Board (1991), the Board was asked by Lothian Council for details of the names and addresses of the employees so that the council could identify poll tax defaulters. The court granted the employee an injunction to prevent this. The information was confidential between employer and employee. This case goes to confirm the employee's right of privacy and the employer's duty not to infringe it by wrongful disclosure.

10.3.2 Duties Owed to the Employee by the Employer

To Provide a Safe System For Working:
The employer has an implied duty to exercise reasonable care to ensure that the employee is provided with a safe system for working.

Provision of Work:
An employer is under no duty to provide his employee with work. Provided he pays him the agreed wage, he can retain him on his staff. There are, however, exceptions to this general rule. If the employee is dependent upon doing work to earn his remuneration, e.g. he relies upon commission for having accomplished a result; he must be given a reasonable opportunity to earn that commission.

Itemised pay statement:

Under the ERA, an itemised pay statements must be provided for all employees, including part-timers. Before these provisions (now in the ERA) came into force, an employer could simply state the amount of take-home pay with no details of how it had been arrived at. Under the ERA, the employee must receive a statement at the time of or before receiving pay, showing gross pay and take-home pay and the variable reductions, for example, Income Tax and National Insurance Contributions.

Time Off:

Pregnant employees are entitled to be paid time off for ante-natal care. The employee must notify the employer in or before the fifteenth week of pregnancy.

Maternity Leave (The right to return): Regulations allow for the right to return to the same job, following a period of maternity leave and protection from detriment and unfair dismissal in connection with maternity leave.

Time off for dependants:

A worker can take time off to arrange for care or take care of a dependant, where the dependant is ill, injured, assaulted, gives birth or dies. Dependants are a spouse, child, parent or guardian. The worker is allowed a reasonable time off and it is paid. Workers who take time off in the above situations are protected against dismissal, detriment and victimization.

Temporary Workers:

Responsibility for and to temporary workers depends on whether they have a contract of employment or have worked sufficiently long for you to be considered by their employer. If engaged through an agency, you are responsible for them only if there is a personal obligation to do the work or the agency is a placement bureau.

Supplying a Reference:

Unless there is a specific provision in the contract of service relating to an employer's duty to supply references or testimonial in respect of his employee, the employer is at Common Law not obliged to do so. If he does decide to make any oral or written comment upon an employee's efficiency and character which is false, he must be careful that he does not make any statement which might lead to an action for defamation. Defamation is a tort, and is defined as a statement which tends to bring the person to whom it relates into contempt, hatred or ridicule, in the opinion of the reasonable thinking members of the public.

Defamation can be either *Libel*, that is, a permanent record of the reference, e.g. in writing, on tape, picture or film, or *Slander*, which form of reference is of a transitory nature, e.g. an oral statement made directly or made by a telephone message.

In each case, the aggrieved employee must show that the statement had the effect that makes it defamatory; the statement was intended to refer to him and the statement was published to a third party. This would obviously include an intended second employer or anyone representing him.

It is obvious then, that, extreme care should be taken when a reference is supplied. Fortunately, the law provides defences that the employer, who has acted wrongly, can use to combat an action for defamation. He can prove that the statement, although based upon opinion only, was made honestly and without malice to be received by a person who has a justifiable interest in its contents. The defence is called 'qualified privilege' and would cover a statement detrimental to the employee based upon suspicion and not on fact.

10.3.3 Duties Owed to a Third Party by the Employer (Vicarious Liability)

This is the liability which arises because of one person's relationship with another. Thus, in tort, a master is generally liable for the acts which his servant performed in the course of his employment. *Case Law* – Harrison v. Michen tyre Co. (1985)

In criminal law, a master may sometimes be held liable for a servant's offences, e.g. Trade Descriptions Act 1968. *Case Law*– Ferguson v. Weaving (1951).

An employer can be liable in tort for the actions of his employee which causes injury to a third party, even though he had no knowledge of those acts and perhaps had actually forbidden their performance. This is known as vicarious liability. The injured person of course, has a right of action against the offending employee and the question is asked, "Why should the employer also bear the responsibility?" Many reasons have been put forward to explain the doctrine of vicarious liability. The most practical explanation, however, is that the employer should be responsible because he has made it possible for the employee to do the injurious act, therefore, he should bear the financial consequence as a part of the costs of running his business. A wise employer should be insured to cover such incidents. What does matter is that, it must be proved the employee performed the 'injurious act' whilst acting in the course of his employment. That is, he was employed to do that act even though he did it in a negligent or even in an unauthorized manner.

10.4 TERMINATION OF CONTRACT OF EMPLOYMENT BY EITHER PARTY

Fig 10.4 –Diagram of Termination of Contract of service by either party.

10.4.1 Termination by Notice

The contract may be terminated by either party giving notice to the other. The length of notice must be stated in the initial contract agreement and the "written particulars" when issued.

The notice is given by an employer to terminate the Contract of employment of a person who has been continuously employed for thirteen weeks or more. The notice required to be given by an employee who has been continuously employed for thirteen weeks or more, to terminate his contract shall not be less than one week. Very often, the agreement will provide that the notice to be given by the employee is the same as that to be given by the employer.

10.4.2 Termination by Agreement

The parties to a contract of employment may end the contract by agreement. Thus, if an employer and employee agree to new terms and conditions on, for example, a promotion of the employee, the old agreement is discharged and a new one takes over.

10.4.3 Termination by Passage of Time

In the case of a fixed-term contract, as where an employee is engaged for example three years, the contract will terminate at the end of the three years, though there may be provisions for notice within that period. If no arrangement has been made as to notice, they can legally be dismissed at the end of the period. If dismissed within the period, they are entitled to their salary; but if the ground for dismissal is misconduct, they cannot recover their salary for the time they have served.

The grounds on which a hired servant may be dismissed are:

- Incompetence,
- habitual negligence,
- wilful disobedience to lawful orders,
- gross misconduct,
- dishonesty,
- drunkenness,
- and permanent disability from illness.

If after you have given notice to the servant or employee and he or she refuses to quit, you may turn him or her out by force. But it is wiser to use experienced security personnel and also call in a constable to see that no breach of the peace occurs. The constable will not assist you in ejecting the employee or servant, but will be there to see that no more force is used than is reasonably necessary.

As mentioned earlier on, an employee who has been caught stealing or in cases of gross misconduct, may be dismissed at once without wages. Unless the misconduct of the servant is very gross and in fact is capable of distinct proof by at least one independent witness, it is safer for you to pay or tender the wages in lieu of notice

The question of whether a dismissal is fair or not is a matter of fact for the particular tribunal hearing the case, and one cannot predict what a particular tribunal will do on hearing the facts of a particular case. The ultimate question for a tribunal is, "Was the dismissal fair and reasonable?" Earlier legislation also removed the burden of proof from the employer in showing reasonableness, so that there is now no 'presumption of guilt' on the employer, and the tribunal is left to decide whether or not the employer acted reasonably.

10.5 TERMINATION FOR BREACH (REASONS JUSTIFYING DISMISSAL)

A total breach of the contract by either the employee or the employer will allow the other party summarily to terminate the employment. The breach must however, be one which completely undermines the original purpose of the contract. The employer may summarily dismiss the employee in the following circumstances:

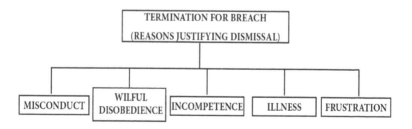

Fig 10.5 – A Diagram of Termination for Breach.

10.5.1 Misconduct

Generally, it is that behaviour that fundamentally impairs the employees recognized performance of work. Whether or not the behaviour would warrant summary dismissal is dependent upon the standard of duty expected of the employee and the degree of responsibility within the employing organization.

10.5.2 Wilful Disobedience

Wilful disobedience can include an unwarranted refusal to obey a lawful order given by an employer or someone in a supervisory capacity or wilfully neglecting to carry out an agreed task, appreciating that this conduct could result in loss or injury. An employee could certainly refuse to carry out an order which is not part of those duties assigned to him, or one which he recognizes could endanger his life or health, unless, of course, the nature of his work is such and he recognized this when he took up the employment.

10.5.3 Incompetence

Incompetence will be a good reason for summary dismissal, only when the employee obtained his employment by claiming competency in the relevant field. So an employee cannot be summarily dismissed if he shows a lack of ability in a field of work he never claimed he was able to do.

10.5.4 Illness

Only when the employer can show that it was essential to employ a replacement to do the work, will the court hold that the termination of the employment was justified.

10.5.5 Frustration

A contract of service must obviously end, when either party, for some reason is incapable of performing his obligations; for example, if the employee is convicted and sentenced to imprisonment, or if he dies. In the case of an employer in the form of a partnership or a corporate body, i.e. a company, if there is dissolution of the former or liquidation of the latter. When a business is sold to another, the contracts of its employees will not be immediately terminated.

The employee has a corresponding right to terminate his contract without notice where the employer has been guilty of misconduct; e.g. improper advances towards a female employee where the employer has caused the employee to become ill, a return to work would be detrimental to his health or when the employer has neglected to carry out his obligation under the contract.

If the employee leaves his employment without giving the required notice and not having good cause as authorized above, theoretically, he can be sued by his employer for breach of contract.

Nevertheless, a delinquent employee would not be able to claim wages or benefits such as accrued holiday remuneration for the part of the agreed wage period which he had completed before he summarily terminated his employment.

10.6 TERMINATION OF CONTRACT OF EMPLOYMENT (DISMISSALS)

An employee cannot claim unfair dismissal unless there has first been a dismissal recognized by law.

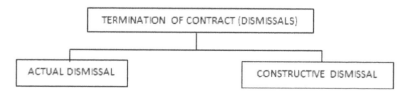

Fig 10.6 – A Diagram on Termination of Contract (Dismissals)

10.6.1 Actual Dismissal

This does not normally give rise to problems since most employees recognize the words of an actual dismissal, whether given orally or in writing.

10.6.2 Constructive Dismissal

This happens when the employee who leaves the job is compelled to do so by the conduct of the employer. The employer's conduct must be a fundamental breach so that it can be regarded as a repudiation of contract. For example, if a male employer were to sexually harass a female employee, then this would be a fundamental breach so that it can be regarded as a repudiation of contract. This would be a fundamental breach entitling the female employee to leave and sue for her loss on the basis of constructive dismissal.

10.7 GROUNDS FOR DISMISSAL

If an employer is going to escape liability for unfair dismissal, he must show that he acted reasonably and indeed, the ERA S.92 requires the employer to give reasons for dismissal to the employee in writing.

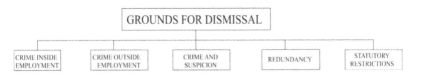

Fig 10.7 – A Diagram on Grounds for Dismissal.

10.7.1 Crime inside Employment

Crime inside employment will normally justify a dismissal on the grounds of misconduct. For example, ETA has decided that an employee was dismissed fairly on the grounds of theft from the employer, even though the employer could not specifically prove loss of stock but had only a reasonable belief in the employee's guilt. No specific stock loss could be proved but the employee had been seen by a security guard loading boxes into his car at night at the employer's warehouse.

Dismissal on the grounds of theft may also be fair even though what was stolen is of little value. An employee was dismissed for misappropriation of cigarettes from a petrol station where he worked. His dismissal was held to be fair even though the cigarettes were from damaged stock due for return to the manufacturer.

If you suspect that an employee is guilty of theft, you should not give your employee into custody or search her boxes. The proper procedure is, if reasonable grounds of suspicion exist, is to apply to a magistrate for a search warrant. If a police station is near, you should mention the facts of suspicion to the police leaving it to the police to take what steps they think fit, and then you will not be liable in trespass or assault.

10.7.2 Crime Outside Employment

It can be difficult for the employer, but the employer will have to show damage to his organization. Example: A teacher has been convicted of shoplifting (stealing from a shop) where it is located near her working environment. If she works for a local authority, it can be a disgrace to the local authority.

The use of drugs or excessive drinking may constitute a fair reason for dismissal where the employer believes on reasonable grounds that the behaviour makes the employee unsuitable for the position held. An employer who wishes to dismiss employees for a drink or drug misconduct should have a drink and drugs policy and make it as part of the employees contract.

10.7.3 Crime and Suspicion

If dismissal is based on suspicion of crime, the suspicion must be reasonable and in all cases, the employee must be told that dismissal is contemplated and in the light of this information, be allowed to give explanations and make representations against dismissal. Where an employee has been charged with theft from the employer and is awaiting trial, the best course of action is to suspend rather than dismiss him, pending the verdict. Employees who are in breach of contract are likely to be regarded as fairly dismissed.

10.7.4 Redundancy

Under the ERA, redundancy is presumed to occur where the services of employees are dispensed with because the employer ceases or intends to cease carrying on business at a place where the employee was employed, or does not require so many employees to do the work of a certain kind. Employees who have been laid off or kept on a short time without pay for four consecutive weeks (or for six weeks in a period of thirteen weeks), are entitled to end their employment and to seek a redundancy payment if there is no reasonable prospect that normal working will be resumed.

10.7.5 Statutory Restriction

Statutory restriction placed on an employer or employee is when, for example, the employer's business was found to be dangerous and was closed down under Act of Parliament or ministerial order, the employee would not be unfairly dismissed.

10.8 REMEDIES FOR UNFAIR DISMISSAL

An employee who has been dismissed unfairly may seek re-instatement, reengagement or claim compensation.

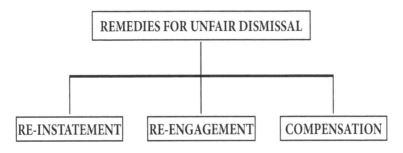

Fig 10.8 – A Diagram on Remedies for Unfair Dismissal

10.8.1 Re-instatement

This means being taken back by the employer on exactly the same terms as before.

10.8.2 Re-engagement

This means being taken back but on different terms.

10.8.3 Compensation

To make up for the loss of something by a guilty party; usually in a form of money. For example when an employer is found guilty of unfair dismissal of an employee, the tribunal orders the employer to compensate the employee by giving the employee money.

As a rule, it is up to the employer to pay the full amount of any award of compensation for unfair dismissal.

There are three types of awards for compensation for unfair dismissal. They are as follows:

- Basic award
- The compensatory award
- The additional award.

It should be borne in mind that an order for compensation can only be made against a party who appears or is represented before a tribunal.

Basic award

A redundant employee held to have been unfairly dismissed and having unreasonably refused an offer of suitable alternative employment will nonetheless receive a basic award of compensation, which is equivalent to two weeks' pay (ERA 1996, s.s 121, 138 and 141).

Compensatory award

The compensatory award for unfair dismissal is such amount as an employment tribunal considers to be "just and equitable having regard to the loss sustained by the complainant" subject to a 2001/02 upper limit of £51,700. However, that upper limit may be exceeded to the extent necessary to enable the award fully to reflect the losses (including arrears of pay) sustained by the employee for the period between the date on which his (or her) employment ended and the date on which he was reinstated or re-engaged.

If an employee has not been reinstated or re-engaged in compliance with a tribunal order to that effect, the upper limit on the amount of the compensatory award may likewise be exceeded to the extent necessary to enable the aggregate of the compensatory and additional awards fully to reflect those same losses.

The compensatory award includes:
The estimated loss of wages (net of tax and other deductions) up to the time the employee secured employment elsewhere; or, if the employee's new job pays less than he (or she) was earning in his previous job, up to the date of the tribunal hearing. As a rule, the employee will not be given credit for income received during the notice period, but any money paid in lieu of notice will be taken into account.

Case Law – (Fentiman v. Fluid Engineering Products Ltd. (1991)

The estimated future loss of earnings, based on the employee's age, personal circumstances, qualifications and skills, state of health, likelihood of obtaining work elsewhere with a 'reasonable' time, and so on.

Case Law – (Fougere v. Phoenix Motor Co. Ltd. (1976) ; and Morris v. Accro Co. Ltd. 1985)

The loss of any benefits, including pension rights and expenses. Pensions can form a big item, raising the total award to well above the maximum. It is extremely complicated, and where necessary, actuarial advice should be sought.

Case Law – The loss of Statutory rights –S.H. Muffet Ltd. V. Head (1987). Any expenses reasonably incurred in consequence of the dismissal, e.g. costs incurred in consequence of the dismissal, e.g. costs incurred in seeking a new job but not legal expenses.

All of the above are subject to a reduction for contributory fault together with a reduction for any failure on the part of the employee to mitigate his or her loss. This would include a person removing himself from the labour market by taking a training course for 12 months. Although if for a short period with little prospect of getting a job during that period, it may not apply.

The amount of the compensatory award may be reduced or increased by a period of up to two weeks' pay if the employee declined his employer's invitation to appeal against his dismissal (in accordance with his employer's internal appeal procedures) or if his employer refused to allow such an appeal (ibid section 127A).

If, following an employee's dismissal, the firm for which he (or she) worked closed down, the compensatory award cannot run beyond the date of closure. It is of no consequence that it would have been economically viable for the business to have continued.

Case Law – (Wivenhoe Ltd. v. Tipper and Others (1990)

Additional Award

- If an employer refuses or fails to comply fully with an order for reinstatement or re-engagement, the tribunal in question will order him to pay such amount of compensation as it thinks fit, having regard to the loss sustained by the employee in consequence of his employer's failure to comply fully with the terms of the order.
- But if the employee is not reinstated or re-engaged in compliance with the order, the tribunal will not only order the payment of basic and compensatory award for unfair dismissal, but will also order the employer to pay in addition not less than 26 nor more than 52 weeks' pay, – unless the employer satisfies the tribunal that it was not practicable to comply with that order. However, it is no defence for an employer to argue that he had already engaged a permanent replacement for the dismissed employee.
- There are, for the most part, statutory limits on the amount of compensation that the tribunals can award. For example, for 2001/02, the maximum statutory redundancy payment that can be awarded is £7,200. The maximum basic award of compensation for unfair dismissal (calculated in much the same way as the statutory redundancy payment) is likewise £7,200; the maximum compensatory award of £51,700 and so on. However, in equal pay, unlawful discrimination cases, there is no upper limit on the amount of compensation that may be awarded.

- The tribunals are now dealing with a great many cases brought by employees alleging either that there was no genuine redundancy situation at the time of their dismissal, or that they had been unfairly selected contrary to an agreed redundancy procedure, or that their selection had been for an inadmissible or unlawful reason (e.g. on ground of sex, race, disability, trade union membership, etc.).
- An employee who believes that he has been unfairly or unlawfully selected for redundancy (or that there was not a genuine redundancy situation) may present a complaint of unfair dismissal before an employment tribunal. If the tribunal upholds his complaint, the employer will be directed to pay compensation comprising a basic award (calculated in much the same way as the statutory redundancy payment), a compensatory award (current upper limit £50,000) and, very possibly, an additional award (of between 26 and 52 weeks' pay).

10.8.4 Powers of the Enforcement Officers

If the employer refuses to pay compensation to an employee after being ordered by the High Court Judge, he could be issued a writ by the court. The Enforcement Officers also known as the Sheriffs working on behalf of the High Court could enter his premises and seize goods from the employer to recover the debt. First, the Sheriffs or enforcement officers will contact the employer to negotiate with him to make payment. If the employer agrees to pay by instalment, a deposit will be required as an initial payment. Secondly, the employer will be required to pay the rest at an agreed date. If he still refuses to pay by the date promised, the officers will make a forced entry at his business premises and seize his goods. A car belonging to the company could even be clamped outside the property and taken for sale to pay the employee. The Enforcement officers has the power to break into an employer's commercial establishment and seize goods to recover a debt, but not at a residential property if the door is locked. The enforcement officers are after the assets of the company and not the employer's personal assets.

Chapter Eleven

THE LAW OF AGENCY

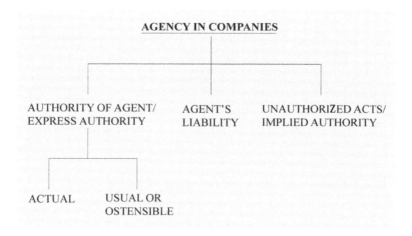

Fig 11.1 – A diagram for Agency in Companies

11.1 THE AUTHORITY OF AN AGENT

11.1.1 Who is an Agent?

Agents are people who bring their principal into contractual relationships with the third party. In other words, they make contracts with people; but these contracts will be binding not on themselves but on people they are representing. In a typical agency relationship, the agent makes the contract and then disappears. In other words, he drops out leaving the contract proper between the principal and the third party. He is just a mere link.

Sometimes, a person (the principal) wishes to have certain tasks carried out. He may wish to sell a house or buy shares in a company.

He therefore employs an estate agent or a stockbroker to carry out these duties on his behalf. Sometimes, the agent has wider powers, and may even be able to bind the principal in all the ways the principal could bind himself, as where the agent has a power of attorney.

The actual and usual or ostensible authority should be known, though the situation of usual or ostensible authority is more likely to be required. Situations where the agent generally may be liable on a contract made for the principal should be noted. i.e. Contract by Deed.

11.1.2 What is an Express Authority

An agency can be created by *express* agreement verbally or in writing, by implication or conduct, where the agent has clear authority from his principal to act for him. An agent may be specifically appointed as such, but in some cases an agent acquires his status without specific authority being given to him, and such an agent may bind his principal by what is called usual authority.

If Mr. White appoints Jones to be the manager of a hotel, Jones may be able to bind Mr White in a contract although he had no actual authority to make it. For the law is not solely concerned with the actual authority of an agent but regards him as having the usual powers of an agent of his class.

It follows that the usual powers of a hotel manager will be relevant in deciding the sort of agreement which Jones can make on behalf of Mr. White. The doctrine of usual authority does not apply where the third party knows that the agent has no authority to make the contract.

As always the law seeks to determine the rights and liabilities of the parties. If the agent himself is liable, should the third party sue the principal or should the principal sue the third party?

Under normal circumstances, the agent must inform the third party (customer) that he is an agent acting for a certain principal. In that case the third party knows the position and the contract will be between the principal and the third party.

As a general rule, it all depends on whether the agent is authorized to enter into a contract and the third party knows that he is dealing with an agent, and knows the identity of the principal, then the contract when made will lie between the principal and the third party. The agent will have neither rights nor duties under the contract.

On the other hand, if a third party who does not know he is dealing with an agent, because the agent has not informed him of the fact, then the third party will naturally conclude that he is dealing with the person who is the agent in his own right.

Consequently the third party may only sue the agent, if the need arises. However if he later discovers the existence of the principal and his identity then he may sue him. He cannot of course sue both agent and principal. This is sometimes referred to as the doctrine of the undisclosed principal.

11.1.3 What is Implied Authority?

By necessity:
An agent's powers may also be extended in an emergency, where the agent cannot contact his principal for instruction, but acts to the best of his ability, e.g. an agent assisting a minor *for necessaries.*

By ratification:
This means to accept or confirm (agreement made in one's name) by formal consent, signature, etc. If an agent makes a contract without authority and the principal takes it over, the ratification dates back to the time of the act.

Such ratification is only valid where: –

i. The principal has received full information from the agent as to what has to be done.
ii. The agent's act must have been legal.

Case Law – **Watteau versus Fenwick**

Where a businessman employs a manager in his shop and instructs him as to the type of contracts he can make, the manager's actual authority is so limited, but his ostensible authority (i.e. as far as outsiders are concerned) is that of a normal shop manager.

The third party with no knowledge of these arrangements can presume he has normal authority. Further, where a husband has normally paid his wife's bills, he will be liable to pay again unless he has given direct notice of cancellation to a person entitled to rely on this.

At one time if a person appointed an agent to manage his or her affairs, the appointment became invalid when the person making the appointment lost mental capacity. However, under the Enduring Powers of Attorney Act 1985, it is possible to enter into an agency agreement which does not terminate on the principal's loss of mental capacity.

11.1.4 What is Meant by Power of Attorney?

The power of attorney is required by the agent if it may become necessary for him to make a transaction by deed. In this case the attorney or agent must himself be appointed by deed. The law has always treated a transaction by deed in a special way. A deed is quite simply a document to which had been affixed a seal. It was necessary for the person executing the deed to state with his finger on the seal, "I deliver this as my act and deed". The deed appointing the agent is called the Power of Attorney. Often old people incapable of acting for themselves appoint some other person to deal with their affairs.

Powers of Attorney Act 1971

Signature and sealing may be by one person other than the donor in his presence and by his direction. In this case two witnesses are necessary. The power of attorney must be stamped within 30 days of its execution.

11.1.5 What is the Significance of Signatures?

An agent may be liable if he signs a document. But it depends on the manner in which he signs it. The agent may sign in his own name. In that case it is probably true to say that the agent has accepted liability unless of course he makes it clear that he is signing as an agent.

- If a person signs 'per procurationem' then it indicates that he has only a limited authority. Often a person will sign in this way on behalf of a company. The principal therefore will only be liable if the agent is acting within his actual authority.
- The principal may of course authorize the agent to sign using his (the principal's) name. This is in order.
- In determining whether a signature on a bill is that of the principal or that of an agent by whose hand it is written, the construction most favourable to the validity of the instrument shall be adopted. The effect of this is that, where an agent signs, in his name, a deed or a bill of exchange then, he will be liable on these documents. An exception would be if the agent signed a deed and was authorized by a power of attorney.
- There is one case when an agent must be appointed by a deed and that is when his principal expects him to execute a deed.

11.2 THE RESPONSIBILITIES OF THE PRINCIPAL AND THE AGENT

11.2.1 The Liability of the Agent

Care and skill

A paid agent is liable to the principal if he fails to do the work and as a result, the principal suffers loss. A paid agent must use the skill he claims to possess, or may be implied from his profession. As held in Turpin v. Bilton (1843). A gratuitous agent is not liable for nonfeasance (failure to perform) However, once he commences the work, he will be liable, if he does not exercise appropriate care and skill.

Case Law – N. Cogg v Bernard. (1703). A gratuitous agent must use the care and skill he will give to his own affairs. This means, he must use such skill as he possesses.

The agent's liability
Generally, there is no liability. The agent is a mere intermediary. Under the law of agency, where an agent misrepresents himself as having authority he does not possess, the third party will not obtain a contract with the principal and if he suffers loss as a consequence, he may sue the agent for breach of warranty of authority. The agent can be sued for damages:

- Where the agent has no authority because it has expired – The third party can claim against the agent for a breach of warranty of authority and he will be personally liable, because he never had authority.
- Where the agent acted on behalf of an undisclosed principal, the third party may choose to sue either the agent or the principal.
- Where the agent entered the contract without clearly indicating that he is acting solely as agent, he may personally be liable.

11.2.2 The Agents Duties to His Principal

- The Agent must perform his duties with care.
- The Agent must perform his duties without personal interest, e.g. if the agent is to sell goods, he must not buy them himself without his principal's agreement.
- The Agent must not make a secret profit nor take a bribe.
- The Agent must not disclose secret information acquired during agency.
- The Agent must submit proper accounts to his principal. An agent must be trustworthy.

11.2.3 The Principal's Duties to His Agent

- To pay agreed commission
- To indemnify the agent against any liabilities he may have incurred in connection with his duties, i.e. compensation for *loss suffered* as well as expenses incurred.

11.2.4 The Agent's Rights

- Rights of re-imbursement: Any reasonable expenses necessarily incurred by the agent in performing his duties must be repaid to him by his principal.
- Set-off: A set-off is a defence to the whole or part of a claim. The defendant acknowledges the claimant's demand but sets up one which counterbalances it. The amount to be set off must have been due at the time of the issue of the claim.

Case Law – In Richards v. James (1848).

If the principal brings an action against the agent for breach of duty, the agent may exercise his right of set-off for any sums due to him either as commission or as indemnity for expenses incurred.

Lien: –As already mentioned in chapter six, a lien is a right to hold and retain someone's property until a claim is satisfied. If the principal has failed to pay the agreed commission or an indemnity to the agent and the agent has any goods of the principal in his possession, then subject to certain conditions, the agent may exercise a lien on such goods and retain possession until the principal has honoured his obligation.

11.2.5 Termination of Agent's Authority

As the agency relationship is usually based upon agreement between the principal and an agent, then it follows that it may be terminated;

- By mutual agreement.
- An agent authority may be terminated on completion of the task.
- Automatically on the bankruptcy of either party.
- By operation of the law: this means if a certain event occurs, such as the death or insanity of either the principal or agent, or the bankruptcy of the principal, the agent's authority will be terminated. They should know that any of these events will take away the agent's authority whether or not he knows that the event has occurred. If the event occurs unknown to

the agent, he may be acting without authority and this will result in him being made liable for any contract he makes after the event has occurred.

- Automatically, where the principal becomes an enemy, alien on outbreak of war.
- The principal can at any time withdraw the agent's authority.

Note: He should inform third parties (doctrine of Estoppel).

11.3 TOUR OPERATORS, TRAVEL AGENCIES AND THE LAW

11.3.1 Tour Operators versus Travel Agencies

'Tour' is the name usually given to a booking made by travel agents for a number of people – it could be five, thirty or more persons booking at one time. Usually, tour members have a set period covering their stay, arranged by the travel agent, often to places of interest in the locality. A tour is usually made up of holidaymakers. It could also be a tour arranged specifically for a football match, a theatre visit or to a particular event being staged in the town.

Several months before the date of arrival, a travel agent will request accommodation at the hotel for a specific tour, stating the type and number of rooms required, and although changes may occur later, this advance request is reasonably accurate. After the booking has been made, and the cost has been ascertained, the agent will then 'sell' his tour. When he has the names of all the people wishing to travel, he will send a voucher to the hotel, giving all the relevant details, including the names of tour members and the cost of the rooms with meals before embarking on the trip. This information will be sent to the hotel in a form of a voucher. Care must be taken by a reservation clerk to see that the arrival and departure of the tourists as well as the dates are well noted.

This confirmation voucher is usually sent within thirty days of the original request for accommodation. If such confirmation is not received within that period, the hotel has the right to refuse to hold the booking any longer without assurances from the travel agent that confirmation is imminent. Lack of such assurance generally means that the agent has been unable to sell his tour and he would probably be cancelling it. No hotel, during a busy period, is able or willing to hold a large booking without it being confirmed as definite within a reasonable period of time.

Many tours include a tour leader, who will be the spokesman for the tour members during their stay at the hotel. The agency will notify his name to the hotel when a confirmation voucher is sent, but no correspondence must take place with him as all queries concerning the tour prior to its arrival must be addressed to the agent.

On the day prior to the arrival of the tour, a list, showing the names of all members with their allocated room numbers and any relevant details i.e. the name of the tour leader and his room number, the time of arrival and departure if known, with meal included "will be sent to the tour leader". Copies of this list are distributed to the various departments of the hotel. Any alterations and amendments to the list, after this distribution, must of course be passed on to the departments concerned.

In some hotels, the Hotel Receptionist has no contact with the tour members themselves on their arrival, but only the tour leader or agent's representative accompanying the guests. It is he who sees that the registration forms are completed, tells the guests the room numbers allocated to them, answers queries that they may have and hands the final details of the tour and its members to the receptionists after the guests have gone to their rooms.

Tour arrivals often cause congestion at the reception area; the front hall must work quickly and efficiently to clear them as quickly as possible.

Often, a tour member may wish to change his room in order to share with someone other than the person allocated by the travel agent, or he or she may require a different room. Both requests make extra work for the receptionist. No matter how harassed the receptionist is, it must be dealt with in the normal courteous manner. He or she must remember to notify the alteration to all departments to whom the tour list has previously been distributed. The luggage porter must be aware of these to ensure that, the luggage is delivered to the right room.

When they all go to their rooms, the reception notifies all departments of the tour arrival, tour number, name of agency and the number of people who have arrived. Should there be any last-minute cancellations in the tour party, it is usual to charge the travel agent for a fee, i.e. one night's accommodation charge for each non-arrival. On the day of departure, the tour leader generally clears his tour with the cashier ensuring that all other extra bills are settled.

It is usual for hotels to give commission to accredited travel agencies; the percentage often varies between countries and agencies. With overseas travel agents, the settlement of the account may be in a foreign currency, so rates of exchange must be carefully calculated.

Travel Agency Reservation

This is made through a travel agent by many people going on holiday or travelling on business, particularly when travelling to places outside their normal country of residence. This type of booking is not included under the tour, because they will travel independently. However, the travel arrangement and bookings may be made in the normal way by the travel agency on behalf of the guest, who receives a reservation coupon, the duplicate of which is sent in advance to the hotel.

The hotel receptionist checks with the guest on arrival that his stay is for the number of nights indicated on the voucher.

Commission to travel agencies are usually paid in the same way as for tour bookings. The title 'travel agent' can cover a number of operators in this field. It can include airlines, shipping lines, and the travel departments of big companies. Before a hotel enters in any agreement or transactions with a travel agency, it is advisable if possible to check its credentials. Agencies usually belong to agents' organisations within their own country or global area which give their members accredited names. In order to safeguard themselves against any loss, some hotels insist that payment in full is made by the agency prior to the arrival of the guests.

11.3.2 Consumer Law Relating to Package Holidays

Consumer Protection on Package Holidays
The main area of consumer protection in the case of package holidays are the Package Travel, Package Holidays and Package Tour. The Package Tours Regulations 1992 and the ABTA Code of the practice were introduced to comply with EU (European Union) Directive 90/314 on the Package Holidays and Package Tours. The directive was inevitable because of the level of tourism across EU member states. Most consumer problems related to holidays, concern differences between the holiday description on the booking and the actual reality. It is possible in these circumstances that there is also an offence under the S. 14 Trade Descriptions Act 1968.

Misrepresentation Act 1967
The Misrepresentation Act 1967 protects consumers from false or fraudulent claims that induce you to enter into a contract. The Consumer Regulations were introduced to help consumers with their problems. We therefore need to acquaint ourselves with the main areas of consumer legislation.

Compensation due to flight delay
The Court justice of the European Union in October 2012 introduced the ruling that if your flight is delayed, you may be able to claim compensation. However you can only claim compensation if the delay means you arrived at your destination more than three hours later than the original scheduled arrival time. There is an exception to the right of compensation if the carrier can prove that cancellation was caused by circumstances beyond their control, which could not have been avoided even if all reasonable measures had been taken. For example, a technical fault which might have

developed suddenly or 'act of God' like an earthquake or a volcanic eruption.

If your flight is delayed for at least two hours, for a flight of 1,500 kilometres (932 miles) or less, you should be entitled to meals, refreshments, phone calls and e-mails. If a delay is at least five hours, then the right to reimbursement is justifiable.

11.3.3 The Package Tour Regulations 1992

The Regulations do not alter the existing Common Law protections but add significant duties on tour operators. The Regulations apply to all Package Holidays, but the word 'Package' is given very broad definition in Regulation 2 (1) the prearranged combination of at least two of the following components when sold or offered for sale at an inclusive price and when the service covers a period of more than 24 hours or includes overnight accommodation: transport and other tourist services not *ancillary* to transport or accommodation and accounting for a significant proportion of the package.

11.3.4 Provision of Information to the Consumer Before the Contract is Concluded

The basic Common Law rules on formation can apply. The brochure is generally seen as an invitation to treat. Regulation 9, provide certain safeguards, by ensuring that certain information is given to the consumer before the contract is concluded and that information is *comprehensible* to the consumer as follows:

- The intended destination.
- The intended means of transport.
- The exact dates and the place of departure.
- The locality of accommodation and its classification.
- Meals that are included in the package.
- The minimum number of travellers to allow the holiday to go ahead.
- Any relevant itineraries, visits or excursions.
- The names and full addresses of the organiser, retailer and insurer.

- The price and any details with regard to revising the price.
- The payment schedule and method of payment.
- Any other necessary details, such as specific arrangements for diet etc. that have been indicated.
- The method and period for complaints to be made.
- The information must be given to the consumer before the contract is made and in the contract itself. This will not apply to late bookings. Failure to comply is a breach under Regulation 9 (3).
- Holiday Brochures: – Holiday operators will be liable if they supply misleading information in their descriptive matter.

11.4 TERMS AND PERFORMANCE OF THE CONTRACT

11.4.1 The Operator's Liability

By Regulation 15 (1), the operator is liable for the improper performance of the contract by other service providers. The only exception is where the improper performance is neither the fault of the operator nor any of the other service providers. For example:

- where it is the fault of the consumer.
- or, where it is caused by the unforeseeable and unavoidable act of the third party; and where there is war, an earthquake or hurricanes. The ABTA Code of Practice also requires that it should be a term of contract for Package Holidays and that the operator will accept liability for the acts or omissions of their employees, agents, sub-contractors and suppliers, which results in death, injury or illness and that the operator will offer advice, guidance and financial assistance of up to £5,000 to consumers in case of death, injury or illness.

11.4.2 Alteration to the Holidays

Alterations depend on the terms of the contract; a common term allows alteration to the itinerary. If an alteration amounts to non-performance then it is a breach of the contract by the operator and will be classed as a breach of the condition allowing the consumer to repudiate and claim back the cost of the holiday. The ABTA Code Clause 2.4 requires operators to offer suitable alternatives in case of cancellation or alteration.

11.4.3 Overbooking of Flights

Passengers who are denied travel because of overbooking are entitled to a choice of reimbursement of the cost of the ticket, re-routing to destination at the earliest moment, or re-routing at a later date, at the passenger's convenience.

11.4.4 Insolvency of the Tour Operator

The Package Travel, Package Holidays and Package Tours Regulations 1992 apply. Under Regulation 16 (1) tour operators must at all times be able to satisfy evidence of sufficient funds to be able to return deposits in the event of insolvency.

Consumers who pay by credit card are also protected under the Consumer Credit Act 1974. Under ABTA bonding arrangements Tour Operators must ensure that a consumer is not left stranded when a tour operator goes into insolvency during his or her holidays.

11.4.5 Remedies

Damages are usually awarded on the basis of difference in value between what was contracted for and what was provided. Incidental losses are also possible. Claims are also possible for physical discomfort. Operators are basically, liable for all losses that arise from the breach.

11.4.6 The Office of Fair Trading

The Office of Fair Trading (OFT) issued guidance to tour operators in March, 2004. The OFT believes that many standard terms in contracts fall short of the requirements of the Unfair Contract terms in Consumer Contract Regulations 1999 and has suggested alternative wording for operators to avoid liability, these include:

- Standard terms on responsibility for errors and changes in invoices or brochures.
- The acceptance of responsibility for statements made by agents, employees and representatives.
- Right to transfer holidays when prevented from travelling.
- Price revision clauses.
- Rights on cancellations and alteration.
- The right to compensation and alteration.
- Cancellation by the consumer.
- Cancellation charges for failure to pay deposits or balance.
- Rights where services not supplied during the holiday.
- Reporting of complaints.
- Reading and understanding declaration.

Exclusion clauses

Exclusion clauses are very common in the booking forms and the holiday maker is well advised to read the form carefully before signing as he or she is taken to have agreed to any conditions on a document to which they have put their signature.

Case Law – In Cook v. Spanish Holidays Tours (1960), the court helped a holidaymaker. Mr. Cook booked a Spanish holiday through the defendants company, but when he and his wife arrived in Spain no room was available for them in the hotel. They were offered a filthy room in an annexe where beetles were running around the floor-boards. They had to spend the night in a park, fly back to England the next day, and the remainder of their holidays was spent in Brighton. Damages for breach of contract were awarded to Mr. Cook. The appeal Court said that the agent could not rely on the argument that his duty was only to book a room and not to provide it. "It isn't much good booking a room if you can't have a room," said the Judge

Some protection has been given to holidaymakers by two recent Acts, namely Misrepresentation Act 1967 and Trade Descriptions Act 1968 both of which enable civil actions and criminal prosecutions to be started against persons who mislead others by false descriptions. One false statement in a brochure can give rise to any number of prosecutions; R. v. Thomson Holidays Ltd (1973). Travel agents in October, 1974, agreed a voluntary code giving more protection to the customer.

At the moment, anyone can set up in business as a travel agent, there being no form of registration. The only control comes under the Civil Aviation Act 1971. Agents who need an air travel organisers licence will have to prove that they have adequate financial resources.

Chapter Twelve

HEALTH AND SAFETY

An employer or occupier has a legal responsibility to provide for the safety and welfare of employees and anyone else who may be lawfully on or near the premises.

12.1 TO PROVIDE SAFE PREMISES

The premises include all parts that make up the fundamental structure of the building, i.e. the floors, walls, roof insulations, power installations and ventilations.

12.1.1 To Provide Safe Plant, Equipment and Maintenance

Plant, is defined as 'fixed assets' as opposed to fluctuating stock and includes such assets as counters and things that are physically fixed and form part of the permanent establishment which could be replaced when worn out. The duty of care does not prohibit an employer from installing apparatus which could cause injury, but he must take care to reduce the risk to a minimum by providing protective equipment or at least by giving warning of the danger to his employees. It would be an act of negligence to let the employee handle dangerous apparatus without giving him adequate training as to its use.

On the other hand, the equipment must be suitable for the purpose for which it is intended to be used. Also the equipment must be free from any defect, and any defect drawn to the attention of the employer must be immediately repaired. The Employer's Liability

Act (Defective Equipment), provides that the responsibility must be borne by the employer who must pay compensation, whether the defect which caused the injury was concealed or not. The employer is also required by the Employer's Liability (Compulsory Insurance) Act, to cover all future claims in respect of personal injuries to employees by an approved insurance company. There can of course, be an agreement between the employer and the manufacturer in case the equipment happens to be defective.

12.1.2 To Provide a Safe Environment

The employer's Common Law duty under this heading can be broadly divided into two sections. To provide safe environment for fellow employees, an employer is liable to pay compensation to an employee who has been injured as a result of the foolish behaviour or incompetence of a colleague. This duty comes within the employer's vicarious liability. Obviously, an employer cannot initially guarantee that a new employee will not endanger his fellow employees, but as soon as he has evidence that his behaviour is likely to do so, he must warn him to correct that behaviour, but if no heed is taken of the warning, he should dismiss him.

12.1.3 To provide Reasonable Protection Against Unnecessary Risks

Where the employment is likely to be dangerous, an employer has the duty to provide protective measures to reduce the danger to a minimum, and to make these measures readily available. However, he is not obliged to supervise the use of the appliance as long as his employees are aware of the necessary protective measures.

12.2 GENERAL HEALTH AND WELFARE

The conditions which must be observed in all relevant premises can be classified as follows:

12.2.1 Cleanliness

The Act requires that all premises, furniture, fittings and furnishings must be kept in a clean state, accumulation of dirt and refuse must be eliminated. Floors and steps must be cleaned everyday by the most effective means possible, i.e. washing, sweeping, mopping, polishing or by some other method.

12.2.2 Overcrowding

Workrooms must solely be used by employees and out of bounds to the public. It must not be overcrowded to a degree that would cause a risk to injury or health. After fittings (cabinet, machinery), there must be enough space for workers to move freely.

12.2.3 Temperature

Reasonable temperature must be maintained in the workroom, especially where staff are present. The standard temperature must not be less than 16°C.

12.2.4 Ventilation

All workrooms must be effectively and suitably ventilated to allow the circulation of fresh or artificially purified air.

12.2.5 Lighting

There must be a suitable and efficient lighting system; it concerns the whole of the premises in which people work or commute and can be either natural or artificial, provided it is efficient. To achieve the required efficiency, windows and skylights must, as far as practical, be cleaned to keep them free from obstruction.

12.2.6 Sanitation

Occupiers (proprietor) must provide suitable and sufficient sanitary facilities for both sexes. Such facilities must be properly maintained and kept in a clean condition. The requirement also includes the availability of adequate washing facilities; i.e. hot and cold water, soap and drying materials or equipment and a sufficient supply of water.

12.2.7 Seating Arrangements

Employees, who have reasonable opportunities for sitting without detriment to their work, should have available for their use suitably situated seats.

12.2.8 Accommodation for Clothing

Arrangements for accommodation of clothing must be made. This applies to clothing not worn during working hours as well as for clothing not taken home. Also, practical reasonable provision must be made for drying clothing.

12.3 SAFETY

12.3.1 Floors, Passages and Stairs

Floors, passages and stairs etc. must be of sound construction and properly maintained and where practical, kept free from slippery substances and obstacles. Suitable handrails must be provided on every staircase on both sides if possible. If there is a special hazard, it must be sufficiently well constructed to prevent people from accidentally falling through.

12.3.2 Fencing Dangerous Parts of Machinery

All dangerous parts of machinery must be fenced to prevent the operator from coming into contact with that dangerous part. This can be accomplished by either a fixed guard-rail or by an automatic device. The rail must always be in position when the dangerous part is in motion, or in use, to guard against all foreseeable injuries. Operators of dangerous machinery must be trained to operate the machinery and warned of its potential danger. All persons under 18 years must be prohibited from cleaning any machine which might expose them to injury from a moving part of that machine.

12.3.3 First Aid and Fire Prevention

- First Aid: An adequate first-aid box or cupboard must be made readily accessible to employees. The box must be placed in charge of responsible persons. One of the responsible persons must be trained in first aid administration and must be available during working hours. If this is in place, then the premises may be exempted from the need to maintain a first aid box.
- Fire Prevention: Fire precautions must be observed in all premises and the laid down standard of satisfaction must be

achieved following inspection. To enable premises employing staff to obtain fire prevention certificate, without which it would be unlawful to operate as a business, the premises must provide a means of escape from fire which is adequate in the circumstances. What is adequate is determined not only by the number of employees on the premises at any one time, but also the number of other people, i.e. residents or customers who may reasonably be expected to be on the premises. General precautions must be observed, e.g. doors of meal rooms must not be locked when unoccupied, and washrooms should be organized so that there will be no obstruction to free passage and there must be recommended fire equipment readily available and properly maintained. In order that a fire certificate can be issued, the local fire authority must be satisfied with the adequacy of the means of escape.

The following precautions must be observed:

The specified means of escape in the certificate must be properly maintained and free from obstruction; fire exits mentioned in the fire certificate (other than ordinary means) must be conspicuously marked; the fire-alarm system of the premises must be capable of being operated without risk to any person and must pass an examination at least once every three months. The means of escape and its routine must be known to all employees.

12.3.4 Safety and Welfare of Employees and the Safety of Third Parties

The employer, in this case, the owner of a hotel or restaurant, is not under the same duty to protect other persons who enter his premises as he is to his employees. However, the law does place some responsibility upon him for the safety of his guests and other persons, such as independent contractors, who come into his premises to work. Also, an employer can be liable for injury caused to a third party by his employee when that employee is conducting the employer's business. This liability is imposed upon him through the doctrine of vicarious liability.

12.3.5 The Occupiers' Liability Act 1957

Section 2 of the Occupiers Liability Act 1957 provides that, to persons entering on his land with his permission, whether expressed or implied, the occupier has a duty; "to take such care as in all the circumstances reasonable to see that the visitor will be reasonably safe in using the premises for the purpose for which he is invited or permitted by the occupier to be there".

12.3.6 The Duty is Owed to Everyone, Except a Trespasser

The Occupier (proprietor) has the duty of care of his guests and workmen carrying out repairs, tradesmen delivering commodities to the premises and entertainers contracted to perform on the premises. In the case of contractors, the 1957 Act provides that an occupier may expect that a person in the exercise of his duty will guard against any special risk ordinarily incidental to his job, as far as the occupier leaves him free to do so.

So where the occupier employs for example an electrician to carry out his work in connection with his trade, he is entitled to expect the electrician to be competent to deal with and guard himself against dangers which could arise from working with electrical installation. The Act also anticipates the fact that injury could be caused to a guest due of the faulty work of an independent contractor, and relieves the occupier who employed him from liability. The occupier had satisfied himself that the contractor was competent in his professed trade. Where injury is caused to a guest in these circumstances, his action should be taken against the contractor.

Therefore, the occupier's duty involves only those factors which are under his control, except where the doctrine of vicarious liability is concerned and includes the security and proper maintenance of safe carpet, stairs, banisters, lifts and efficient lighting. Whether or not an occupier will be liable in any case will depend upon the relevant facts. Normally, an action for negligence will succeed if a guest is injured in a part of the premises to which access is allowed.

The occupier, therefore, must give clear notice that certain parts of the premises are not accessible to persons other than staff. If no notice is given, he could be liable for an injury caused to a guest irrespective of the situation of the accident.

Case Law – Campbell v. Shelbourne Hotel Ltd (1939)

The lights in a hotel were switched off at 11 pm. Campbell, a guest walking down the unlit passageway opened a door leading into a private part of the premises. He fell down some steps and was injured. It was held that the hotel management had been unreasonable in switching off the lights in the passageway, which might be used by a guest; therefore, the guest was entitled to damages. The same degree of care must also be observed with notices explaining procedures to be followed in an emergency, especially, in the event of a fire.

Case Law – McLenan v. Segar (1917)

Fire broke out in a hotel at night. A guest who had arrived late and had been taken immediately to her bedroom had no knowledge of the emergency procedure to be followed, and was injured when she tried to escape from the premises through the second floor window. It was held that the proprietor was liable.

A duty of care is owed by an occupier of a hotel premises to children allowed on the premises. Dangers which may be obvious to an adult may be concealed or be a temptation to a child. It is therefore not sufficient to give a warning if the child would not profit by it. The occupier must take due care to protect the child from all dangers to which he might be exposed in entering the premises. However, this greater duty of care applies only to obvious dangerous situations. This apart, the occupier's duty as in all other cases is a duty of reasonable care as stipulated by law. There is nothing with which a child cannot hurt himself. Even in the case of trespassers, especially children, the occupier has a duty to afford protection against known potential dangers. *Case Law* – British Rail Board v. Herrington (1972).

12.4 HEALTH AND SAFETY ACT WITH PARTICULAR REFERENCE TO THE HOSPITALITY INDUSTRY

12.4.1 Hotel and Catering – A High Fire Risk Industry

Hotel and catering establishments inevitably contain areas of high fire risk. A high percentage of fires occurring on such premises are attributable to electrical faults, heating and cooking appliances, or to smoking. In hotels, there is the problem of the 'sleeping risk' where customers and staff may be unaware of a fire having started until it is well advanced. There is then an additional risk from smoke and from toxic gases produced when some plastics burn. The poisonous effect of these gases on a semi-conscious mind can in some cases make a perfectly normal person act irrationally.

In order to reduce fire risk, there must be a constant awareness on the part of management and staff, with repeated fire drills, maintenance checks and training. These procedures must be backed up by notices informing the public of the procedure to be adopted in the event of an outbreak. In the event of a fire, the smooth efficiency of the organization for evacuation and the obvious demonstration of control by the staff are the best means of ensuring that members of the public do not panic and also, that goods and the building itself are protected. It is necessary to ensure the containment (shutting off) of areas of high fire risk and routes of escape, and the limitation of the spread of fire and smoke by the installation of fire doors are in strategic places. There are various Acts of Parliament and possibly Local Acts and Bye-Laws which require a control of fire safety in hotels and catering establishments.

THE FIRE PRECAUTION ACT

The Fire Precaution Act 1971 came into force in 1972, when hotels and boarding houses were the first class of premises to be designated. Under the Fire Precaution (Hotels and Boarding Houses) Order 1972, Statutory Instrument (SI 1972/238)(and an equivalent Order for Scotland), any premises where sleeping accommodation for more than six persons (staff or guests), or any sleeping accommodation above the first floor or below the ground floor, required a fire certificate issued by the fire authority.

The Fire Precaution Act 1971 and its Fire Certificates were totally repealed and replaced by the Regulatory Reform (Fire Safety) Order 2005, which came into full force on 1 October 2006 (in England and Wales).

12.4.2 Regulatory Reform (Fire Safety) Order 2005

In 2000, the Government in the form of the Office of the Deputy Minister (OPDM) set up a review of the fire safety legislation led by the Deputy Prime Minister John Prescott found out that there were some Acts of Parliament or parts of Acts which specified fire safety legislation. In order to revamp the whole thing and bringing it up to date, they decided to place all the odd bits of fire legislation under the umbrella of the Regulatory Reform (Fire Safety_ Order 2005), which became law in October. It applies to England and Wales only. The major change in the legislation was that it brought in the concept of risk assessment rather than prescriptive codes.

The Fire Precaution Act had relied on codes and guides for its implementation, and the Fire Precaution Regulations had changed by introducing risk assessment as a way of complying. The requirement for a fire certificate was never repealed; the guides and codes were still used as prescriptive means of applying the law.

The Fire Safety Order lays out the foundation of the risk assessment by saying that the responsible person (employer, person in control of the building, or the owner) must take into account for the safety of their employees and anyone else that may lawfully be in or near their premises.

The following must be provided (to protect their employees and anyone else who may lawfully be on or near their premises):

- means of detection and giving warning in case of fire.
- the provision of emergency lighting to escape routes.
- means of fighting fire (where necessary).

- the training of staff in fire safety.
- the publication of an emergency plan and the fire safety procedures for a specific building.

The Fire Safety Order then tells the responsible person (employer, person in control of the building, or owner) how they must assess these items in order to protect their employees and anyone else who may lawfully be on or near their premises:

- Carry out a fire risk assessment of the workplace and the communal areas in blocks of flats or maisonettes.
- Identify the significant findings of the risk assessment and the details of anyone who might be at risk in case of fire. Under the Management of Health and Safety Regulations, these must be recorded if more than five persons are employed.
- Provide and maintain such fire precautions as are necessary to safeguard those who use the workplace.
- provide information, instruction and training to employees about the fire precautions in the workplace.

The Fire Safety Order 2005 now requires the responsible person for each building to carry out or commission from a competent person, a Fire Risk Assessment to ensure that the general fire precaution within the particular building are fit for the purposes that the building is being currently put to use. The current use of an old building by today's occupiers and users has to be taken into account, in arriving at the appropriate general fire precautions. Thus, both proportionate and appropriate remedial fire safety works may be necessary to discharge the responsible person's legal duty, to control or reduce the risk to life from fire building.

Early Legislation
The first designating order became operative on the first of June 1912 in the U.K. and applies to all hotels and boarding houses. The order required everyone owning or occupying hotel or boarding house accommodation to fill a form supplied by the fire authority

registering their premises. Once the premises were registered, they could continue to trade there. At a later date, the fire authority would make an inspection and either issue a fire certificate or recommend alterations required to make the premises conform to the Fire Precautions Act by a stated date. Provided the work was done within the time, they would get their certificate and could continue to trade – if not, then they could no longer use the premises for the designated purpose.

Means of Escape

Definition: A 'protected route' for persons escaping from fire that is separated from the rest of the building by fire resisting doors and by walls and partitions which are built from fire resisting materials. Fire resisting materials should have a resistance of not less than half an hour, doors not less than 20 minutes, although half an hour is generally specified.

Stage 1: Specifies maximum distance into a room from a door (9 metres or 6 metres in a kitchen) in larger rooms, the number and width of exits is specified. Exit doors, not in normal use should be clearly marked.

Stage 2: Specifies the maximum distance of the route taken from a room to a 'protected route' or an 'external route' (fire escape), and the fire resistance required of the walls, doors, fanlights, etc., bordering the route.

Stage 3: Deals with stairways and specifies fire resisting constructions, means of access, e.g. through fire resisting self-closing doors. N.B. Lifts are not acceptable means of escape.

Stage 4: Covers the isolation of ventilation systems from protected routes, types of closing device which may be used on doors, the use of panic bolts only marked 'push to open' on exit doors, the provision of direction and exit signs illuminated where necessary, and the resistance of floors for half an hour.

Stage 5: Specifies the forms which emergency lighting must take.

12.5 CLASSIFICATION OF FIRES

In the early stages of fire in a building, the personal hazard to the occupants can be severely affected by the materials used as internal linings and finishes of walls and ceilings. These materials have been broadly classified into four groups with an indication as to where each may be used: Class A:- Fires in ordinary combustibles, e.g. wood, textiles, paper

Class B:- Fires in flammable liquids
Class C:- Fires involving gases
Class D:- Fires in special risks (metals)

Modern building require not only means of escape, access for the fire brigade and structural protection, but also first aid equipment for occupants to use on small fires while waiting for the arrival of the brigade and in some cases fixed installations to help contain the fire until the arrival of the fire brigade. In very large and high buildings, special installations may also have to be provided for the fire brigade. Expert advice on the appropriate provisions and the maintenance desirable for particular cases may be obtained from local fire brigades, which normally maintain an office for this purpose.

12.6 FIRE FIGHTING EQUIPMENT

Fires are extinguished by removing the fuel; excluding oxygen or cooling the materials involved to below ignition temperature. Removal of combustible materials is carried out manually in case of need. Water is cheap, readily available and acts extremely efficient as a cooling agent. It is therefore used, except in cases where electricity or oil or other special features, which render it hazardous, are present or where its use would cause damage that could be avoided by other means.

HAND EXTINGUISHERS

Buckets were widely used before chemical extinguishers and hose-reels were developed. They are cheap and their use is well understood. On the other hand, they are liable to be empty unless well maintained. Projecting the water to any point above floor level is difficult and the main application of buckets will be to fires at floor level. Fire buckets should be painted red, have round bottoms to prevent use for other purposes, be fitted with covers and be fixed at a convenient height. A better method is to have galvanized steel tanks filled with water.

BUCKETS: WATER

Sand is non-conducting and can be employed for small fires associated with electrical apparatus where water would not be possible and also for small liquid fires, which are covered or absorbed by the sand. The technique can only be applied on flat surfaces. In tanks, the sand will merely sink to the bottom.

BUCKETS: SAND

SODA – ACID

For fire-fighting purposes, this type of apparatus acts as a water extinguisher. The chemicals merely provide the power to produce the jet. The advantages of soda-acid extinguishers compared to buckets are the freedom from evaporation and risk of inappropriate use as well as the jet delivery which enables the water to be carefully directed at a fire from some distance away. Soda-acid extinguishers must be protected against frost. A similar performance is given by an extinguisher operated as compressed gas cartridge. This type has the additional advantage that antifreeze can be added to the water.

Soda – acid

FOAM EXTINGUISHERS

Chemicals dissolved in the water in the inner container mix with those in the outer container when the extinguisher is forced out of the nozzle by the pressure. A gas pressure type is also available as in the case of soda-acid extinguishers. Foam extinguishes fire by excluding oxygen.

They can be used in most cases where water is appropriate but are especially suitable for burning liquids since the foam can float upon the surface. The usual scale of provision is the same as that for soda-acid extinguishers.

Foam extinguisher

Vaporising liquids

A number of liquids that vaporize rapidly when applied to a fire are used in extinguishers. They act by excluding the oxygen. They are non-conducting, do not spoil most materials on to which they might be sprayed and dispense by vaporization after use. They are widely used for electrical apparatus and motor vehicles. There are some serious disadvantages; they are to varying degrees toxic, either before or after use. When used externally, winds may disperse the vapour and allow the fire to re-establish itself.

CARBON DIOXIDE EXTINGUISHER

Carbon dioxide gas can be compressed to a liquid and stored in pressure cylinders. When the pressure is released, the liquid vaporizes and expands very rapidly and the gas will extinguish fires by excluding oxygen. It causes no damages to materials on which it is used and for this reason is often used for machines, libraries, museums and similar situations. It is non-conducting and well suited for use on electrical equipment, and it is effective on small liquid fires. It is not toxic but can cause suffocation by excluding oxygen from the lungs. The discharge, which is made through a nozzle, has an effective range of only 1 to 2.5m. Many CO_2 extinguishers have a control valve so that complete discharge is not inevitably made immediately the extinguisher is used. An extinguisher containing 3 kg of carbon dioxide is regarded as the equivalent in extinguishing capacity to 3 water buckets.

Carbon dioxide extinguisher

DRY POWDER

These extinguishers deliver a cloud of inert powder expelled by carbon dioxide or nitrogen. The powder cools the flames, separates them from the combustible material and to some extent excludes oxygen. The powder is non-conducting so that use on electrical equipment is possible and it is also effective on small fires or liquids.

Dry Powder

FIRE BLANKET

Fire blankets can be used to wrap around people whose clothes are on fire and also to cover small fires or fires in small open containers.

Fire Blanket

FIXED APPARATUS

Hose-reels

Small diameter rubber hoses for use by the occupants of a building provide a very much more effective measure than buckets or soda-acid extinguishers and in many circumstances will be competitive in price. Rubber hose is used, usually of 18 or 25 mm internal diameter. Up to 22 mm of unreinforced hose or up to 36 mm of reinforced hose is wound on to a drum. The hose is connected to a water supply serving the spindle of the drum and fitted with a small diameter nozzle with a control cock.

Hose reels in recess

Hose reel in recess installed, as usual, in a recess of corridors or landing wall. In case of need the control valve is turned on, then the person using the hose takes the nozzle end of the hose and moves towards the fire, pulling out the hose as he goes. A superior arrangement is the use of a swinging arm hose-reel where the drum automatically swings to follow the line of movement of the hose.

Hose-reel installations must be taken into account when buildings are being planned. They should be sited near means of escape so that they are readily available to people leaving the building and if the floor is full of smoke after the hose-reel has been in use, the hose itself can guide its users to safety. There should be sufficient hoses to enter every room and all floors.

SPRINKLERS

There is clearly great advantage, particularly for buildings involving special fire risks such as very large or high buildings, underground car parks, warehouses or stores. Sprinkler installations fulfil such a purpose. They consist of a grid of water pipes fixed under the ceiling with delivery heads normally on a 3 m square grid. Water is prevented from emerging by a glass bulb containing liquid. When the temperature rises, the liquid expands, breaking the bulb, which is preventing the water passing.

The flow of water is arranged so that it works a turbine-operated fire alarm. The sprinkler installation therefore both sounds the alarm and helps to minimize and contain the fire. In an unheated building, there would be danger of freezing in the winter. It is possible to overcome this by means of the dry pipe system where special valve arrangements enable the delivery pipes to be filled with air under pressure. When this pressure drops, due to the opening of a sprinkler head, the water is admitted to the delivery pipes.

Sprinkler systems require central control and test gear. This is often arranged in the basement, but there is much to be said to having this gear, or at least the alarm and stop valve in a prominent position near the entrance to the building. This will enable the water to be shut off quickly before too much damage is done as soon as the fire is under control. Two independent water suppliers are generally thought desirable for sprinkler installations. In towns, it is sometimes possible to have supplies from water mains served by two independent trunk mains. When this is not the case, storage on the site is necessary.

The regular grid required for sprinklers for which complex standards exist depending on the fire protection of the building and the nature of the activities, and the need for control gear and storage space means that installations must be planned for, in the early stages of building design.

A special type of sprinkler can be used for oil fires. Although a jet of water would do more harm than good, a fine spray falling on the surface of burning liquid cools the surface and also, by turning into steam, excludes oxygen.

It is also possible to obtain valves which open on the bursting of a sprinkler bulb. They then admit water to a series of sprinklers. This technique is sometimes used in the case of rooms containing electrical equipment. Sprinklers cannot discharge over the apparatus but they can be used to protect door and window openings to prevent the spread of fire if the water supply is controlled by the temperature within the electrical room itself.

DRENCHERS
They are devices similar to sprinklers which deliver a curtain spray usually used to protect the external face of a building from some adjacent fire risk. Since they would inevitably be subject to freezing they are not normally provided with frangible bulbs but have open waterways. The water supply is turned on manually when required. Periodical flushing of the pipe work is required.

Drencher system.

OTHER FIRE EXTINGUISHING MEDIA
Both hose reels and automatic systems using fixed pipes can be provided for delivering carbon dioxide, foam or, in rare cases, powder from a central reservoir.

Fusible links
Two strips of brass soldered together with low-melting point solder can be used as a link in a straining wire system. The solder will melt

and actuate the system as do sprinkler bulbs. A wide variety of situations can be dealt with by this method. Projection room shutters are held open by a wire running over the projectors with a fusible link over each valve controlling the entry of oil to a boiler room, may be operated by a lever and weight and held open by a wire passing over the boilers with a fusible link over each.

FIRE ALARM

The simplest form of fire alarm is a series of manually operated switches, usually installed behind glass which has to be broken in order to gain access. The operation of any one switch sounds alarms on all floors and records at a central indicator which alarm was operated. Automatic devices which will give warning in case of need can be used. They operate either by being affected by sharp rises in temperature or by being able to detect smoke. In both cases, the detector units are placed at strategic points and wired back to a central indicator. Each type of alarm can, if desired, be arranged to repeat at the local fire station.

Fire Alarm

12.7 THE FIRE BRIGADE

In buildings of modest size, hard access for fire appliances to a reasonable proportion of perimeter is required but no special installation for use by the fire brigade is normally needed. Water for fire-fighting purposes is taken from hydrants in the highway.

Fire brigade hydrants

If the building is extensive or sited a long way from the road, one or more fire brigade hydrants may be needed. Fire brigade hydrants are 65 mm in diameter with a valve and a special type of coupling for hoses.

Access by fire brigade appliances

For fire-fighting and emergency escape to take place effectively, fire brigade appliances such as pumps and escape ladders must be positioned close to buildings. It is usual for the local authority to insist that an appropriate proportion of the perimeter of the building is accessible in this way. In buildings remote from the highway with only access roads on the site, it may be necessary to construct special roadways or hard standing to meet this requirement.

High buildings

Until comparatively recently the height of buildings in England was limited to 24 metres in height plus a further 6metres in the roof space. This requirement is related to fire-fighting and escape. The move towards high buildings necessitated the provision within the building of adequate means of vertical access for fire-fighting, which would not be interrupted even when several floors were on fire. The lobby approach staircase or more colloquially the 'fire tower', equipped with wet or dry riser and firemens' lift, has been developed to meet this need.

The stairs and lobby have to be vented to prevent smoke accumulating in case of fire. In a tall building with internal stairs, considerable cost and space will be involved. Recent high buildings have been provided with pressurized stairs and lobbies. Provided an adequate pressure can be maintained, smoke will not be able to enter the pressurized area. The cost of fans and input ducts is less than the value of space occupied by the natural draught vents, and the mechanical system appears to give a better performance. The most popular arrangement seems to be one where the stair is moderately pressurized at all times and this is automatically increased when any fire detector registers an outbreak.

Means of conveying water for fire-fighting up the building are needed and this is achieved by permanent pipe installation with fire brigade hydrant connections at each floor level. In buildings up to 45 m high, a 100 mm diameter 'dry riser' is required. This is equipped with an inlet at ground level to which the fire brigade pumps may be connected. An automatic air vent is needed at roof level and provision for draining down without flooding at ground level is desirable. Between 45 m and 60 m, a 150 mm diameter riser is used, while over 60m in height 'wet risers' are required. These have their own water reserves on site and are supplied by duplicate pumps in the building itself. An alternative power supply is needed. A standby generator or diesel power for one pump is normal. In buildings higher than 69 m, pumping in stages up the building may become necessary.

Emergency control of services
It should be possible for the fire brigade to turn off the main electrical and gas intakes at a readily accessible spot so that firefighting may be easier and safer.

Advice from fire brigade
Local fire brigades are normally very pleased to be asked for advice about firefighting provisions for proposed buildings and it is sensible to take advantage of this at an early stage in design.

12.8 SUMMARY: THE HEALTH AND SAFETY ACT

The Health and Safety Act objectives

The Health and Safety Act has two main objectives:

1) To secure the health, safety and welfare of people at workplaces; and to protect people, other than employees at workplaces against risks to health or safety arising out of or in connection with the activities of employees at workplaces.

2) The Act is designed to protect, not only your employees, but also the public who come on your business premises. The employer is given a general duty to; "ensure, so far as is reasonably practicable, the health, safety and welfare at work, of all his employees."

The Act specifies the duty under five headings:

- The provision and maintenance of safe and satisfactory plant and systems of work
- Safety and the absence of risks to health in connection with the use, storage, handling and transport of articles and substance
- The provision of all necessary instruction, training and supervision
- The maintenance in a safe and satisfactory condition of the place of work, as well as means of access to and egress (exist) from it; and
- The provision and maintenance of safe and satisfactory working environment for employees' welfare at work.

Breach of the rules will be a criminal offence
Normally, employer will have to provide and bring to the notice of their employees written statements of their general policy with respect to health and safety at work and especially as to; "the organizations and arrangements for the time being in force for carrying out that policy." It shall be the duty of every employer to conduct his undertakings in such a way as to ensure, so far as it is

reasonably practicable that persons not in his employment who may be affected thereby are not exposed to risks to their health and safety. Those who have control of any place where the public may use any plant or substance, may take all reasonable practical steps to see that the public are kept safe and without risk to their health. Any person who designs, manufactures, imports or supplies an article for use at work, must take all reasonable practical steps for tests, examinations, or otherwise to see that such articles will not cause injury to those who use it.

As for an employee at work, he has two duties:

To take reasonable care for the health and safety of himself and the people who may be affected by his acts or omissions at work; and to cooperate with his employer or others so far as is necessary to see that statutory duties are performed or complied with. But employers will not be permitted to levy any charge on employees in respect of anything done or provided in pursuance of any duty requirement if the relevant statutory duties are performed or complied with. It may be that employees will have to be provided with any relevant safety clothing at no charge to them.

The job of the Health and Safety officials; The job of the health and safety officials is to:

1   Ensure that adequate advice and information on health and safety matters is made available and that research and training is undertaken as often as is necessary, and to make proposals and regulations.
2   The officials will arrange for investigations and inquiries into accidents. They will generally control the comprehensive and integrated system of law dealing with health, safety and welfare of the employees.

Anyone who fails to discharge his duties contravenes the Health and Safety Act; and anyone who obstructs in the course of their duties, may in most cases, be fined by a magistrate's courts, an unlimited amount, if convicted by a jury. Or in the case of individuals in certain cases, they may be imprisoned for up to two years.

Offences and defences
Anyone charge under the Act may prove that the offence was committed due to the act of default or some other person, and in that case, the 'other person'; may be charged and (if he was indeed at fault) convicted. Worse, where any offence is proved to have been committed with consent of, or connivance of, or to have been attributed to any neglect on the part of any director, manager, secretary or other similar officer of a company, or anyone purporting to act in any such capacity, he, as well as the company shall be guilty of the offence and liable to be punished accordingly.

APPENDIX A: CASE STUDIES

The following case studies are real. They are drawn from countries all over the world. These are practical incidents, which confirm the theoretical aspect of this book. These case studies will serve as a guide for the personnel in the hospitality industry and help them to be cautious when discharging their duties. And above all, boost their confidence.

1. Holidaymakers Hit By Bug

It was reported in the newspapers that holidaymakers were hit by vomiting and diarrhoea in a five-star Sunrise Resort Hotel. Most of the holidaymakers were admitted to hospital and some of the holidaymakers made their way home at their own expense. They had gone on a package holiday. A package holiday is when transport and accommodation and other services are purchased or offered for sale at one inclusive price. The trip must also be longer than 24-hours.

Holiday firm Kovosa was forced to suspend bookings for ten days while hygiene experts were sent to the hotel. Guests claimed the representatives of the tour firm were told of the seriousness of the problem two weeks ago but continued to allow new guests to arrive.

A meeting was held between more than 100 guests demanding action from representatives of the tour firm. The Head of Holiday Law, M. and J. solicitors represented more than 30 of the holidaymakers. He said, "It is offensive to anyone, especially those with a young family, that a tour operator can be so mercenary as to send hapless victims to a hotel where the customers had no confidence with the hygiene and overall standard of the hotel".

The company also contacted customers who had since returned to their countries to address any concerns they had. A spokesperson said, "'The health and well-being of our customers is our top priority and we take all reports of illness very seriously." The company immediately arranged for an independent Hygiene consultant to carry out a comprehensive review of the hotel and the cause was believed to be viral. The hotel has put in place a number of preventative measures to minimise any further illness. The company also said their team in the resort were providing assistance to their guests and they would continue to monitor the situation. And as a precautionary measure only, new arrivals would have their holiday in alternative accommodation.

Law That Protects Tourists
Regulations are in place to protect guests while on package holiday.

These include regulations such as ensuring the food at a hotel is fit for consumption and the pool is safe to use.

- If you fall ill during your break, let your holiday company know immediately and inform them if you want to be moved to different accommodation.
- The Package Travel Regulations of 1992 provides you with legal protection and places a duty on your tour operator to offer you prompt assistance.
- As a matter of fact, the holiday representative must help you as a customer. If the representative cannot or, will not move you, then, you can ask them to get you back home.

Refund
Many companies will make you pay for flights back. And there is no guarantee that they will refund the cost of your holiday. When you have returned, you need to raise a complaint with them. Your insurer may cover the bill for getting you home and may even pay part of your lost holiday. Always check that your travel insurance covers medical fees.

2. A Tourist Flees from a Sex Attacker In a Hotel.
A woman was recovering in a hospital in Fameko after leaping out of a second floor hotel balcony to escape a suspected would-be

rapist. The backpacker fled when a hotel manager entered her room and tried to massage without her consent. She told the police, she had ordered a 4a.m. wake-up call but a man came to her room and allegedly offered to give her a massage and refused to leave.

The woman who was believed to be travelling around the world by herself suffered head injuries and a broken leg in the fall, but she managed to flag down a rickshaw to take her to the police station so she could report the alleged attack. Detectives have arrested Mr. M, the hotel manager in connection with the incident. He denied the allegations and claims he only knocked on the woman's door after staff failed to call her on the intercom.

But police said, the woman, who is understood to be a pharmacist, claims Mr. M had pestered her for three days to give her a free massage. Deputy Superintendent Amoko said the woman was in police protection, but added, "She is very scared and has cancelled her plans to stay in the country".

Comment

A Hotel proprietor/manager is responsible for the safety of his guest, her belongings and her valuables. Even if his employees lose the belongings of the guest through wilful neglect, the Hotel Proprietor is still responsible. The employee represents his employer in anything he does or says whilst at work. Let the master answer or (vicarious liability). As the saying goes, 'you cannot get blood out of stones,' so if a guest sues the hotel for negligence, which has been caused by the employee, the employee may not be able to pay compensation out of his wages. It would be the responsibility of the employer to pay. The proprietor would also have to pay if he wants to stay in business.

For a Hotel manager to behave in this manner, it becomes a serious matter. It goes to prove how naïve he is about the industry. The question is, is he insane? Shall we call it lust? Or lack of knowledge?

In order to protect the hospitality industry, some requirements must have to be laid down worldwide which potential proprietors must satisfy before being given a licence to operate. Those already operating should be encouraged to attend workshops to update their knowledge.

3. Unfair Dismissal

Madam Amma joined the company in 2004. In December 2005, she revealed her pregnancy. She started maternity leave in March 2006. Madam Amma returned to her post after the birth of her daughter to discover that the colleague who was filling in for her had been given her job.

At first, she shared the work with her cover, Mr. Kofi, but seven months later, in December 2007, she was made redundant. The company claimed they did not need two people.

After an eight-day hearing, the Employment Tribunal found Madam Amma had suffered unfair dismissal. Judge Mr. Bernard Brew said; "The fact that the claimant had taken maternity leave and had on-going responsibilities as a mother contributed to her selection for redundancy. The panel decided the size of her award. The tribunal found her bosses made assumptions about her ability to work and travel as a young mother, claiming during redundancy consultations that, she would not be able to; "put in the hours." It concluded, "Had a fair procedure been adopted during redundancy selection, it would have helped the company."

Mr. Kofi would not have been in a position to take her job, had he not been employed for maternity cover.

4. Holiday Representatives cleared over a case concerning the death of two children in a hotel

Two representatives of a travel agency company were cleared of the deaths of a brother and sister who died of carbon monoxide poisoning whilst spending holidays with their father. Nina, seven, and her brother Jay, nine, died after a faulty boiler leaked gas into their bungalow in October 2006.

The two representatives of the travel agency company were found not guilty of manslaughter by negligence by a court. Whilst on holiday with their dad, fumes leaked into their rooms at the hotel.

Outside the Court, the childrens' mother said she was disappointed with the verdict, adding, "the travel agent put our children in a gas-filled bungalow and let them die, claiming they did not know, but they should have."

The boiler was described as being in a 'repulsive' state and decrepit with rust corrosion.

After the trial of eleven people, including hotel staff, builders and boiler engineers, they were found guilty of manslaughter and for breaching regulations. Hotel staff and engineers blamed each other for the deaths.

The hotel manager and two senior technical staff were each sentenced to seven years. A civil engineer was given two year probation. The Hotel lost its licence and was closed down.

The children's father said, "If just one person had done his job correctly my kids would be here today. This was no accident. Their deaths could have been avoided."

The firm said, "This tragic accident was the result of unique circumstances, none of which could be the responsibility of the company or the representatives." After an investigation that lasted for ten years, the travel agency was accused by the Court for breach of duty of care. The directors of the travel agency therefore negotiated with the children's parents as to how to resolve the matter between them.

Learn Tragic Lessons
The deaths were a horrific tragedy – but the court verdict was the right one. Guilty parties should always be held accountable. However, blaming the two lowly representatives for this was a mistake.

Understandably, the grieving family wanted answers. We can only hope that authorities and other hoteliers will learn lessons from this awful accident and ensure it does not happen again.

5. Constructive Dismissal.

"Horrible Ms H. left me in tears" says Nanny

Ms. T, a former nanny accused her employer Ms H. of being 'unpleasant' and behaving 'horribly' as she allegedly forced her out of her job in favour of another woman.

Ms T is claiming constructive dismissal and sexual discrimination against Ms H. She started baby-sitting Ms H's daughter in April 2004 and was then offered the job of a nanny.

Ms T said the working relationship took a turn for the worse in 2007 when she took six months' maternity leave. Ms H, once called Ms T and left a rude, angry message asking when she would be returning to work. Ms T. said she was later side-lined by the arrival of a new nanny and was asked to carry out cleaning duties instead, at which point she quits.

Ms T. sought compensation over allegations of sex discrimination and constructive dismissal.

6. Unfair Dismissal

A lady spoke out against: 'Scandalous' conditions.

A woman won her whistle blowing claim against her former employer. Mrs Kay was sacked after being branded a troublemaker in her job, organizing services for disadvantaged people.

In January, she took the company, which provides vocational training, to an employment tribunal. It was ruled that she was unfairly dismissed. During the hearing, Mrs Kay told the tribunal how she was subjected to vile abuse by senior management for speaking out against what she saw as scandalous conditions and attitudes.

These included:

- Member of staff buying pornographic material
- The absence of health and safety training for staff and no system for sounding the fire alarm

- Lack of structure and punctuality for activities which left students bored
- A lack of funds for even basic materials such as pens and paper In its ruling, the tribunal made it clear that Mrs Kay was made redundant as a direct result of having voiced these concerns. She spoke of her relief at being vindicated, saying it put the spotlight on failing education services. "This experience has strengthened my determination to stand up for other people's rights and to work tirelessly to achieve justice for them." she said.

Mrs Kay's solicitor said, "Today's judgement sends a very clear message to employers that they cannot resort to silencing measures against employees who raise legitimate concerns."

7. Dismissed for Being Unwell

A lady has been working for a company for many years. She fell whiles rushing to catch a bus to work. She was given a week off by her doctor, covered by a sick certificate, which she sent to her employer.

She was at home when she received a telephone call from her employer, saying she has been suspended. Shortly after the phone call, she had another call that she has been dismissed.

8. Two Women in Hospital

After an Explosion in a Hotel, the women, believed to be in their forties, were staying at a three-star hotel. An ambulance spokesman said: "Our understanding is, pipes carrying hot water from a boiler have exploded and the women were hit by flying shards of metal." Could this have happened if there had been frequent checks or periodic maintenance on the heating system?

Who should be held responsible?

9. Problem with "Do Not Disturb Sign"
Hotel Guest starves to Death
A hotel guest was found starved to death in his room two weeks after he checked in and ordered staff not to disturb him. Mr. Tay, 40,

who was a loner, had paid two months in advance at the Haley Hotel.

The operations manager at the hotel told an inquest, "he was adamant he didn't want to be disturbed. "He did not go out and come back but we didn't check on him".

The operations manager at the hotel said he thought Mr. Tay; "looked pretty ill". He again said he can't believe he starved to death, because there was breakfast laid out every morning and he had the chance to eat as much as he wanted.

The Assistant Deputy Manager said Mr.Tay had all his worldly goods' with him. They include a notebook containing spidery, paranoid scrawls – all in capital letters.

Police identified the former analyst from his bank cards and passport details but found little information about his family, the coroner's court heard. His widowed mother Grace, 72, said she last saw him when he left the family home more than three years ago. After being told of his death, she said, "I'm, shocked and don't understand why the police didn't find me." Dr. David's, who recorded an open verdict said: "There are lots of unanswered questions".

What went wrong?

(1) Could his death have been prevented?
(2) Has the hotel been negligent in ensuring the safety of Mr. Tay?
(3) Were the police negligent for failing to use all modern techniques (e.g. the media) to find the relatives of Mr. Tay, since his mother was alive?
(4) When Mr. Tay was providing information for check in, did he provide a name for his next of kin?
(5) When the staff realized he was not going out and coming in, why did they not use all means to find out earlier what was going on? For example, ringing the phone in his bedroom to see if he would answer.

(6) If the Hotel Manager said, "he looked pretty ill," why did they not talk to him and call a doctor or the paramedics to send Mr. Tay to the hospital?

10. Holiday maker Dies in Balcony Plunge

A holidaymaker plunged to his death after a balcony stunt at his hotel went tragically wrong. He fell more than 30ft after losing his grip as he dangled from the fifth floor veranda and asked friends to count how long he could hold on.

He had just returned from a night out with four friends. He was seen hanging on the balcony moments after he got back in at 7.40 a.m. on Saturday. An onlooker said, 'It all happened so quickly. He clambered over his balcony and only held on for a few seconds before he dropped." He fell head first like a lead weight and smashed on to a concrete ramp leading down to an underground car park next to his hotel garden. "His friends saw everything. They were in tears when ambulance workers told them their friend was gone". A police source added, "His friend told us he wanted to show off and hung off his balcony to see how long he could hold on for." He fell before they could talk him out of it. They had been drinking most of the night but they sobered up pretty quickly. Pathologists were due to carry out a post-mortem.

11. Fallen from a Hotel

Doe aged 20, has been in an induced coma for a month after falling from his hotel room on an island. He took a last-minute decision to go on holiday and did not take out travel insurance. Friends and well-wishers raised money to fly him home by air ambulance when he was well enough.

Many hotel falls involving foreign tourists, (especially the young ones) have been blamed on a craze dubbed "balconying", where holidaymakers try to leap between rooms or jump from their room into a swimming pool.

Hotel owners on the islands are discussing measures to combat the craze including fines, repatriation and video campaigns. Could this be contributory negligence?

12. Compensating Travellers.

An airline encountered growing pressure to fully compensate travellers stranded during a volcanic ash cloud crisis. The airline has been warned to pay hotel and meal bills or risk legal action by the European Commission.

The airline said, it would pay only 24-hours' worth of accommodation and food bills to passengers affected, despite EU legislation stating that 'reasonable costs should not be time limited'. Frustrated travellers set up a Facebook page venting their anger.

The European Commission wrote to the airline reminding them of EU regulations which do not allow for limiting compensation to a single night. The EU commission said, they expected to seek clarification from the airline on their policy so that it is in line with EU law.

The airline said it had decided to pay out for one day and one night pending the outcome of compensation discussions by the European Commission. Thousands of passengers had their travel plans ruined after ash from an Icelandic volcano closed European airspace.

Note: The above case goes to prove that the travel agents were not held responsible, even though most passengers bought their tickets from travel agents. In most cases, the travel agent drops out leaving the battle between the passenger and the principal, which is the airline.

13. Worker Stabbed to Death at Golf Club

A Golf Club worker died after allegedly being stabbed in the neck during a row with a co-worker. Another employee is being questioned by the police after the incident at a prestigious Golf Club.

The 32-year-old victim suffered 'severe neck injury' after the argument broke out in the club's kitchen. Suddenly, one of them attacked the other with a knife and there was blood everywhere and it was instantly clear nothing could be done to save him.

Officers arrived within minutes and arrested a 33-year old man on suspicion of murder. The victim was pronounced dead at the scene. He was formally identified and the police were waiting to inform all close family members.

The course was cordoned off for forensic examination. According to the police, a post mortem test showed the victim died from 'serious stab wounds to the neck'.

The Police also said that it was clearly upsetting for the staff and guests who were there and thanked them for their cooperation.

Note – What measures can employers take to ensure a safe working environment in order to prevent such incidents?

14. Thieves Breaking Into a Hotel Room at Night

A tourist checked into a hotel and thieves managed to break into his room at night and stole his money and his belongings.

- How did the thieves manage to break into his room?
- Where were the security personnel and the staff when the thieves broke in?
- Who should be held responsible?
- How are you going to deal with this case as a hotel Manager/ Proprietor?
- How are you going to prevent this happening in future?

15. Unpaid Bill by a Guest

An eighteen-year-old lady checked into a hotel. Payment was made by her fiancé for two weeks. She stayed an extra week without paying any more money. The hotel manager therefore demanded payment for the extra week spent. She said her fiancé will be coming to pay within the following week that will be the fourth week.

The fiancé never checked in with her and he did not promise to pay for the extra two weeks and had not called at that time or sent payment to cover the extra two weeks in advance. He travelled abroad the very day he checked her into the hotel. It was later discovered that the lady's belongings were disappearing from her room gradually. The hotel manager then alerted staff in the hotel, especially the front office personnel to keep an eye on the lady's movements. She was taking the last of her belongings, which was a transistor radio when a member of the staff cautiously seized the radio from her. She left the hotel leaving the radio behind and never returned.

Who should be held responsible for the rest of the payment and why?

Did the hotel have the right to seize her property? Did the hotel have the right to detain her?

16. To Search or not to search when suspicious of a guest when checking in".

Staff smelt the scent of marijuana on the fourth floor of a hotel. On close examination it was confirmed that a guest was smoking it in a room. However, there were clear notices at the reception and in the bedrooms informing guest not to smoke in their rooms. When the security personnel told him to refrain from smoking in the hotel room, he pulled a pistol and threatened to shoot. He was overpowered by the security and the gun was taken from him and the police were informed.

How would you handle a case like this and how would you stop this happening again?

17. Hotel Staff to be Vigilant at all Times.

A former wrestler shot a policeman and went into hiding in a hotel. After several weeks of search by the police, his description by the police in the media reminded the hotel receptionist of such a guest in the hotel. He informed his employer and the employer reported the case to the police. This led to his arrest. The police found the gun under his mattress when they came to search his room.

Had it not been the receptionist who was vigilant and intelligent, an incident could have happened in the hotel as well. This man could have shot anybody in the hotel and cause a big problem for the hotel proprietor. The loyal employee saved his employer from trouble.

18. Two Sailors Found Dead In Their Hotel Rooms

Two sailors aged, 22 and 35, were found dead in their hotel rooms. They went to town and returned to the hotel with two ladies who they entertained in their rooms.

It was discovered that they had some drinks with the ladies in their bedrooms. The two ladies left the hotel before the sailors were found dead.

This brought a big problem for the hotel proprietor. Until this matter is investigated, the hotel proprietor is considered responsible. He has to prove he is not responsible by co-operating with the police until the problem is solved. A doctor must come to pronounce them dead before the bodies can be removed from the hotel. An autopsy has to be done and the cause of death concluded.

What measures does the hotel need to put in place to reduce or to prevent such an incident happening again?

If these two ladies had given some information about themselves to reveal their identities, the hotel would have been able to trace them quickly to help with the investigation. If the hotel is found guilty or partly guilty, the proprietor and some hotel staff may be fined or may be imprisoned. It should be at the discretion of the hotel and the hotel guest to allow or not allow certain visitors to visit hotel guests' in their rooms. If possible, some form of identity must be required.

Some house rules can also help solve or prevent problems like these. We must learn from our mistakes with many murder cases occurring all over the world. It is high time proprietors of sleeping establishments (hotels or private hotels) design some house rules to help solve these atrocities.

19. The Problem With the 'Do Not Disturb' Sign

In September 2009, a businessman visited his millionaire girlfriend in a top hotel. A 'Do not disturb' sign was hung outside the door. It was later discovered that the woman had been murdered in her room and the visitor had gone. The man was hunted down by police. He was later discovered in the woods after a police chase. The police found him hanging on a tree in the woods. He had committed suicide.

In the light of the above case studies, Hotels and private hotels must be on their guard to reduce such incidents in their establishments. In recent times, there has been an increase of murders in sleeping accommodations especially in hotels all over the world.

For instance, some ladies pose as prostitutes all over the world. They have a way of getting guests to drink heavily. Afterwards, they steal their money and valuables and then sneak out of the hotels.

Since the safety of the guests lies in the hands of the hotel proprietors, it becomes necessary to put in place serious measures so as to prevent or minimize these problems, and in turn maintain a good reputation so as to maximize sales.

After all, everyone wants to lodge at a safe haven.

20. Tragedy at a Hotel

A mother of two was questioned on suspicion of murdering her two young children on holiday in Kabana Hotel. She was arrested after her five-yearold daughter and one-year-old were found dead in a hotel room in a popular resort Kabana Hotel.

The woman, aged between 30 and 40, has not been named. The whereabouts of the children's father was not known. It was reported in the newspapers that the children, who arrived at the resort some few days back, had been suffocated. A police spokeswoman said, "There was no blood, cuts, bullet wounds or other signs of external injury".

21. Prince Held Over Murder at Hotel.

A Prince was being questioned on suspicion of murder after his assistant was found strangled in his hotel room. The 33-year-old was arrested after a room attendant found the body of a 32-year-old man in a suite at a five star hotel.

Police arrested the man some hours later. Officers kept the suspect in custody for some time. It was understood that, the prince who travelled to Lapaloma as a tourist, did not have diplomatic immunity. His link to the Sabana royal family may be 'minor', said sources.

The victim had serious head injuries but a post-mortem examination showed that he died from manual compression of the neck. Officers believe they know the identity of the deceased, who is from Sabana and awaited formal identification.

22. Fallen of a Gardener from 60 feet

A gardener fell 60 feet down a shaft while doing routine landscaping work. He broke his back, shattered his ankle and broke a bone in his foot in the freak accident. He now says he is out of work and struggling to survive on benefits. The 23-year-old had been tending to plants on a traffic island near a hotel premises and when the metal grill gave way and plummeted down the shaft into an underground car park.

He had to wait in agony for 20 minutes to be treated because ambulances could not get into the carpark. The gardener, said; "I cannot describe the pain. All the doctors and surgeons said I was lucky to have survived; but the doctors could not guarantee that there will not be any lasting pain or physical changes".

The gardener was working for a sub-contractor employed by a Transport Company in Kumasi. He is now unemployed and says his mother has been forced to take time-off to care for him.

His solicitors G. and J. are preparing to launch a personal injury claim for compensation.

The Health and Safety Executives are still investigating the incident. When it happened, Mr Bonsu, Director of Roads said, "We are saddened by the news that one of our subcontractors has been injured."

APPENDIX B: QUESTIONS ON THE CONTRACT OF ACCOMMODATION

1. Outline the essential steps in making a valid contract for accommodation.

    Mrs Smith writes to the Sunway Hotel asking whether they have accommodation available for the first week in July. The hotel replied that they do have the accommodation she requires and state their terms. Mrs Smith does not answer this letter but shows up in July expecting to find the accommodation available. The hotel is full. Advise the proprietor.

2. Explain the legal position regarding the return of a deposit in the event of cancellation of a contract by a guest.

3. Mrs Brown writes to the Cross Inn to enquire about accommodation for the first week in September. The Cross Inn replies that they have accommodation available at that time and state their terms. Mrs Brown accepts the offer by return of post. However, when she arrives at the Cross Inn, she finds no room reserved for her and the hotel was full. The hotel claims they did not receive her second letter. Advise Mrs Brown.

4. In answer to Paul's enquiries, the Coventry Hotel offers him the accommodation he requires subject to his confirmation 'as soon as possible'. Paul waits a day or two to hear from another hotel and then posts a letter of acceptance. By the time this reaches the hotel, the accommodation had already been let to another guest.

5. In April, the Sun Hotel advertises that 'owing to cancellations, accommodation is available during July. Mary writes to the

Hotel saying she will take a single room from the 1st to the 14th of July but gets no response. Is it a valid contract?

6. In January Henry reserves accommodation in a London hotel for the last week in July. He later writes to cancel the reservation because of work pressure. What legal action may the hotelier take?

7. Mr. & Mrs Bright walk into a private hotel and book a room for a week. On a wall in their bedroom is a notice saying the hotel will not be liable for any valuables unless these are deposited with the housekeeper. While the Brights were out the next day, Mrs Bright's fur coat was stolen. Advise Mrs Bright.

8. Where accommodation is booked in advance, when does the contract come into existence? The Murphy family book a hotel for a holiday that is advertising special facilities for families including a games room and a new swimming pool. On arrival, they find that the games room is being redecorated after a flood the previous week and the new swimming pool is unfinished and not ready for use. The brochure contained an exclusion clause. Advise Mr Murphy.

9. The Lucas family wish to spend a quiet walking holiday. They apply for the brochures of countless hotels and, after careful study, book at the Rose and Crown at Little Marsh. The brochures contain photos of a small inn with country view and states that it is on the edge of the moors. On arrival, the Lucas family find that the new town of Brickstone now stands between the Rose and Crown and open country. In fact the Inn is surrounded by new town buildings. Advise Mr. Lucas.

10. The manager of the Hotel Splendid is rewriting his hotel brochure. Advise him on the importance of accuracy in describing the hotel's facilities and the possible legal repercussions of any misleading statements.

11. In January, Mrs H. books accommodation at the Sunway Hotel in a popular resort for a fortnight in August. Later she changes her plans and cancels her booking. Advise the hotel.

12. Mr Stern booked accommodation at the Imperial Hotel at $30 a week. On his bill were the following extras:
   i. $3 a day for early morning tea
   ii. $5 for laundering shirts
   iii. $2 for shoe cleaning.

In addition, there is a service charge of 15% on the entire bill. Must Mr. Stern pay these extra charges on top of the $30 a week?

Under what circumstance can a guest refuse to pay a service charge at a hotel?

APPENDIX C

GLOSSARY

Inn – In Common Law, the owner of a house who holds himself out as being willing to receive travellers who are willing to pay an appropriate price for accommodation. Reference case - Hotel Proprietor Act 1956 (William v Linnit 1951) 1KB. For limitation of an innkeeper's liability.

Hotel – An establishment held out by the proprietor as offering food, drink and if so required, sleeping accommodation, without special contract, to any traveller presenting himself who appears able and willing to pay a reasonable sum for the services and facilities provided and who is in a fit state to be received; Hotel Proprietor's Act. 1956.

Ultra vires – Beyond the powers. Term relating generally to the excess of legal powers or authority; specifically, the exercise by a corporation of powers beyond those conferred on it explicitly or implicitly. (subject matter not included in the memorandum and on which the contract was based was held to be ultra vires)

Ultra vires rule and companies – The ultra vires doctrine was modified extensively in relation to the company and a third person by Cos.A.1989, s 108 substituting a new s 35 in Cos. A. 1985. By Cos. A.2006,s39(1), the validity of an act done by a company shall not be called into question on the grounds of lack of capacity by reason of anything in the company's constitution. By Cos. A 2006,s 40(1), in favour of a person dealing with a company in good faith, the power of the directors to bind the company, or authorize others to do so is deemed to be free of any limitation under the company's constitution. For this purpose a person 'deals with' a company if he is a party to any transaction or other act to which the company is a party:

    I. is not bound to enquire as to any limitation on the powers of the directors to bind the company or authorize others to do so;

   II. is presumed to have acted in good faith unless the contrary is proved; and

  III. is not to be regarded as acting in bad faith by reason only of his knowing that an act is beyond the powers of the directors under the company's constitution

The references above to limitations on director's powers under the company's constitution include limitations deriving:

- From a resolution of the company or of any class of shareholders; or
- From any agreement between the members of the company or of any class of shareholders; Cos.A.2006, s 40(3).
- This section does not affect any right of a member of the company to bring proceedings to restrain the doing of an action that is beyond the powers of the directors. But no such proceedings lie in respect of an act to be done in fulfilment of a legal obligation arising from a previous act of the company; Cos. A. 2006, s40(4).
- This section does not affect any liability incurred by the directors, or any other person, by reason of the directors' exceeding their powers; Cos.A. A2006,s 40(5).

Rescission – Remedy for inducing a contract by innocent or fraudulent misrepresentation where by the contract is abrogated. A party intending to rescind must notify the other party.

Assert – declare; state clearly [assert one's belief; assert that it is so. Insist on one's rights or opinions; demands recognition.

Undertaking – A promise, especially a promise in the course of legal proceedings by a party or his counsel, which may be enforced by attachment or otherwise in the same manner as an injunction.

Void–Of no legal effect: a nullity; e.g. an agreement for an immoral consideration. A contract may be void on the face of it, or evidence may be required to show that it is void. But when an illegal contract has been executed, money paid either in consideration or performance cannot be recovered back.

Voidable – An agreement or other act which one of the parties to it is entitled to rescind an e.g. in the case of fraud in a contract, if however, the party entitled to rescind the contract affirms the contract, or fails to exercise his right of rescission within reasonable time, so that the position of party becomes altered, or if he takes a benefit under the contract of a third party, acquires rights under it, he will be bound by it.

Vindicate – clear of blame or suspicion. Justify a person by evidence or argument.

Culpable – deserving blame.

Inferred – deduce or conclude from facts and reasoning; imply, suggest.

Tudor times – Relating to the English royal dynasty which held the throne from 1485 to 1603.

Affirmation – an affirmative answer; a word or phrase indicating agreement; an affirmative agreement; such as 'yes.'

Floatation –the process of offering a company shares for sale on the stock market for the first time.

Trivial – of little importance; a trivial matter.

Peer – a member of a nobility; a person who holds any of the five grades of the British nobility; duke, marquis, earl, viscount and baron.

Perjury – criminal law, the act of deliberately giving false evidence while under oath; a false oath.

Treason – betrayal of one's sovereign of country, especially by attempting to overthrow the government.

Coronation – the ceremony of crowning a Monarch.

Set-Off –Pleading by way of defence to the whole or part of the plaintiff's claim. The defendant acknowledges the plaintiff's demand but sets up one which counterbalances it. Amount to be set off must have been due at the issue of the writ.

Set Aside – To annul, make void, over rule.

Writ – Instrument under seal issued in the name of the Sovereign, declaring some command; A judiciary writ is issued by a court, ordering to originate some actions. A writ is generally valid for four months from date of issue.

Winding Up – process whereby a company is brought to an end, e.g. following insolvency. It may be compulsory winding up by the court, winding up under the court's supervision.

Voluntary Winding up – Thus, a company may be wound up; when the period fixed in the articles for the company expires.

Legacy – A money or personal property left to someone by a will; something handed down to a successor.

Legal tender – currency that a creditor must pay by law. Accept to pay a debt.

Conveyance –A method by which property in the mainland is transferred or the document by which this is done.

Covenant –A promise set out in a deed.

Deliberations – long and careful consideration; slow and careful action.

Exculpate – to free from blame or guilt.

Imposition – something imposed unfairly on someone.

Pretentious – trying to impress by pretending to be more important or better than one actually is.

Contravention – commit an act that is not allowed by (a law, treaty etc.); conflict with (a right, principle, etc.)

Judicature Act –Judicature Acts 1873, came into operation on November 1875 and consolidated the pre-existing superior courts into one Supreme Court, consisting of the High Court and the Court of Appeal. The 1925 Act Consolidates the judicature Acts 1873–1910, and other enactments relating to the Supreme Court and the administration of justice therein; the Act has been amended in some minor particulars by the Administration of Justice Act, 1928 and subsequent Acts. Courts of Appeal, Supreme Court of Judicature. (Judges) are not bound to explain the reason of their decision.

Express –Distinctly stated, rather than implied.

Express Term – An express statement of undertakings and promises contained in a contract other written instrument. A deviation from such a term may constitute a breach of contract.

Tender – **to offer for sale** – To offer money, etc., in payment or satisfaction of a debt other obligation. Payment extinguishes the debt; tender does not. There must be actual production of the exact sum of money, or dispensation of such production.

An offer relating to the supply of goods – Thus X requires 1,000 ingots and invites tenders. If he accepts Y's tender, there is a contract for the sale of 1,000ingots by Y to X.

Tender of Performance – Express readiness to perform an act in accordance with an obligation.

Firm	Company, business, concern, enterprise, organization, corporation, conglomerate, office, bureau, agency, consortium, outfit, set-up.
Culminate	Come to climax; come to a head; peak; reach a pinnacle; build up to; lead up to; end with; finish with; conclude with;
	Highest point; top; summit; crowning moment; apex; consumption; completion; finish; conclusion.

Rights	Having a legally or morally just claim.
Liabilities	Accountability (Legal) responsibility, answerability, blame, blameworthiness, guilt, fault, liable for negligence (Legally).
Ratification	To give formal approval.
Vicarious	Performed by one person as a substitute for, or for the benefit of, another. Secondary; surrogate; empathic; substitute; derivative.
Conspicuous	Easily seen, clear; visible; noticeable; obvious; evident, prominent; crystal clear; patent; striking; overt; eyecatching.
Licensee	A person who holds a licence, esp; one to sell alcoholic drink.
Encumbrance	Hindrance, obstruction, obstacle, impediment, constraint, handicap, inconvenience, nuisance, disadvantage, drawback, burden, responsibility, obligation, liability, weight, stress.
Fictitious	False, fake, sham, fabricated, bogus, assumed, made up, informal, pretend.
Shareholder	The owner of one or more shares in a company.
Director	A person who directs and controls, e.g. Business.
Compensation	Repayment; reimbursement; remuneration; requital; indemnify; redress; damages.
Putrid	Sickening or foul; deficient in quality or in value.
Decomposed	To rot.
Delusion	A mistaken idea or belief.
Toxic	Poisonous substances.
Indemnity	To secure against loss or damage or liability.
Implied	Suggested or understood by implication or deduction from the circumstances.
Implied contract	A contract inferred from the conduct of parties or from some relationship existing between them.

Liquidation	The dissolving of a company by selling its assets to pay off its debts (of a business or firm) to have its affairs terminated.
Dissolution	The act of officially breaking up an organization or institution; the act of officially ending a formal agreement, such as marriage; the formal ending of a meeting or assembly such as Parliament.
Imminent	Likely to open soon.
Manipulation	To handle or use skilfully to control something or someone cleverly or deviously.
Defamation	To attack the good reputation of; to spread by unfavourable report.
Detrimental	Disadvantaged or damaged.
Belligerent	Aggression or warlike behaviour.
Slander	False and damaging statement about a person; the crime of making such a statement.
Malice	The desire to do harm or cause mischief to others.
Repudiate	Refuse to accept or be associated with; deny the truth or validity of.
Inchoate	denoting the beginning of an action.
Duress	Consists at Common Law of threats of violence to person or threats to property. Note its effect which is to make the contract voidable; forcible contract; threatened in a contract; other forms of coercion; undue influence and economic duress must be looked at. Note that undue influence is equitable in origin and is applied chiefly to cases where some fiduciary relationship exists between the parties but is not limited to these situations.

Economic Duress Is a form of commercial pressure as where a contractor refuses to perform a contract unless the price for his work is increased in a situation where the other party to the contract may suffer penalty if it is not completed on time

APPENDIX D: ABBREVIATIONS FOR THE ACTS OF PARLIAMENT

The titles of some Acts which are referred to repeatedly are abbreviated in accordance with the list below. In every case, the abbreviation is followed by the appropriate date of the Act, thus: Th.A. 1968; E.R.A. 1996.

A.E.A. Administration of Estates Act

A.J.A. Administration of Justice Act

B.Ex.A. Bills of Exchange Act

C.C.A. Consumer Credit Act

Ch.A. Children Act

C.J.A. Criminal Justice Act

C.J.J.A. Civil Jurisdiction and Judgements Act

C.J.P.O.A. Criminal Justice and Public Order Act

C.L.A. Criminal Law Act

C.L.S.A. Courts and Legal Services Act

Cos. A. Companies Act

County C.A. County Courts Act

C.P.A. Consumer Protection Act

C and Y.P.A. Children and Young person's Act

C.P.I.A. Criminal Procedure and Investigations Act

E.P.A. Employment Protection Act E.R.A. Employment Rights Act

En.P.A. Environmental Protection Act

H.A. Housing Act

H.S.W.A. Health and Safety at Work Act

H & P.A. Housing and Planning Act

L.G.H.A. Local Government and Housing Act

L.P.A. Law of Property Act

L.R.A. Land Registration Act

S.C.A. Supreme Courts Act

S.G.A. Sale of Goods Act

S.S.A. Social Security Act

T.U.L.R.A. Trade Union and Labour Relations Act. *Source:* Acts of Parliament

APPENDIX E: TABLE OF STATUTES

Employers and Workmen Act 1875 (90) S10

Employers Liability (Compulsory Insurance Act 1969)

Employers Liability (Defective Equipment) Act 1969

Equal Pay Act 1970

Factories Act 1961

Fair Trading Act 1973

Fire Precautions Act 1971. Repealed and replaced by Regulatory Reformed (Fire Safety) order 2005, which came into effect on 1 October 2006.

Food and Drugs Act 1955

Food Hygiene Regulations S.I. 1970

Health Services and Public Health Act 1968

Labelling of Food Regulations (S.I. 1970)

Hotel Proprietors Act 1956

Industrial Relations Act 1964

Wages Regulations (Licensed Non-Residential Establishment)

Innkeepers Act 1878

Innkeepers Liability Act 1863

Judicature Act 1873–5

Landlord and Tenant act 1954

Law of Property Act 1969

Law Reform (Contributory Negligence) Act 1945

Lease Reform Act 1967

Licensing Act 1872

Licensing Act 1904

Licensing Act 1964

Young Person's Act 1938 & 1964

Local Authorities Act 1972

Misrepresentation Act 1967

National Insurance Act 1965

National Insurance (Injuries) Act 1957

Occupiers Liability Act 1957

Office, Shops and Railway Premises Act 1963

Partnerships Act 1890

Public Health Act 1875

Race Relations Act 1968

Redundancy Payments Act 1965

Refreshment Houses Act 1964

Registration of Business Names Act 1916

Road Traffic Act 1972

Sales of Goods Act 1893 Shops Act 1950

Social Security Act 1973

Supply of goods (Implied Terms) Act 1973

Terms and conditions of Employment Act 1959

Theft Act 1968

Town and Country Planning Act 1971

Trade Descriptions Act 1968

Trade Union and Labour Relations Act 1974

Wages Council Act 1959

Weight and Measures Act 1963 Wine and Beer

houses Act 1869 Food Safety Act 1990.

APPENDIX F: BIBLOGRAPHY

- *The Acts of Parliament* – UK
- *Ghana Legal System* – the Judicial Service Council of Ghana
- *English Legal System* – Martin, J.
- *Black's Law Dictionary* – Garner, A.B. (Editor-in-Chief)
- *Legal Aspects of the Hotel and Catering Operations* – Richards, M. And Stewart, S.W.
- *Understanding Law* – Adams, J. And Brownsword, R.
- *Hotel Catering Economic Development Committee* (EDC)
- *Industrial and Welfare Catering* (1970–80) HCIMA Review, Volume one. U.K.
- *A study in Industrial concentration* Review, Volume 2 – Koudra, M. Catering Contractors.
- *Profile of the Hotel and Catering Industry* – Medlick, S. with Airev, D.W., BA, MSC
- *Standard Industrial classification,* 1968 U.K.
- *Business Dictionary and Official Hotel Guide*
- *State Insurance corporation of Ghana* 0 – SIC
- *Dictionary of Insurance* 2nd Edition, 1995 – Bennett, C.
- *English Law* – Eleventh Edition. Smith and Keenan
- *Marketing Orientation in the Hotel and Catering Operations* – Kotas, R.
- *Law for Business,* 12th edition 2003 – Keenan, D.
- *The Enforcement of Morals* 1968 – Devlin, P.
- *The elements of Jurisprudence* – Hollard, E.T.
- *Contract Law* – Richards, P.
- *Hotel and Catering Institutional Managers' Yearbook*
- *National Fire Service* – U.K.

- *Law of Small Business,* Eight Edition, 1995 – Clayton, P.
- *Butterworth's Food Law* – 2nd edition, Atwood, B. LLB Solicitor.
- *The Sheriffs are Coming* – BBC Television Programme Some case studies from the Daily Newspapers.

Milton Keynes UK
Ingram Content Group UK Ltd.
UKHW020620261123
433289UK00010B/31